Korea 2010: Politics, Economy and Society

Korea 2010:
Politics, Economy and Society

Volume 4

Korea Yearbook

Edited by

Rüdiger Frank
James E. Hoare
Patrick Köllner
Susan Pares

BRILL

LEIDEN • BOSTON
2010

This work was supported by the Academy of Korean Studies (publication grant AKS-2010-P-01).

This book is printed on acid-free paper.

ISSN 1875-0273
ISBN 978 90 04 18535 7

Copyright 2010 by Koninklijke Brill NV, Leiden, The Netherlands.
Koninklijke Brill NV incorporates the imprints Brill, Hotei Publishing, IDC Publishers, Martinus Nijhoff Publishers and VSP.

All rights reserved. No part of this publication may be reproduced, translated, stored in a retrieval system, or transmitted in any form or by any means, electronic, mechanical, photocopying, recording or otherwise, without prior written permission from the publisher.

Authorization to photocopy items for internal or personal use is granted by Koninklijke Brill NV provided that the appropriate fees are paid directly to The Copyright Clearance Center, 222 Rosewood Drive, Suite 910, Danvers, MA 01923, USA.
Fees are subject to change.

PRINTED BY DRUKKERIJ WILCO B.V. - AMERSFOORT, THE NETHERLANDS

CONTENTS

Preface xi

Chronology of Events in the Korean Peninsula 2009 1
   South Korea 1
   North Korea 4
   Inter-Korean relations and Six Party Talks 8

South Korea in 2009: Domestic Developments and the Economy 13
   Patrick Köllner
   1   Introduction 13
   2   South Korea loses two former presidents 14
   3   Parliamentary (in)action 18
   4   A new cabinet and the travails of the
        'Sejong City' project 20
   5   South Korea's middle class under pressure 22
   6   South Korea's economy in 2009: the big picture 23

North Korea in 2009: Domestic Developments and the Economy 29
   Rüdiger Frank
   1   Introduction 29
   2   The joint New Year editorial 30
   2.1 Leadership 30
   2.2 Ideology 31
   2.3 Economy 32
   2.4 Unification 33
   2.5 Military affairs 34
   3   The budget report 35
   4   The SPA elections 37
   4.1 Supreme People's Assembly 37
   4.2 The National Defence Commission 39
   4.3 The cabinet 39
   5   Policies 40
   5.1 The 150-day battle 40
   5.2 The currency reform of November 2009 43

6	Ideology	46
6.1	Return to orthodox, conservative socialism	46
6.2	Problems	47
7	Other economic policies	48
7.1	Kaesŏng	48
7.2	International economic exchanges	49
7.3	Innovation	50
7.4	Further policies	50
8	Structural changes and personnel policy	51

Relations Between the Two Koreas in 2009 55
Sabine Burghart and James E. Hoare

Introduction		55
1	A period of adjustment?	55
2	Lee's 'creative pragmatism': a solution to the North's sabre-rattling?	56
3	Kaesŏng Industrial Complex: a pawn in the DPRK's hands?	58
4	Humanitarian assistance: over to private organisations	60
5	Other developments	62
6	Outlook	64

Foreign Relations of the Two Koreas in 2009 67
James E. Hoare

Introduction		67
1	Republic of Korea	67
1.1	Relations with the United States	67
1.2	Relations with China	69
1.3	Relations with Japan	71
1.4	Other relations	72
2	The Democratic People's Republic of Korea	74
2.1	The Six Party Talks, the nuclear issue and relations with the United States	74
2.2	Relations with China	79
2.3	Relations with Japan	80
2.4	Relations with Russia	81
2.5	Other relations	82

Conflict Management in Urban Planning:
The Restoration of the Ch'ŏnggyech'ŏn River in Seoul....................85
Annette J. Erpenstein
1 Introduction..85
2 Historical background of the Ch'ŏnggyech'ŏn river..........86
2.1 Function and maintenance..87
2.2 Coverage work and negligence 88
2.3 Modern times 89
3 Excavating a layered reality 90
4 Strengths and weaknesses of the current democratic
 process of urban planning 91
5 Stakeholder and conflict management in the
 Ch'ŏnggyech'ŏn project..95
5.1 Political strategy: participation, utilisation, complicity......95
5.2 Traffic issues 97
5.3 Co-operation and participation...98
5.4 Downtown business issues...100
5.5 Historical issues..101
5.6 Conflict management and outcome..................................103
6 The power of geographical imagination in planning
 decisions...105
7 Conclusion..106

The Role of Think Tanks in the South Korean Discourse
on East Asia 113
Thomas Kern and Alexander Ruser
1 Introduction..113
2 Analytical relevance of regionalisation............................115
3 Think tanks and political discourse..................................118
4 The discourse on regionalisation in South Korea.............121
4.1 Growing influence of think tanks....................................121
4.2 Institutional isomorphism...125
4.3 Political relevance 128
5 Conclusion..131

South Korea's Economic Policy Response to the Global Financial Crisis 135
Werner Pascha

1 Introducing the issues 135
2 The South Korean economy on the eve of the global financial and economic crisis 136
3 The crisis and economic policy reactions 140
3.1 Effects of the crisis 140
3.2 Policy reactions 141
3.3 'Green New Deal' 145
3.4 How the measures are viewed 148
3.5 Labour and social policy measures 150
3.6 Organisational aspects 152
4 The preliminary impact of the policy response to the crisis 153
5 Political-economic boundary conditions 156
6 An effect of 1997-1998? 159

'Green Growth': South Korea's Panacea? 165
David Shim

1 Introduction 165
2 Initiatives and implications of 'Low Carbon Green Growth' 168
2.1 Domestic policy 168
2.2 Foreign policy 171
3 Evaluation of 'Low Carbon Green Growth' 173
3.1 New policy? 174
3.2 Ambitious policy? 174
3.3 'Green' policy? 176
3.4 Trouble-free policy? 178
4 Conclusion 181

South Korea's Economic Relations with India: Trends, Patterns and Prospects 189
Durgesh K. Rai

1 Introduction 189
2 Trade relations 191
2.1 Trade policy 191
2.2 India and Korea in global trade: a comparative picture ... 195

2.3	Bilateral trade	198
3	India-Korea investment relations	205
3.1	Korean investment in India	205
3.2	Indian investment in Korea	208
3.3	Technical collaboration	210
4	Co-operation and future prospects for bilateral economic relations	212

On the Trail of the Manchurian Western 217

Mark Morris

1	Prologue	217
2	Introduction	218
3	The Good, the Bad and the Weird	219
4	Representative films from the Manchurian westerns	221
4.1	Lessons from popular culture	221
4.2	Korean heroes, Chinese bandits, Japanese soldiers, patriotic armies and some very patient women, and horses, too	223
4.3	Towards a genealogy of action heroes	235
5	The appeal of genre films	239
6	Running into the future: some conclusions	241

A Meta-Analysis of North Koreans Migrating to China and South Korea 247

Daniel Schwekendiek

1	Introduction	247
2	The political economy of North Korean migration	250
2.1	Terminology	250
2.2	Historical migration	251
2.3	Migration in the post-Cold War era	253
3	Migration surveys in China	256
4	Migration surveys in South Korea	258
5	Comparative meta-analysis of migrants surveyed in China and South Korea	262
6	Conclusion	267

Textual and Visual Representations of the Korean War in
North and South Korean Children's Literature..................................271
    Dafna Zur
    1   The Korean War in North and South Korean
          children's books 271
    2   Ideology in post-war South Korean
          children's literature 273
    2.1   Emergence of an anti-communist rhetoric 275
    2.2   Anti-communist rhetoric in texts.......................................277
    2.3   Anti-communist rhetoric in illustrations 279
    3   Post-1980s South Korean children's literature.................280
    4   The Korean War in North Korea......................................286
    4.1   The Korean War in text..287
    4.2   The young hero: transcendental courage and
          martyrdom 288
    4.3   The Korean War in illustrations 291
    5   Aesthetics of violence 298

About the Authors and Editors 305
Map of the Korean Peninsula 311

PREFACE

Alert readers will note that the title of this publication has changed a little. After detecting some confusion among the readership, for whom the term 'Yearbook' conjured up a misleading image, the editors and the publishers have agreed that in future the title will be *Korea: Politics, Economy and Society*, plus the year in question. So this is *Korea 2010: Politics, Economy and Society*. In all other respects, however, the publication remains the same mix of survey articles and a chronology, which are the responsibility of the editors, and additional papers that, we hope, represent a wide range of current scholarship on issues of concern and interest. They include three essays on aspects of South Korean politics: Annette Erpenstein's paper on conflict management and urban planning examines the restoration of the Ch'ŏnggyech'ŏn river in Seoul, a pet project of President Lee Myung-bak when he was Mayor of Seoul, Thomas Kern and Alexander Ruser look at aspects of the role of South Korean think tanks, and David Shim examines what 'green growth' really means. Werner Pascha and Durgesh Rai deal with South Korean economic matters, and Mark Morris returns with another entertaining examination of the South Korean cinema. North Korean issues are covered in papers by Daniel Schwekendiek and Dafna Zur. Feedback about any of these papers, or about the volume as a whole, would be most welcome. We are grateful to those of our readers who have done so for past volumes. For the next edition, the editors hope for a similar set of wide-ranging contributions. As has been said before, we are particularly interested in papers dealing with North Korea and inter-Korean affairs or those that analyse Korean affairs from a comparative perspective. Contributions are welcome from both junior and senior scholars. What we are looking for is clear thinking, well expressed.

Charles Armstrong in the United States and Sung-hoon Park in the Republic of Korea continue to provide support as associate editors. They were joined in 2010 by Stephen Epstein from Victoria University of Wellington in New Zealand, who will serve as associate editor in the Oceania region. The editors would like to express their gratitude once again to the Academy of Korean Studies for providing a publication grant, and to thank Albert Hoffstädt and Patricia Radder and their colleagues at Brill, who have encouraged the project from its first inception. We remain grateful to Emeritus Professor Keith Pratt and the Design and Imaging Unit at Durham University for making available the map reproduced in the yearbook. Special thanks are as always due to Siegrid Woelk who has once more done a fine job of producing the camera-ready copy.

James E. Hoare, Rüdiger Frank, Patrick Köllner, Susan Pares

London, Vienna, Hamburg, May 2010

CHRONOLOGY OF EVENTS IN THE KOREAN PENINSULA 2009

SOUTH KOREA

03.01.09	Vice-Foreign Minister Lee Yong-joon visits Myanmar and Laos to discuss issue of North Korean defectors seeking shelter there.
12.01.09	President Lee Myung-bak and Japanese Prime Minister Taro Aso meet in Seoul.
16-28.01.09	Speaker of National Assembly visits Jordan, Turkey and UAE.
05.02.09	National Assembly gives voting rights to South Koreans living abroad in presidential and parliamentary elections, starting in 2012.
16.02.09	Death of Cardinal Kim Sou-hwan (Cardinal Stephen Kim).
19-20.02.09	US Secretary of State Clinton visits ROK as part of 4-nation Asian tour, meets President Lee.
24.02.09	Iraqi President Jalal Talabani visits South Korea, meets President Lee. Agreement on oil-for-development deal.
01.03.09	90th anniversary of March First Movement celebrated.
02-08.03.09	President Lee visits New Zealand, Australia and Indonesia, announces New Asia Initiative to improve relations with Asian neighbours.
09-20.03.09	Joint US-ROK annual military exercise, Key Resolve and Foal Eagle.
02.04.09	2nd G20 summit held in London, ROK one of co-chairs.
10.04.09	ROK and ASEAN sign FTA on services.
19-21.04.09	Prime Minister Han Seung-soo attends opening of Hannover fair, Germany, 19.04.09; visits Czech Republic, 20-21.04.09.
01.05.09	FTA on services between ROK and 6 members of ASEAN enters into force.

10-14.05.09	President Lee visits Uzbekistan and Kazakhstan. Agreement with both countries to develop energy sources.
21.05.09	Seoul High Court acquits 6 people wrongfully convicted in 1981 of forming anti-government group.
23.05.09	Former President Roh Moo-hyun commits suicide.
01-02.06.09	ROK-ASEAN commemorative summit on Cheju island. FTA on bilateral investment signed, 02.06.09.
11.06.09	ROK's 1st space centre opens at Kohŭng.
15-17.06.09	President Lee visits US, meets President Obama, 16.06.09. US undertakes to use all necessary means, including nuclear weapons, to defend ROK against DPRK military threats.
22.06.09	Prime ministers of ROK and UAE sign agreement in Dubai on co-operation in nuclear energy.
27.06.09	World Heritage Committee inscribes 40 Chosŏn-dynasty tombs located in South Korea on list of UNESCO World Heritage sites.
28.06.09	President Lee and Japanese Prime Minister Aso meet in Tokyo.
07-09.07.09	ROK websites, including the Blue House, and US government websites come under cyber attack. DPRK involvement suspected, but not proved.
07-14.07.09	President Lee visits Poland, Italy and Sweden. Attends G8 summit in Italy and meets Pope Benedict XVI.
13.07.09	President Lee announces conclusion of negotiations on ROK-EU FTA.
13.07.09	Deployment of ROK troops in Lebanon as part of UNIFIL extended until end 2010.
17.07.09	ROK Foreign Ministry condemns renewed Japanese claim to Tokto, carried in 2009 Japanese defence white paper.
21.07.09	Cia-Cia language textbooks written in *han'gŭl* distributed to elementary school students on Buton island, Indonesia, as Cia-Cia tribe adopts *hang'gŭl* as official writing system for its language.
06-08.08.09	Indian Minister of Commerce Sharma visits ROK, signs Comprehensive Economic Partnership Agreement with ROK, 07.08.09.

17-27.08.09	Joint ROK-US annual military exercises, Ulchi Freedom Guardian.
18.08.09	Death of former President Kim Dae-jung.
23.08.09	State funeral for Kim Dae-jung in Seoul.
25.08.09	ROK launches 1st satellite-carrying rocket from Naro space centre, but fails to establish contact with satellite.
03.09.09	Chung Un-chan designated as new prime minister. National Assembly gives approval, 28.09.09.
20-26.09.09	In US, President Lee attends UN summit on climate change, meeting of United Nations General Assembly (UNGA) and 3rd G20 summit.
15.10.09	ROK and EU initial FTA in Brussels.
20-25.10.09	President Lee visits Vietnam and Cambodia, attends 2009 ASEAN summit and ASEAN+3 meetings in Thailand.
22.10.09	In Seoul, US Secretary of Defence reaffirms US commitment to provide extended deterrence for ROK, including US nuclear umbrella, if needed, against DPRK.
31.10.09	Death of Lee Hu-rak, former director of KCIA.
18-20.11.09	President Obama visits ROK as part of 4-nation Asian tour. He and President Lee discuss North Korean nuclear issue and ratification of ROK-US FTA, 19.11.09.
24.11.09	2nd Korea-Africa Forum, held in Seoul, attended by President Wade of Senegal and other leading African officials. ROK pledges to double aid to Africa by 2012.
06-07.12.09	Canadian Prime Minister Harper visits ROK, discusses negotiations on Canadian-ROK FTA.
16-19.12.09	Chinese Vice-President Xi Jinping visits ROK.
17-18.12.09	President Lee attends Copenhagen climate change conference.
26-27.12.09	President Lee visits UAE, meets President Khalifa bin Zayed Al Nahyan, signs nuclear energy deal after ROK secures UAE project to construct 4 nuclear reactors.

NORTH KOREA

01.01.09	Joint new year editorial from *Rodong Shinmun*, *Chosŏn Inmingun* and *Ch'ŏngnyŏn Chŏnwi*.
08.01.09	21,000 metric tons of US food aid arrives in DPRK.
13.01.09	DPRK releases Yoshiaki Sawada, a Japanese citizen held as suspected drugs dealer since 2003, on humanitarian grounds.
17.01.09	US scholar Selig Harrison says DPRK reports it has weaponised the 30.8 kg of plutonium listed in its formal declaration.
21-24.01.09	Wang Jiarui, director of International Liaison Department of Chinese Communist Party's Central Committee, visits DPRK, meets Kim Jong Il, 23.01.09.
03-07.02.09	7 former US government officials and experts, including Stephen Bosworth, visit DPRK.
04.02.09	KCNA reports Chinese government decision to offer free aid to DPRK.
14.02.09	UN Population Fund says 2008 census data show DPRK population had reached 24.05 million as of 01.10.08. Report confirmed by KCNA, 16.12.09.
16.02.09	Kim Jong Il's 67th birthday marked in DPRK.
26.02.09	4 DPRK officials leave for 10-day trip to US at invitation of US humanitarian aid organisations.
01.03.09	90th anniversary of March First Movement marked.
08.03.09	Elections for deputies to Supreme People's Assembly (SPA).
12.03.09	DPRK informs International Civil Aviation Organisation (ICAO) and International Maritime Organisation (IMO) that it plans to launch a satellite between 04.04.09 and 08.04.09. It also announces that it has recently signed up to 2 international treaties on space exploration.
17.03.09	2 US journalists detained on Sino-DPRK border, allegedly for intruding into DPRK territory.
17.03.09	US reports DPRK has said it no longer wishes to receive US food aid. NGOs supported by USAID announce, 19.03.09, that DPRK has asked them to close food aid distribution programme agreed in May 2008.

17-21.03.09	Premier Kim Yong Il visits China, launches Year of DPRK-China Friendship with Chinese Premier Wen Jiabao, 18.03.09.
31.03.09	DPRK announces it will indict 2 US journalists detained on 17.03.09 on charges of illegal entry and hostile acts.
05.04.09	DPRK launches 3-stage rocket over East Sea, described as satellite launch vehicle.
09.04.09	At 12th SPA, Kim Jong Il re-elected chair of National Defence Commission. Constitution revised. New ministers of railways, forestry, electric power, agriculture and metal industry named.
09.04.09	Japan extends existing sanctions against DPRK for a year.
15.04.09	97th anniversary of Kim Il Sung's birth marked.
24.04.09	DPRK announces it will refer 2 US journalists to trial.
25.04-19.05.09	Foreign Minister Pak Ui Chun visits Cuba, Peru and Brazil. Attends ministerial meeting of Co-ordination Bureau of Non-aligned Movement (NAM) in Cuba, 27-30.04.09; signs agreement on co-operation with Cuba, 04.05.09.
04.05.09	*Rodong Shinmun* announces national '150-day battle' in support of economy.
06-15.05.09	President of SPA Presidium Kim Yong Nam visits Singapore, South Africa and Zimbabwe. Attends President Zuma's inauguration in South Africa, 09.05.09.
25.05.09	DPRK conducts 2nd nuclear test and launches 2 short-range missiles. Further 3 short-range missiles launched, 26.05.09.
04-08.06.09	Trial of 2 detained US journalists; sentenced, 08.06.09, to 12 years' labour reform for unspecified 'grave crime against the Korean nation'.
18.06.09	Japan imposes ban on all trade with DPRK until April 2010.
18.06.09	DPRK qualifies for place in 2010 World Cup finals in South Africa.
24.06.09	President Obama extends sanctions on commerce with DPRK for further year.

24.06.09	Pentagon announces it is monitoring several DPRK ships for allegedly carrying weapons of mass destruction.
02.07.09	DPRK test-fires 4 short-range missiles over East Sea.
04.07.09	DPRK test-fires 7 short-range missiles over East Sea.
11-20.07.09	Kim Yong Nam attends 15th NAM summit in Egypt.
22.07.09	Formation of Ministry of Foodstuff and Daily Necessities Industry announced.
04-05.08.09	Former US president Bill Clinton visits DPRK to negotiate release of 2 US journalists. Conveys verbal message from President Obama to Kim Jong Il. Kim announces pardon for journalists, who leave Pyongyang with Clinton, 05.08.09.
27.08.09	DPRK officials reported to have met US relief organisations in Los Angeles to discuss resumption of food aid to DPRK.
03.09.09	DPRK permanent representative to UN sends letter to president of UN Security Council (UNSC) announcing that DPRK has entered final phase of uranium enrichment and of reprocessing of spent fuel rods and that extracted plutonium is being weaponised.
08-12.09.09	Kyodo News Agency delegation visits DPRK.
16.09.09	Completion of first phase of construction of Pyongyang University of Science and Technology marked; 20-member delegation from ROK attends.
16-18.09.09	Dai Bingguo, special envoy of Chinese President Hu Jintao, visits DPRK; meets Kim Jong Il, 18.09.09, delivers letter from Hu.
18.09.09	State Science and Technology Commission revived at cabinet level.
21.09.09	Korean Workers' Party calls for 100-day extension to 150-day campaign launched on 20.04.09 in support of economy.
25.09.09	Food shipment donated by Russian government arrives in DPRK.
28.09.09	Full text of constitution, revised by SPA, made public.
30.09.09	UN Development Programme resumes operations in DPRK.
04-06.10.09	Chinese Premier Wen Jiabao visits DPRK, to celebrate 60 years of diplomatic relations.

12.10.09	DPRK test-fires 5 short-range missiles over East Sea.
13-15.10.09	US pastor Revd Franklin Graham visits DPRK.
17-20.10.09	General secretary of World Council of Churches (WCC) visits DPRK at invitation of Korean Christian Federation.
26-28.10.09	Syrian government economic delegation visits DPRK, signs agreements on co-operation.
09-13.11.09	Jack Lang, special envoy of President Sarkozy, visits DPRK, reports DPRK willing to have exchange on human rights with France.
19.11.09	UNGA adopts resolution condemning DPRK for systemic violations of human rights. ROK one of co-sponsors. Resolution approved, 18.12.09.
21-24.11.09	3 US experts on Korean affairs visit DPRK.
23.11-04.12.09	DPRK delegation attends 26th general assembly of IMO in London.
30.11.09	Reports indicate that DPRK replaces domestic currency with new notes at exchange rate of 1 new note to 100 old ones.
09.12.09	DPRK confirms outbreak of A/H1N1 influenza in Pyongyang and Shinŭiju.
10-15.12.09	Delegation from US-DPRK Scientific Engagement Consortium visits DPRK, discusses opportunities for exchange and collaboration.
12.12.09	Georgian-registered aircraft allegedly carrying DPRK-produced weapons detained by Thai authorities at Bangkok airport.
14-17.12.09	US business delegation in DPRK.
16.12.09	KCNA announces SPA has adopted new economic laws on property management, commodities consumption and import of facilities.
17.12.09	DPRK accepts French proposal to set up permanent office for humanitarian and cultural co-operation in Pyongyang.
25.12.09	DPRK detains US citizen Robert Park when he enters DPRK across border with China.

Inter-Korean Relations and Six Party Talks

09, 16.01.09	Small food shipments arrive in DPRK from ROK non-governmental sources.
12.01.09	US Secretary of State Clinton says she would engage with DPRK bilaterally as well as through Six Party Talks to address DPRK's nuclear programme and proliferation.
15-19.01.09	Nuclear delegation from ROK visits DPRK to explore possibility of buying spent nuclear fuel rods.
17.01.09	KPA General Staff warns ROK of DPRK's military 'confrontational posture'. Repeats warning, 18.02.09.
19.01.09	Hyun In-taek replaces Kim Ha-joong as ROK minister of unification.
30.01.09	DPRK Committee for Peaceful Reunification of the Fatherland states all agreements preventing confrontation between North and South would be nullified and inter-Korean sea border regarded as void.
19-20.02.09	3rd meeting on Northeast Asia peace and security mechanism within framework of Six Party Talks held in Moscow.
20.02.09	Secretary of State Clinton announces appointment of Stephen Bosworth as US Special Representative for North Korea Policy.
23.02.09	ROK Ministry of Defence 2008 white paper terms DPRK armed forces an 'immediate and grave threat'.
02.03.09	1st general-level inter-Korean talks for 6 years held at P'anmunjŏm. DPRK condemns upcoming ROK-US annual military exercises.
02-10.03.09	Stephen Bosworth visits China, Japan and ROK to discuss resumption of Six Party Talks.
05.03.09	DPRK warns it cannot guarantee security of ROK civil aircraft flying though DPRK territorial air space during ROK-US joint military exercises. ICAO issues formal letter of protest to DPRK, 12.03.09.
06.03.09	16th general-level inter-Korean military talks at P'anmunjŏm. DPRK repeats warning over ROK civil aircraft.
09.03.09	KPA General Staff closes military communications channel controlling cross-border traffic at Kaesŏng

	Industrial Complex (KIC) and Mt Kŭmgang tourist zone for 1 day in protest at ROK-US joint military exercises. Border crossing to KIC closed further 2 times, 13.03.09 and 20.03.09, before re-opening for 3rd time, 21.03.09, and military communication line restored.
30.03.09	ROK employee of Hyundai Asan, Yu Sŏng-jin, detained at KIC, accused of criticising DPRK regime and of inciting woman worker to defect.
09.04.09	DPRK abolishes cabinet committee on economic co-operation with ROK.
13.04.09	UNSC urges DPRK to comply fully with its obligations under Resolution 1718, calls for tightening of sanctions against DPRK, urges early resumption of Six Party Talks.
14.04.09	In response, DPRK announces it is leaving Six Party Talks, will not abide by agreements reached at talks, and is restoring its nuclear facilities.
15.04.09	IAEA states its international inspectors have been asked to remove their surveillance equipment and leave DPRK. 4 US monitors also preparing to leave.
21.04.09	1st official inter-Korean governmental meeting for over a year, held in Kaesŏng. DPRK seeks negotiations for operational changes at KIC, announces it intends to review special benefits for ROK firms on land fees and cheap labour.
29.04.09	DPRK calls on UNSC to apologise for having infringed DPRK sovereignty and to withdraw its resolutions on DPRK, otherwise DPRK will take defensive measures.
04.05.09	ROK states it has expanded its nuclear task force established in 2008 to deal with DPRK nuclear programme.
07-12.05.09	Stephen Bosworth visits China, ROK and Japan to discuss stalled Six Party Talks.
12.05.09	ROK Unification Ministry announces closure of its bureau for humanitarian aid to DPRK and creation of new bureau for analysis of DPRK internal politics.
15.05.09	DPRK declares void all contracts and agreements regarding KIC, announces it will raise wages for DPRK

	workers and collect land tax fees from ROK companies.
24.05.09	KCNA reports death of former ROK president Roh Moo-hyun. Kim Jong Il offers condolences, 25.05.09.
26.05.09	ROK announces it will become full member of Proliferation Security Initiative (PSI).
27.05.09	DPRK announces it views ROK participation in PSI as declaration of war and threatens retaliation if ROK attempts to search its vessels.
11.06.09	At inter-Korean talks on KIC at Kaesŏng, DPRK demands quadrupling of wages for its workers and 30-fold increase in rents.
12.06.09	UNSC unanimously passes resolution 1874 following DPRK's nuclear test of 25.05.09: all weapons exports from DPRK and most arms imports banned, UN member states authorised to inspect cargo vessels suspected of carrying military materials into or out of DPRK.
13.06.09	DPRK denounces resolution 1874, says DPRK will weaponise existing plutonium stocks, begin uranium-enrichment programme and take military action if US and allies attempt to isolate country.
19.06.09	At inter-Korean meeting, DPRK offers to lift restrictions on all ROK access to KIC; but meeting fails to reach agreement on wages and rents. Further meeting, 02.07.09, also fails to reach agreement on future of KIC.
06.07.09	UNSC condemns DRPK's firing of 7 ballistic missiles on 04.07.09 as violation of UN resolutions.
12-13.07.09	Chinese Vice-Foreign Minister Wu Dawei visits ROK, expresses support for bringing DPRK back to Six Party Talks, rather than 5-way gathering.
15.07.09	Kim Yong Nam, speaking at 15th NAM summit, confirms DPRK has no intention of returning to Six Party Talks.
01-08.08.09	7 workers from ROK branch of World Vision visit DPRK.
10-17.08.09	Hyundai Group chairwoman Hyun Jung-eun visits DPRK, meets Kim Jong Il, 16.08.09.
13.08.09	Hyundai Asan employee Yu Sŏng-jin released from detention.

17.08.09	Hyundai Asan and DPRK agree to resume inter-Korean tourism projects, re-energise operations at KIC and provide family reunions.
19.08.09	Kim Jong Il sends message of condolence to family on death of former ROK President Kim Dae-jung.
20.08.09	DPRK says it will restore road and rail cross-border traffic to level before imposition of restrictions on 01.12.08.
21-23.08.09	DPRK delegation visits Seoul to join in mourning for Kim Dae-jung; meets President Lee Myung-bak and delivers verbal message from Kim Jong Il, 23.08.09.
23.08.09	Kim Yang Gon, head of KWP's unification front department and member of DPRK delegation, and Hyun In-taek, ROK minister of unification, meet in Seoul.
25.08.09	North-South Red Cross telephone link re-opens.
26-28.08.09	North and South Red Cross officials meet at Mt Kŭmgang for talks on family reunions.
28.08.09	UAE reported to have seized ship carrying DPRK weapons to Iran.
01.09.09	ROK and DPRK lift land border restrictions.
02.09.09	Military communications link in western sector of North-South border re-opened.
04-06.09.09	Stephen Bosworth visits ROK, confirms US would only talk to DPRK within framework of Six Party Talks.
06.09.09	DPRK opens dams on Imjin river, releasing wave of water that kills 6 ROK citizens camping by river. ROK demands explanation for incident from DPRK, 08.09.09; states discharge of dam water violation of international law, 11.09.09.
07.09.09	Inter-Korean joint economic office at KIC re-opens.
16.09.09	Agreement on raising minimum wage for DPRK workers at KIC by 5%.
21, 23.09.09	President Lee offers DPRK 'grand bargain': to give up nuclear weapons in return for security guarantees and aid within context of Six Party Talks. DPRK rejects proposal, 30.09.09.
26.09-01.10.09	17th session of family reunions held at Mt Kŭmgang.

05.10.09	Kim Jong Il tells visiting Chinese Premier Wen Jiabao that DPRK might return to multilateral talks, depending on outcome of bilateral dialogue with US.
14.10.09	Inter-Korean working-level meetings at Kaesŏng to discuss flood control on Imjin river. DPRK expresses regret over deaths of 6 South Koreans on 06.09.09.
21-23.10.09	Delegation from Korean Christian Federation of DPRK attends WCC meeting in Hong Kong together with church representatives from ROK.
24-27.10.09	Sung Kim, US special representative to Six Party Talks, and Ri Gun, director-general of North American affairs bureau in DPRK foreign ministry, hold informal meetings at two locations in US between these dates.
26.10.09	ROK Red Cross offers limited amount of food aid and medicine to DPRK Red Cross. DPRK rejects offer, 10.11.09.
28.10.09	ROK sends communication equipment to DPRK to allow upgrading of telephone and fax lines used to approve border crossings.
18.11.09	ROK rejects DPRK requests to resume tours to Mt Kŭmgang tourist area. DPRK reported, 22.11.09, to have proposed inter-Korean talks on ROK's security concerns.
08-10.12.09	Stephen Bosworth visits DPRK, delivers personal letter from President Obama to Kim Jong Il.
08.12.09	ROK offers DPRK assistance against spread of influenza A virus. Offer accepted, 14.12.09. ROK delivers anti-viral drugs to DPRK via Kaesŏng, 18.12.09.
12-22.12.09	Joint inter-Korean inspection team visits factories in Chinese and Vietnamese industrial parks in effort to improve international competitiveness of KIC.
28.12.09	ROK government announces decision to donate 26 billion won for humanitarian projects in DPRK, via WHO, UNICEF and private aid groups.
30.12.09	Cross-border military lines of communication in east and west sectors opened after modernisation.

Chronologies prepared by Susan Pares from the following sources: Cankor (Canada-Korea Electronic Information Service), *Korea, Korea Focus*, North Korea Newsletter, *Vantage Point*, Yonhap News Agency.

SOUTH KOREA IN 2009: DOMESTIC DEVELOPMENTS AND THE ECONOMY

Patrick Köllner

1 INTRODUCTION

Grief, anger, relief and pride were some of the more intense emotions aroused by political and economic developments in the Republic of Korea (ROK—South Korea) in 2009. Grief and mourning were caused by the deaths of former presidents Roh Moo-hyun and Kim Dae-jung. The death of Roh Moo-hyun, who committed suicide barely fifteen months after he had left office, also aroused an outburst of anger not only among his more ardent supporters. The anger was directed at the government of President Lee Myung-bak, which stood accused of having persecuted Roh by means of bribery charges, thereby putting the former president under enormous stress and eventually leading to his suicide. Protests following on the heels of Roh's death highlighted again political fissures, which characterise today's South Korean society. Deep-seated antagonism dividing government and opposition also shaped parliamentary proceedings in 2009.

In a more positive vein, the global financial and economic crisis, which had hit South Korea will full force in autumn 2008, proved less disastrous than many had feared. On the back of a full set of state-led anti-crisis measures and helped to no small degree by the export-related success of a number of the leading business conglomerates, the South Korean economy even rebounded in the latter part of 2009, much to the relief of policymakers and ordinary citizens. South Korea also scored a diplomatic triumph in 2009, when the country was chosen as host of a high-profile G20 summit meeting scheduled for November 2010, which is set to focus on the architecture of global finance and on coming up with a co-ordinated 'exit strategy' from state-led crisis management. Becoming the first Asian country to co-chair the G20—perceived by some as a new 'global directorate'—has provided many South Koreans with a sense of pride, symbolising as it does full international recognition of the country's phenomenal rise from 'rags to riches' in the course of just a few decades. Since South Korea's diplomatic record in 2009 is covered in some detail in the relevant overview article in this yearbook, this article focuses in the following on domestic developments, starting with the demise of former presidents Roh Moo-hyun and Kim Dae-jung.

2 SOUTH KOREA LOSES TWO FORMER PRESIDENTS

In early spring 2009, former President Roh Moo-hyun, who had retired from politics after his term in the Blue House (2003-08), made headlines when prosecutors investigated accusations that, while in office, he had taken millions of dollars in bribes from the wealthy head of a shoe-manufacturing company located in Roh's former home base of Pusan. Investigations centred on a payment of US$1 million to Roh's wife and another of US$5 million from the same businessman to the husband of one of Roh's nieces. Prosecutors thought that the latter payment finally ended up in the hands of Roh's son Gun-ho. (In a separate bribery case, Roh Moo-hyun's elder brother Gun-pyeong had been sentenced in 2008 to four years in prison.) In a statement on his website released in early April, Roh denied personal wrongdoing but admitted that his wife had indeed taken the money. According to Roh, no bribery had taken place but the US$1 million in question constituted a loan to his wife to pay off personal debts, while the payment of the larger amount involved a legitimate business investment. Still, the former president was summoned for intensive grilling at the Supreme Public Prosecutor's Office in Seoul at the end of the month. Before travelling to Seoul for questioning—his every step from his home in the southeast to the prosecutor's office was covered by reporters and was also televised live on TV—Roh apologised to the public over the corruption probe, declaring that he felt ashamed and that he was sorry for causing them disappointment.

The 62-year-old Roh became the third South Korean ex-president to be questioned on corruption charges. (Former presidents Chun Doo-hwan and Roh Tae-woo had also personally faced a criminal probe.) In total, five former presidents including Roh have been tarnished by cash-for-influence scandals involving either themselves or their family. What particularly took Koreans aback was that such accusations were levelled against Roh Moo-hyun, given that in his campaigning for presidential office he had emphasised his determination to combat corruption in South Korea. While prosecutors were still deciding on whether to arrest and formally press charges against Roh, the former president committed suicide on 23 May 2009 by jumping from a cliff near his residence in the village of Pongha, South Kyŏngsang province. In a suicide note found in his computer, he wrote that 'what is left for me for the rest of my life is just to be a burden to others', adding that no one should be blamed for this death. With his reputation tainted by the corruption probe, Roh decided to end it all.[1]

South Koreans were stunned and reacted with disbelief at the news of the former president's suicide. Even citizens who had never supported him politically were saddened or even overcome by sorrow by the nature of his premature death. Reportedly, about one million citizens paid their respects in Roh's southeastern hometown in the first few days after his death and double that number found their way to makeshift altars set up in different parts of the country or attended the final public funeral ceremony in downtown Seoul on 29 May. Soon after the first shock had settled, however, reactions to Roh's fateful decision diverged. The *Donga Ilbo* in an editorial said 'that the lawyer-turned-president has chosen such an extreme way in the face of questioning leaves something to be desired'. While conservative newspapers in general mourned Roh's death, they also argued that the issue should not be politicised (*Straits Times*, 25 and 26 May 2009). Yet many South Koreans felt angry, believing that the corruption investigation that had come to embroil Roh had been politically motivated. Supporters of Roh insinuated that the investigation against the former president had been an attempt by the government to undermine progressive political forces and some even went as far as accusing President Lee Myung-bak of having driven Roh to his death. Opposition parties joined the chorus, demanding an apology and the resignation of the whole cabinet. They also claimed that the prosecutors had leaked details of the investigation to the press on purpose without showing any respect to the former state leader.

The government, bent on preventing the kind of massive political protests that had shaken South Korea the year before,[2] tried its best at damage control, with President Lee expressing his condolences to his

---

[1] Numerous obituaries covered the life and achievements of Roh Moo-hyun. For international examples, see BBC News (2009) and Foster-Carter (2009).

[2] See the overview chapter on South Korea in 2008 in *Korea Yearbook 2009*, pp. 18-24.

predecessor's family and the government at large emphasising that the investigation had been independently conducted. Roh's death also led the government to put an end to the investigation, and in early June the prosecutor-general quit to take responsibility for his role in the corruption probe. In the end, and in contrast to the year before, public protests remained limited in scope and duration. (According to the police, an anti-government rally on 10 June, the 22nd anniversary of the 1987 pro-democracy uprising, drew only 12,000 people, cf. *Straits Times*, 10 June 2009.) Still, public sympathy over the former president's death boosted, if only temporarily, support for the opposition Democratic Party (DP)—which overtook the ruling Grand National Party (GNP) in a survey on party support released in early June—and also made it more difficult for the incumbent president to push through legislative bills at the extraordinary session of parliament in June (see section 3 below). On a different note, Roh Moo-hyun's death also put the spotlight on South Korea's worsening suicide problem—the ROK already has the highest suicide rate among the 30 member states of the OECD. According to statistics from the World Health Organisation, the suicide rate in South Korea doubled between 1995 and 2006 to about 22 such deaths per 100,000 people, with social workers blaming the high rate on 'heightened pressure to succeed in South Korea's increasingly wealthy society combined with a breakdown of traditional family support systems' (Schuman 2009).

Three months after Roh's suicide, South Korea mourned the death of another former president. The 85-year old Kim Dae-jung, a devout Catholic, who had led the country from 1998 to 2003, died on 18 August after having been taken to hospital with pneumonia the month before. Shortly before his death, Kim had crossed swords with the current president, likening Lee to a dictator. In response, the government had demanded that Kim refrain from inappropriate intervention in politics. Still, at the news of Kim's serious illness, political opponents of Kim Dae-jung, including former President Kim Young-sam but also Lee Myung-bak himself, rushed to the hospital to make their peace with the dying former president. After Kim had passed away, Lee Myung-bak said in a statement that Kim's accomplishments and aspirations to achieve democratisation and inter-Korean reconciliation would long be remembered by the people. Numerous obituaries in local and international media likewise paid tribute to Kim's long and persistent struggle against South Korea's military dictatorships as a pro-democracy activist and opposition lawmaker, and to his role as the president who reached out to the Democratic People's Republic of Korea (North Korea) and tried to bring it in from the cold. (For his efforts at inter-Korean conciliation, epitomised by his 'Sunshine policy' and the 2000 first inter-Korean summit, but also for his efforts to improve relations with neighbouring countries, in particular Japan, Kim had received the Nobel Peace Prize in 2000.)

Kim's legacy was somewhat tarnished by revelations that the Kim Jong Il regime had received US$500 million under the table before the summit. Neither was Kim's policy of providing generous aid to the North without much in (immediate) return well received by everyone in South Korea. In fact, Kim Dae-jung was held in higher esteem abroad, where he was widely seen as the 'Mandela of South Korea', than at home, where many saw him as part of the faction-ridden and unable-to-compromise political establishment. Yet after his death there was widespread recognition that South Korea had lost a great champion of democracy and peaceful development on the Korean peninsula. Obituaries noted that Kim 'remains the country's only politician to have emerged as a truly international figure' (Breen 2009) and that polls had repeatedly shown that South Koreans ranked Kim only behind Park Chung-hee as the Korean who most influenced the nation's modern history (Lee 2009). Kim was heralded posthumously as a 'courageous patriot' and a 'moral hero of modern Korea'.[3] More than 100,000 people visited the 175 mourning altars that had been set up nationwide. An official funeral service was held at the National Assembly to honour Kim Dae-jung's contribution to bringing democracy to South Korea. Even a high-level North Korean delegation visited the South to join the mourning for the former president. Never before had North Korean officials travelled to the ROK to pay tribute to a former South Korean president.

---

[3] See respectively Richard Halloran, 'In Memoriam: Kim Dae Jung', in: *Straits Times*, 24 August 2009; and Gittings (2009). For other English-language assessments of Kim's achievements see e.g. Michael Breen, 'Obituary: Kim Dae-jung', in: *Far Eastern Economic Review*, 25 August 2009, and Christian Oliver, 'Obituary: Kim Dae-jung', in: *Financial Times*, 19 August 2009, p. 2. For a detailed chronology of Kim's life see *Korea Times* (2009).

3 PARLIAMENTARY (IN)ACTION

Despite the fact that the ruling party commanded a comfortable parliamentary majority (see below), fierce resistance from the opposition prevented the government of Lee Myung-bak from passing major reform bills until mid-2009.[4] The death of Roh Moo-hyun led to a deferral of the extraordinary parliamentary session that had been scheduled to start on 1 June. Demands for an apology by Lee Myung-bak for Roh's suicide and an official investigation into the case, which had been tabled by the DP and minor opposition parties as pre-conditions for attending the parliamentary session, were rejected by the GNP and its ally, the Pro-Park Alliance, and the two latter parties decided unilaterally to convene the session on 26 June. In response, the DP initially boycotted the extraordinary session and occupied the hall in front of the main chamber of the Assembly. Only after repeated warnings from the Speaker of the Assembly that he would invoke his right to call for floor votes on disputed bills did the DP decide to take part in the session from 12 July onwards. Lawmakers then passed a motion to extend the deployment of the South Korean military in Lebanon by 18 months but locked horns again over contentious bills on the media and on temporary workers, with both the ruling and the main opposition parties staging sit-ins at the main chamber to prevent the other side from taking over the speaker's podium. DP chairman Chung Sye-kung even went on a hunger strike to protest against three bills tabled by the government to revise the country's media laws. Governing legislators, aided by security guards, had to overcome physical resistance by opposition lawmakers to finally pass the bills on 22 July.

Under the revised laws, newspaper companies controlling less than 20 percent of the local market (in practice, all newspaper companies) and business conglomerates with less than ten trillion won (around US$8 billion) will be allowed to invest in private broadcasters including TV stations and cable news networks. New investors are, however, barred from exercising management rights until 2012. The new laws effectively end the ban on cross-ownerships of newspapers and broadcasters, which had been introduced in the 1980s to prevent monopolies in the media market. The government argued that a lifting of the ban would spur competition in South Korea's media market and

---

[4] See also the overview chapter on South Korea in 2008 in *Korea Yearbook 2009*, pp. 27-28.

help the sector against falling behind internationally. The bills eventually passed were more restrictive than the GNP had originally planned. Modifications of the original bills had taken place to placate intra-party critics and the opposition. The latter however condemned the new laws, believing that the three major conservative dailies would henceforth acquire stakes in broadcasters and help the incumbent government to control public opinion, reducing the opposition's chance to gain power. Government lawmakers also voted on a revision of bank ownership laws, which raised the maximum stake that non-financial companies can hold in financial holding firms from 4 to 9 percent.

Co-operating with minor opposition parties and civic groups, the DP continued its anti-media laws campaign in July and August, but suspended street rallies after the death of former President Kim Daejung. The party also called off a planned boycott of the 100-day regular parliamentary session scheduled to start on 1 September, fearing that it could suffer a public backlash if it continued to resort to divisive tactics. Among other contentious issues to be covered by the parliamentary session, a planned renewal of the law on temporary workers stood out. Under the law, which expired on 1 July, enterprises had been able to hire contract workers for up to two years. Given that South Korea had lost 169,000 jobs in the first five months of 2009 alone, the GNP had proposed to renew the law for another two years. Opposition parties and unions vehemently opposed an extension of the law, arguing that it put job security and decent wages out of reach for an increasing segment of the workforce (*Korea Herald*, 28 August 2009; *Straits Times*, 26 June 2009). The issue remained unresolved at the end of 2009.[5] The confrontation over the law on temporary workers occurred against the background of renewed high-profile labour unrest in South Korea. Hundreds of fired workers at Ssangyong Motor occupied the bankrupt carmaker's paint factory in P'yŏngt'aek, Kyŏnggi province, for 77 days between late May and early August. Finally, agreement was found to reduce the number of redundancies and to retain the rest of the workers on an unpaid basis (*JoongAng Ilbo*, 7 August 2009). While there were repeated clashes with riot police, the Ssangyong episode at least came to a relatively peaceful ending. A clash between riot police and aggrieved workers in Seoul had

---

[5] The National Assembly provides an English-language overview of recently enacted laws at http://korea.na.go.kr/res/tra_list.jsp.

led to six deaths in January 2009. Not the least because of the country's labour problems (as perceived and reported by international media), the 2009 survey on international competitiveness by the World Economic Forum ranked South Korea only at 19th position, six grades down from 2008.[6]

Moon Kook-hyun, the leader of Creative Korea Party, which had won three seats in the 2008 parliamentary election, lost his seat in the National Assembly on 22 October. The Supreme Court upheld an earlier high court verdict and sentenced Moon, a former CEO-turned-presidential candidate, to a suspended eight-month jail term. (Under the ROK's election law, legislators automatically lose their seats if sentenced to a jail term or fined one million won, i.e. around US$850.) The leader of the minority party had been charged in 2008 with having sold, before the general election in that year, a high slot on the party's candidate list for 600 million won (around US$480,000). Moon became the 16th lawmaker since the opening of the 18th National Assembly in 2008 to be stripped of his parliamentary seat because of violations of the campaign law (*Korea Times*, 22 October 2009). In five by-elections taking place on 28 October, the DP was able to regain a seat in North Ch'ungch'ŏng province and to win two more in Kyŏnggi province. The GNP only managed to win the other two seats up for grabs in South Kyŏngsang and in Kangwŏn province.[7] As a consequence of the by-elections, the ruling party retained its number of seats (169), while the DP improved to 86 seats in the 299-seat National Assembly (*Korea Times*, 28 October 2009).

4 A NEW CABINET AND THE TRAVAILS OF THE 'SEJONG CITY' PROJECT

On 3 September, President Lee reshuffled the cabinet. As prime minister-designate he chose Chung Un-chan, a 63-year-old economics professor and former president of Seoul National University (SNU).

---

[6] Christian Oliver and Song Jung-a, 'A militant tendency', in: *Financial Times*, 18 September 2009, p. 7.

[7] The GNP, however, did better than it had at the five by-elections that took place on 29 April 2009. There, the GNP had been unable to get a single candidate through, with the seats going respectively to three independent candidates and one candidate each from the DP and the New Progressive Party (a splinter of the Democratic Labour Party).

The nomination of the Princeton-educated Chung came as a surprise as he had earlier criticised neo-liberal policies pursued by President Lee. Chung is known to advocate an expanded social safety net and a more balanced distribution of wealth. His nomination was thus widely perceived to symbolise a more centrist and integrative policy approach by the government. Still, the nomination process did not go as smoothly as the president might have hoped. The opposition DP and the Liberty Forward Party charged Chung with having dodged military service, receiving substantial additional income courtesy of a businessman-patron and a consultancy agreement with an Internet bookseller run by a SNU alumnus (government employees including SNU professors are not allowed to have jobs on the side), and also with evading taxes. Chung denied all charges levelled against him and was finally confirmed on 28 September, with the opposition boycotting the vote. Some cabinet members retained their posts: Foreign Minister Yu Myung-hwan and Unification Minister Hyun In-taek stayed in office, indicating, together with the appointment of General Kim Tae-young, former chairman of the Joint Chiefs of Staff, as new defence minister, a continuation of both the pro-US and the hardline approach vis-à-vis the North, which has characterised the administration of Lee Myung-bak since its inception. Reshuffling took place at the heads of the ministries of Knowledge Economy, Justice, Labour, and Gender Equality. In addition, a new special minister in charge of handling political affairs was appointed.

One of the reasons why Chung got chosen as prime minister might have been the fact that he is a native of South Ch'ungch'ŏng province, the designated location of a new administrative town called Sejong City. The town project, which had been the brain child of former President Roh Moo-hyun, has experienced many twists and turns. The original idea, as presented to the public in 2002, had been to build from scratch a new capital around 150 kilometres away from Seoul in order to address imbalances in geographic development in the southern part of the peninsula. While the Ch'ungch'ŏng region in central Korea was expected to benefit substantially in terms of growth stimuli and infrastructure from the relocation of the capital, crowded Seoul on the other hand would be given some space to breathe. The relocation had been approved by the National Assembly in August 2004 but was ruled unconstitutional three months later. The Constitutional Court argued that an important national issue such as the relocation of the capital required a revision of the constitution or a national referendum.

In response, the then government redesigned the planned city as an administrative hub which would host 13 national ministries and government agencies. The GNP, then in opposition, at first opposed the administrative-hub plan but changed tack before the local elections in 2005.

When Lee Myung-bak campaigned for the presidency, he also voiced support for the administration-hub plan—not out of conviction, but in order not to drive away voters in the two Ch'ungch'ŏng provinces, which are considered swing regions when it comes to presidential elections. After he had won the presidency, Lee rescinded his support for the relocation of ministries, arguing that such a step was lacking in efficiency. Instead, he proposed to develop Sejong City into a science-and-business town. The challenge of attracting corporations and universities to the new city and of overcoming national and local resistance to the new plan—opposition parties advocate developing Sejong City into a co-capital with Seoul, while a GNP faction led by Park Geun-hye still favours the administrative-hub plan—has rested since September 2009 with the new prime minister. During his first 100 days in office, Chung launched a joint government-civilian panel to review alternatives and also paid a number of visits to the region to sound out people about the government's plans. If Chung manages the challenge well, he might even hope for higher political office. If not, he is likely to go down in oblivion.

5 SOUTH KOREA'S MIDDLE CLASS UNDER PRESSURE

'Middle class continues its contraction' and 'Shrinking of middle class stops' read the headings of two articles in English-language newspapers in South Korea in March 2010 (*Korea Herald* 2010; *Korea Times* 2010). Intriguingly, both readings of statistical data released by the government are correct. According to the Ministry of Finance and Strategy, the disposable income of middle-class households accounted for 66.7 percent of all such household income in 2009, down from the 70.1 percent registered in 2003, but marginally up from the 66.2 percent registered in 2008. Since 2003, both the upper- and the lower-income class have expanded at the expense of the middle class. The upper class's share of disposable income increased by 1.9 percentage points between 2003 and 2009 (reaching 20.2 percent in the latter year), while the lower-income class's share rose by 1.5 percent to reach 13.1 percent in 2003. (The middle class is defined as consisting of households earning between 50 and 150 percent of the nation's medium income. Everything above or below is considered upper- and lower-income class respectively. Households deriving their income from agriculture and fisheries and single-person households are excluded from the relevant surveys. The latter exclusion might in particular lead to a distortion of overall trends, as the proportion of single-person households rose from 15.6 percent in 2000 to 20.2 percent in 2009.)

The Ministry of Finance and Strategy suggested that population ageing and rapid technological advances lay mainly behind the decline of the middle class. While South Korea long epitomised 'growth with equity', the share of the middle class effectively began to shrink in the early 1990s, a development that was accelerated by the 1997-98 financial and economic crisis. (According to the Korea Development Institute, the middle class's share of income had stood at 75.2 percent in 1992.) The decline of the middle class is also reflected in other metrics. In May 2009, Statistics Korea announced that the Gini coefficient[8] had risen from 0.277 in 2003 to 0.293. The figure for urban workers stood at 0.324 in 2009, the highest figure since relevant data were first compiled in 1990. In terms of the interdecile ratio as applied to household earning, the top 10 percent of South Korean households earn 4.7 times as much as the bottom 10 percent. The OECD average is 4.2 (*Korea Times* 2010). While South Korea is still far away from the kind of income inequality that can be found in parts of Latin America or other places, the widening income gulf is worrying, as it lays, among other things, the basis for growing political discontent.

6 SOUTH KOREA'S ECONOMY IN 2009: THE BIG PICTURE

South Korea has weathered the financial and economic crisis, which had hit the global economy with full force in 2008, better than other major economies. While the South Korean economy experienced negative growth of 5.1 percent in the fourth quarter of 2008, the first quarter of 2009 already saw an end of the slump, with the economy registering a plus of 0.2 percent quarter on quarter. The upward trend

---

[8] The Gini index measures how wealth is distributed, with zero indicating perfect equality and one indicating perfect inequality.

quickened in the course of the year, with the third quarter even witnessing growth year on year. The final quarter's substantial growth then enabled the country to end the year in the black: according to provisional figures, the South Korean economy managed to grow—if only marginally—by 0.2 percent in 2009, while most other major economies experienced more or less severe recessions. That the world's 14th largest economy (ranking in 2008 behind Australia but well before Turkey) did much better in the face of the global crisis had, on the one hand, to do with the massive stimulus package the government injected into the economy. In relative terms, i.e. comparing the size of stimulus spending to the size of the overall economy in 2007, South Korea's fiscal spending constituted the second biggest among G20 countries (3.6 percent compared to Russia's 4.1 percent and the G20 average of 2.2 percent). The Samsung Economic Research Institute estimated that government spending alone boosted the South Korean economy by 1.5 percent in 2009. In other words, the ROK would have registered minus growth of 1.3 percent if it had not been for the large-scale stimulus provided from state coffers.[9] On the other hand, South Korea also enjoyed a better than expected foreign trade performance. While exports declined substantially from US$422 billion in 2008 to US$363.5 billion in 2009, imports shrunk even more, from US$435 billion in 2008 down to US$323 billion in 2009, leading to a trade surplus of over US$40 billion. Overall, South Korea registered a plus in the current balance of nearly US$43 billion in 2009 (figures for 2009 are provisional, see also Table 1 below).

The rebound of the South Korean economy did not, however, lead to the creation of many jobs. The unemployment rate, which had stood at 3.2 percent in both 2007 and 2008, rose to 3.6 in 2009 (before briefly reaching a ten-year high of 4.8 percent in January 2010). With many companies reluctant to hire new staff in the face of lingering uncertainties, unemployment has emerged as one of the dark clouds hanging over Asia's fourth largest economy. The South Korean government thinks that new sources of growth and jobs can be opened

---

[9] See Shin Chang-mook, 'Retrospect on the Korean economy in 2009', in: *Korea Focus*, spring 2010, pp. 103-04. The government's crisis management also included such measures as a substantial lowering of the base rate. For an analysis of the government's reaction to the crisis see Werner Pascha's article elsewhere in this book.

Table 1 ROK basic economic data

	2004	2005	2006	2007	2008	2009
GDP (billion won, at current prices)	826.9	865.2	908.7	975.0	1,026.5	1,063.1
GDP (billion US$)	722	845	951	1,049	931	833
GDP growth (%)	4.7	4.2	5.0	5.1	2.3	0.2
Per capita income (GDP base, in US$)	15,037	17,548	19,692	21,655	19,153	17,085
Exports (billion US$)	253.8	284.4	325.5	371.5	422.0	363.5
Imports (billion US$)	224.5	261.2	309.4	356.9	435.3	323.1
Trade balance (billion US$)	+29.4	+23.2	+16.1	+14.6	-13.3	+40.4
Balance of payments (billion US$)	+28.2	+15.0	+5.4	+5.9	-5.8	+42.7
Gross external debt (billion US$, end of year)	172.3	187.9	260.1	383.2	377.9	401.9
International reserves (billion US$, end of year)	198.2	210.0	238.4	261.8	201.2	270.0
Inward foreign direct investment (billion US$, notification basis)	12.8	11.6	11.2	10.5	11.7	11.5
Consumer prices (%)	+3.6	+2.8	+2.2	+2.5	+4.7	+2.8
Producer prices (%)	+6.1	+2.1	+2.3	+1.4	+8.6	-0.2
Unemployed (in thousands)	860	887	827	783	769	889
Unemployment rate (%)	3.7	3.7	3.5	3.2	3.2	3.6

Note: Data for 2010 provisional.
Sources: Bank of Korea, *Monthly Statistical Bulletin*, 4/2010 and earlier editions; Invest Korea, online: www.investkorea.org (accessed 26 April 2010).

up by tapping the potential of 'green industries',[10] by increasing the competitiveness of a number of the country's more domestically oriented sectors and by expanding trade and investment ties with other nations. In relation to the latter undertaking, South Korea, after three years of negotiations, signed a comprehensive economic partnership agreement (CEPA) with India in August and also initialled a free trade agreement with the EU in October.[11] As a bloc, the EU is South Korea's second-largest trading partner (after China) and the most important source of direct investment. Bilateral trade between the EU and South Korea declined to 53.5 billion Euros in 2009 (European Commission 2010).[12]

Both the Korea Composite Stock Price Index and the exchange rate of the won vis-à-vis the US dollar rallied in 2009, gaining 61.4 percent and 32.7 percent respectively, between early March, the low point, and late December. Still, for most of the year South Korean exporters enjoyed a substantial price advantage vis-à-vis competitors from, say, Japan. The world's biggest electronics manufacturer, Samsung Electronics, consolidated its position as the largest flat-screen TV maker and also gained on Nokia, the global market leader in mobile phones. Samsung was also able to supply, at an earlier date than others, innovative products such as light-emitting diode (LED)-backlit LCD television sets. LG Electronics finished 2009 as the world's number two TV maker and number three in terms of mobile telephones. In the car sector, the Hyundai-Kia Automotive Group overtook Ford to become the world's fourth biggest producer (after Toyota, General Motors and Volkswagen).

---

[10] For an assessment of South Korea's 'green growth' strategy see David Shim's article elsewhere in this yearbook. In November 2009, the South Korean cabinet approved a plan to reduce carbon-dioxide emissions by 2020 by 4 percent from 2005 levels (*Korea Times*, 17 November 2009).

[11] A CEPA is similar to a free trade agreement (FTA), but tariffs are reduced in phases. For an analytical overview of ROK-India economic relations, see the article by Durgesh K. Rai elsewhere in this yearbook.

[12] The text of the FTA, which was expected to be signed in the first half of 2010, can be found on the European Commission's webpage (European Commission 2009).

REFERENCES

BBC News (2009), 'Obituary: Roh Moo-hyun', 23 May 2009. Online: http://news.bbc.co.uk/2/hi/asia-pacific/2535143.stm (accessed 29 April 2010)

Breen, Michael (2009), 'Korea Loses Greatest Democrat', in: *Korea Times*, 18 August 2009. Online: http://www.koreatimes.co.kr/www/news/nation/2009/08/116_50300.html (accessed 25 April 2010)

European Commission (2009), 'EU-Korea Free Trade Agreement online'. Online: http://trade.ec.europa.eu/doclib/press/index.cfm?id=443 (accessed 26 May 2010)

European Commission (2010), 'South Korea: Main Economic Indicators'. Online: http://trade.ec.europa.eu/doclib/docs/2006/september/tradoc_113448.pdf (accessed 26 May 2010)

Foster-Carter, Aidan (2009), 'Obituary: Roh Moo-hyun', in: *Guardian*, 24 May 2009. Online: http://www.guardian.co.uk/world/2009/may/24/roh-moo-hyun-obituary (accessed 29 April 2010)

Gittings, John (2009), 'Obituary: Kim Dae-jung', in: *Guardian*, 18 August 2009. Online: http://www.guardian.co.uk/world/2009/aug/18/obituary-kim-dae-jung (accessed 26 May 2010)

Korea Herald (2010), 'Middle class continues its contraction', 17 March 2010. Online: http://www.asiaone.com/News/Latest+News/Asia/Story/A1Story20100317-205156.html (accessed 19 March 2010)

Korea Times (2009), 'Chronology–Life of Kim Dae-jung (1924-2009)', 18 August 2009. Online: http://www.koreatimes.co.kr/www/news/nation/2010/04/116_50287.html (accessed 29 April 2010)

Korea Times (2010), 'Shrinking of middle class stops', 16 March 2010. Online: http://www.koreatimes.co.kr/www/news/biz/2010/03/123_62464.html (accessed 17 March 2010)

Lee, Chang-sup (2009), 'Kim Dae-jung Main Actor in E. Asian Drama', in: *Korea Times*, 18 August 2009. Online: http://www.koreatimes.co.kr/www/news/nation/2010/01/113_50285.html (accessed 25 April 2010)

Schuman, Michael (2009), 'Fallout of Ex South Korea President's Suicide', in: *Time*, 25 May 2009. Online: http://www.time.com/time/world/article/0,8599,1900808,00.html (accessed 29 April 2010)

NORTH KOREA IN 2009: DOMESTIC DEVELOPMENTS AND THE ECONOMY

Rüdiger Frank

1 INTRODUCTION

This overview of domestic developments in the Democratic People's Republic of Korea (DPRK—North Korea) begins with an analysis of two major official publications and events that take place regularly and hence are suited to a continuous examination. The joint New Year editorial, which is studied intensively in North Korea, provides insights into the strategic planning of the leadership, even though these are often cloaked behind repetitive and propagandistic phrases. The annual parliamentary session is the only regular official meeting of the top North Korean leadership that the public is informed about; the last Party congress took place in 1980. At the parliamentary session, rare information on economic issues is provided, most importantly on the state budget. The session is also a time for the announcement of personnel changes.

After having analysed these regular events, we will focus on a few extraordinary developments of the year. In 2009, these include the delayed elections for the 12th Supreme People's Assembly (SPA, the North Korean parliament) and for the powerful National Defence Commission (NDC), and a cabinet reshuffle. The first concrete manifestation of the resuscitated Chollima movement, the '150 day battle', was another expression of North Korea's attempted return to orthodox, conservative socialist policies. At the end of the year, a very unusual currency reform with far-reaching effects was implemented.

The text concludes with an overview of other important developments in North Korea's ideology, in the economy, and regarding changes in personnel and institutions.

2 THE JOINT NEW YEAR EDITORIAL

The most important regular programmatic publication of the year, the 2009 joint New Year editorial published simultaneously by the major media of the DPRK, was relatively balanced; no major policy changes were visible. However, a few interesting details and perspectives were provided. Issues of leadership, ideology, the economy, unification and military affairs are singled out here.

2.1 *Leadership*

The personal leadership of Kim Jong Il was specifically highlighted, especially his 'inexhaustible energy' and on-the-spot guidances 'from the outset towards the end of last year'. This is important for the debate about his health. International speculations about an illness of the top leader seem to have hit a vulnerable spot in North Korea; as a response, state propaganda tries very hard to prove that he is well and active.

Increased activity by Kim Jong Il could also be interpreted as an attempt at generating more of an independent leadership profile, rather than being seen only as his father's son. This, in turn, would mark the beginning of a transfer of power, because in order to do so effectively, Kim Jong Il needs the necessary personal legitimacy. As Graph 1 shows, the frequency of reporting about his personal visits has moved up substantially in both language editions of KCNA.

The two leaders Kim Jong Il and Kim Il Sung are repeatedly mentioned, but so is the central role of the Party: 'The ultimate victory is in store for us as long as there are the plans for the bright future worked out by the great Party and the infinite spiritual strength of our army and people who perform miracles by turning out in hearty response to the call of the Party.' The 'leader-people-united strength' is 'more powerful than a nuclear weapon'. Kim Jong Il is called the 'destiny of the country'. North Korea nuclear arms or other weapons are not specifically mentioned. Rather, 'our strength is the single-minded unity of the entire army and all the people around the leadership of the revolution'.

Graph 1   Number of KCNA articles with the terms 'field guidance/
           spot guidance' in the English (E) and Korean (K) editions
           (1997-2009)

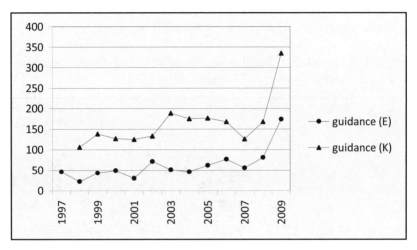

Source: Author's own calculations, based on KCNA.

2.2 *Ideology*

Traditional ideological positions such as 'the invincibility of the socialist cause of *Juche*' were emphasised. The year 2009 is supposed to mark a 'new revolutionary surge', a 'historic leap', and a 'Chollima upsurge' for the building of a great, prosperous and powerful nation (*kangsŏng taeguk*). The victory of 'Korean-style socialism' is predicted and the great revolutionary tradition emphasised. Success is to be achieved by 'relying on our ideology' and on the basis of the advantages of 'the independent socialist economy'. Ideology is described as 'our inexhaustible spiritual strength'. All problems should be solved 'our own way'. Collectivism and self-reliance are described as

> our peculiar mode of revolution and nothing is better than this ... Self-reliance is our strength and the key to a thriving nation ... We should always base ourselves on the socialist soil, develop our strength and open the route of advance to victory by relying on our resources, technology and the advantages of our system. At any time, in the future as well as the present era of advanced science and technology, we should constantly inherit the revolutionary spirit of self-reliance.

In the editorial alone, the word *songun* is used 26 times, the word *juche* 14 times, and 'socialist/socialism' appears 27 times.

A quantitative analysis of KCNA articles (see Graph 2) shows an on the whole synchronous and positive development of all three terms in North Korean propaganda since around 2004.

Graph 2   Number of English KCNA articles with the terms 'socialism', *'juche'* and *'songun'* (1997-2009)

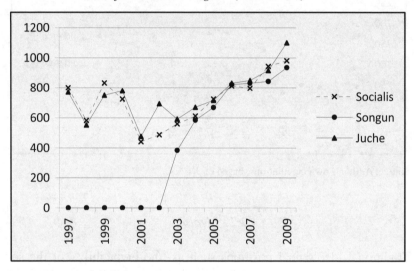

Source: Author's own calculations, based on KCNA.

2.3 *Economy*

Reflecting the routine of official news in other socialist countries, the editorial was full of reports about successes. Technological updating was undertaken in industry, new power stations were completed, co-operative farms were developed. Pyongyang is to be further beautified. Socialist planning is emphasised: 'push the effort to put production on a normal track and the modernization in close combination by taking advantage of the socialist planned economy'. The metal industry is singled out as the most important sector of the economy. In addition, the development of 'promising mines on the principle of bringing profit' is urged, an exhortation with a special implication as

China's investment in North Korean mineral extraction has been substantial.

It is not unusual for North Korea to admit difficulties: 'To relieve scarcity of food is a pressing problem'. Production of consumer goods is to be 'sharply increased'. The construction of residential houses in Pyongyang and afforestation are stressed. Obviously, the state's control over the economy is to be strengthened: 'Economic management should be improved to give full play to the advantages of the socialist planned economy. The centralized and unified guidance of the state over the economic construction should be strengthened and planning improved in line with the requirements of the developing reality.' Technological innovation is emphasised, including a 'mass-based technological innovation drive'. In particular, the stress on central planning and on the indigenous development of technology is reminiscent of similar public statements and policies of former socialist countries of Europe.

2.4 *Unification*

The unification of Korea remains the supreme task of the DPRK. The grave challenge to unification posed by the conservative authorities in the Republic of Korea (ROK—South Korea) is highlighted. The implementation of the 15 June and 4 October agreements[1] is demanded. Both are seen as closely connected; the 4 October declaration is interpreted as the action programme of the 15 June declaration. 'By our nation itself' is the fundamental idea for unification. South Koreans are asked to 'put an end to the fascist rule of the sycophantic and treacherous conservative authorities and remove the danger of war'. The attack against South Korea has become particularly harsh since the current government took office in Seoul, as a bilingual quantitative analysis of the term 'puppet' (usually reserved for South Korean authorities) shows:

---

[1] This refers to the summit meetings between Kim Jong Il and South Korean Presidents Kim Dae-jung and Roh Moo-hyun respectively.

Graph 3   Number of KCNA articles with the term 'puppet' in the English (E) and Korean (K) editions (1997-2009)

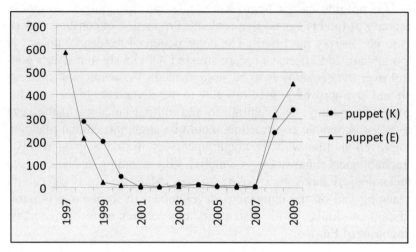

Source: Author's own calculations, based on KCNA.

As if to respond to claims of a disintegrating society in the wake of a failed economy, ideological poisoning and a looming leadership crisis, political stability in North Korea is stressed: 'In the present world no other country is more politically stable than our Republic whose people are all filled with a great hope, ambition and confidence about the future.'

2.5 *Military affairs*

Closer unity and comradeship is urged between soldiers and officers; the KPA should assist the people and become a model for the whole of society in the fields of ideology, spirit, morality and culture. Society in its entirety is to be more firmly militarized. 'The habit of giving priority to arms, military affairs, should be established more thoroughly in the whole of society. Great efforts should constantly be put to the development of the defence industry as required by the line of economic construction in the Songun era and everything necessary be provided for it on a preferential basis.' The editorial repeated the statement that North Korea is committed to the goal of denuclearization of the Korean peninsula, as long as this is not done unilaterally by

Pyongyang. It is ready to develop relations with countries that are friendly towards North Korea and to 'make a positive contribution to achieving the cause of global independence', a euphemism for the international fight against dominance by the United States and its allies.

3 THE BUDGET REPORT

Kim Wan Su, Minister of Finance, delivered the report on the results of the implementation of the DPRK state budget for 2008 and delivered the state budget for 2009 during the regular annual session of the Supreme People's Assembly on 9 April. Table 1 summarises the verbal statements in his report and contrasts them with the plans laid out in the 2008 budgetary report before the SPA.

Table 1   Comparison of state budgets 2008/2009

	Plan for 2008	Achieved 2008	Plan for 2009
State budgetary revenue	+4%	101.6% (+5.7%)	+5.2%
Profits of state enterprises	+4.7%		+5.8%
Profits of co-operative organisations	+0.4%		+3.1%
Fixed asset depreciation			+6.1%
Real estate rent			+3.6%
Social insurance			+1.6%
Local budgetary revenue		117.1%	
State budgetary expenditure	+2.5%	99.99%	+7%
National defence	15.8%	15.8%	15.8%
Priority sectors of the national economy			+8.7%
Coal and mining	+49.8%		
Development of science and technology	+6.1%		+8%
Agriculture	+5.5%	+5.4%	+6.9%
Light industry			+5.6%
City management			+11.5%
Education	+4.2%		+8.2%
Culture and arts			+3.2%
Public health	+5.9%		+8%
Sports			+5.8%

Source: Author's own compilation, based on KCNA.

The Korean and the English version contain the same information. As usual, the selection of data has been somewhat arbitrary, and no absolute numbers are provided. A comparison with the planned data from the 2008 budget helps to reveal a number of deviations. Planning of revenue has become more detailed for 2009 if compared to 2008; income from fixed asset depreciation, real estate rent and social insurance was reported in 2008 but not planned. Despite the unusually high planned increase in coal and mining, it is conspicuous that there has been neither a report about achievements in those areas nor a new planned figure. However, despite the emphasis on the 'commanding heights' of a socialist planned economy and on the defence industry, there is a planned figure for growth in light industry that was not provided in 2008. The newly added position of city management can be explained by the new emphasis on the beautification of Pyongyang. The same could be true for culture and arts and for sports, reflecting the preparations for the 2012 celebrations.

The budgets reflect what we could call macroeconomic data on the DPRK. Since there is almost no private economic production in North Korea, there are only the state sector and the military sector. The latter is usually perceived as being relatively large and including all kinds of enterprises. However, data on this part of the economy are unavailable, for obvious reasons. But with the rest of the economy including trade under state ownership and control, the state budget is comparable to the Gross National Product minus the military sector. The rate of increase of budgetary revenue would hence be an equivalent of the GNP growth rate. From this perspective, Graph 4 shows that the economy (or the official picture thereof) had been growing at an extraordinary pace since the beginning of the reforms in 2002, but declined sharply in 2006.

For the year 2009, a certain moderate growth in the expectations of the North Korean planners is discernible. The projected data for revenue and expenditures are respectively 1.2 percent and 4.5 percent higher than the anticipated growth rates for 2008. The growth rates for the single sectors reflect this development, being between 1.4 percent and 4 percent higher than the year before.

Graph 4   Economic growth in North Korea according to the DPRK budget (growth rates in %)

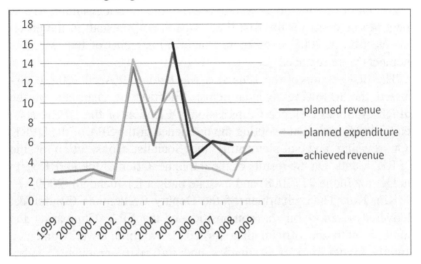

Source: Author's own calculations, based on KCNA.

4 THE SPA ELECTIONS

4.1 *Supreme People's Assembly*

The parliamentary elections were originally expected to be held in 2008. The delay in arranging them has been interpreted by outside observers as having some connection with the health of Kim Jong Il. They took place on 8 March 2009. On the occasion of the SPA elections, KCNA pointed out the superiority of the election system in North Korea, emphasising its elements of equality, direct elections, secret elections and absence of coercion, surveillance or threat. Socialist democracy was described as the highest form of democracy.

In preparation for the elections, a meeting of the Central Committee of the Democratic Front for the Reunification of Korea was held in Pyongyang. The DFRK consists of the Workers' Party of Korea (WPK), the Korean Social Democratic Party, and the Ch'ŏndoist Party. The results of the elections were published on 9 March. Countrywide, 99.98 percent of registered voters participated in balloting and 100 percent of them voted for the registered candidates. This was interpreted as an expression of the single-minded unity of the Korean army and people united around the leader.

A total of 687 members were elected to the 12th legislature, 316 of them (46 percent) for the first time. This is not unusual; in the previous election in 2003, even more (about 50 percent) of the assembly members were replaced.

The first session of the 12th SPA was held on 9 April 2009. It discussed the following agenda items: 'Election of chairman of the DPRK National Defence Commission', 'Election of the DPRK state leadership body', 'On adopting the ordinance of the SPA of the DPRK "On revising and supplementing the Socialist Constitution of the DPRK"', and 'On the results of the implementation of the DPRK state budget for Juche 97 (2008) and its state budget for Juche 98 (2009)'.

Kim Kuk Thae, chairman of the Deputy Credentials Committee, delivered a report on the composition of the SPA. Comparing the numbers with the official data for 2003, we find fewer women, a slightly higher rate of academics and university graduates, and a higher average age of the deputies. The most striking difference is in the class background of members; the proportion of workers dropped from around one-third to around a mere tenth. Military service personnel were a newly added category in 2009 (16.9 percent).

The gender ratio in the North Korean parliament is similar to that of the National Assembly of the ROK. Out of a total of 687 deputies, 15.6 percent are women (2003: 20.1 percent). Regarding age, 1 percent of the deputies are below 35 years (2003: 2.2 percent), 48.5 percent between 36 and 55 years (2003: 50.1 percent) and 50.5 percent above 56 years (2003: 47.7 percent).

Despite the great emphasis on the military and the working class, both groups are heavily underrepresented; bureaucrats seem to take almost two-thirds of all seats. Of all SPA deputies, 16.9 percent are service personnel, 10.9 percent workers (2003: 33.4 percent), and 10.1 percent co-operative farmers (2003: 9.3 percent). The remaining 62.1 percent were not accounted for but are most likely to be bureaucrats and party officials. Of the SPA deputies 90.4 percent hold academic degrees and titles including professorships and doctorates or are scientists, technicians and experts (2003: 89.5 percent). University graduates account for 94.2 percent of the deputies (2003: 91.9 percent).

Choe Thae Bok was elected SPA chairman, Kim Wan Su and Hong Son Ok vice-chairpersons. Kim Yong Nam was elected president of the Presidium of the SPA of the DPRK. Yang Hyong Sop and Kim

Yong Dae were elected vice-presidents, Kim Yong Ju honorary vice-president, and Choe Yong Rim general secretary of the Presidium of the SPA of the DPRK.

4.2 The National Defence Commission

Not surprisingly, Kim Jong Il was (re-)elected Chairman of the National Defence Commission (*kukbangwiwŏnhoe*, NDC). The Commission was enlarged from eight to thirteen members. On proposal by Kim Jong Il, the session elected the first vice-chairman, vice-chairmen and members of the NDC of the DPRK. Jo Myong Rok was elected first vice-chairman, Kim Yong Chun, Ri Yong Mu and O Kuk Ryol vice-chairmen and Jon Pyong Ho, Kim Il Chol, Paek Se Bong, Jang Song Thaek, Ju Sang Song, U Tong Chuk, Ju Kyu Chang and Kim Jong Gak members of the NDC. The latter five are newly appointed members. In addition to Kim Jong Il, there are now five civilians in the NDC, although all of them hold security-related posts.

The most noted person among these was Jang Song Thaek (Chang Sŏng-t'aek), Kim Jong Il's brother-in-law. In general, the enlargement of the NDC reflects not only more responsibilities incurred in upgrading this commission in the context of the overall steering of North Korea, but also a more balanced combination of military and civilian members.

4.3 The cabinet

A few changes have been made to the structure of the cabinet since 2003. The Ministry of Power and Coal Industries was split up into two new ministries (Electric Power Industry and Coal Industry). The Ministry of Metal and Machine-Building Industries has also been divided into two ministries (Metal Industries and Machine-Building Industries). Two further ministries have been newly created: the Ministry of Oil Industry and the Ministry of Capital City Construction.

Table 2 in the appendix to this overview lists the names of the newly elected or confirmed administrative elite and, more importantly, the names of the administrative units. Since neither in English nor in Korean has the alphabet been used to order the single ministries, we can expect that the listing shown in that table reflects a certain ranking of the units in the eyes of the North Korean state leadership. The highest ranks are taken by the chair of the State Planning Commission, followed by the ministers of Foreign Affairs, People's Security, Electric Power Industry, Coal Industry, Mining Industry, Oil Industry and Metal Industry, in that order. The low rank of the Ministries of Commerce and of Finance is noticeable.

5 POLICIES

5.1 *The 150-day battle*

In the context of the general trend of the past years—the return to orthodox conservative socialist positions and policies—Kim Jong Il started a new round of the 1958 Chollima movement in December 2008. The major emphasis of this softened North Korean version of the Chinese Great Leap is on the intensified use of labour in lieu of other production factors such as capital or technology. Because Kim Jong Il explicitly referred to his father's campaign of half a century ago when he visited the same steel works at Kangsŏn where his father had started the original movement and urged the workers to create miracles by working harder, I call this new campaign *chollima* 2. The official North Korean term is 'great revolutionary upsurge' (*hyŏngmyŏngjŏk taegojo*); the expression 'great leaping advance' (*piyŏgŭi p'okp'ung*) is also found. On 27 March 2009, KCNA described the current time as 'the era of great leap forward' (*widaehan piyŏgŭi sidae*).

Experience with 'work-harder campaigns' in North Korea, China and the socialist countries of Europe has shown that these can indeed produce initial high results, at the cost, however, of other factors such as machinery and equipment, reserves and so on, and also at the expense of those sectors that were not included in the campaign. Furthermore, it became obvious that such campaigns were not sustainable. Individuals learn and react by withholding performance, so that eventually, they might deliver close to their full capacity during campaigns, but will strongly underperform between campaigns.

The *chollima* 2 movement was raised to a new level by the (re)introduction of a work-harder campaign in 2009, called the 150-day battle (*150il chŏnt'u*). Such major 'battles' were conducted regularly until the famine and the reform period of the 1990s. They are in principle a mini-plan at high speed. Within a relatively short (as compared to a five-year plan) period of time, a number of specific targets are to be reached through extraordinary input from the workforce.

The 150-day battle was initiated by Kim Jong Il who provided an example of self-sacrifice for the nation by radically increasing the frequency of his guidances (see Section 2.1 above). This may even have its implications for a possible leadership succession, along the logic of: 'Kim Jong Il has worked himself to death for the country.' Anecdotes about Kim Il Sung, who shortly before his own death urged officials not to pay attention to him but rather to alleviate his son's burden, were repeatedly published by KCNA.

On 21 September 2009, the Central Committee of the WPK issued a report on the successful conclusion of the 150-day-battle: 'The period of the campaign witnessed the further consolidation of the single-minded unity of our party and the revolutionary ranks; the leader believes in the people and they absolutely trust and follow their leader. This is the most shining success achieved in the 150-day campaign ...' The 150-day campaign seamlessly merged into a 100-day campaign.

Outlining the achievements of the 150-day battle, KCNA reported a number of specific data presented in the typical form of central planning propaganda:

Box 1   Quantitative achievements of the 150-day campaign

- the overall campaign plan was carried out at 112 percent
- industrial production showed a 1.2-fold increase over the same period last year
- production of steel, rolled steel and Juche iron jumped 'several times'
- the workers of the Pukchang Thermal Power Complex generated 1.4 times as much electricity
- coal production swelled 1.5 times
- railway freight transport assignment was carried out at 118 percent
- the quota for the production of machine tools was honoured at 126 percent
- that of generators at 114 percent
- that of motors at 122 percent
- that of transformers at 120 percent
- timber production rose 1.5 times
- cement production increased 1.4 times

Source: KCNA, 25 September 2009.

For outside observers, the relevance of these reports is twofold: they allow a better idea of the main targets and target areas of the campaign to emerge, and they provide a rare occasion to learn more about specific economic development projects that are otherwise only mentioned randomly, or not at all.

In addition to numbers, institutions were mentioned that had achieved the targets of the campaign. These were the ministries of Mining Industry, Machine-Building Industry, Electronics Industry, Chemical Industry, Forestry, and Land and Marine Transport; the Mining Machine-Building Industry Guidance Bureau, the Tideland Reclamation Guidance Bureau, the Salt Industry Guidance Bureau and 'other units'. Other fields or successes that were mentioned included:

Box 2   Qualitative achievements of the 150-day campaign

- rice transplanting
- maize planting
- weeding
- the construction of the Hŭich'ŏn power station
- the construction of the Kŭmyagang power station
- the Ryesŏnggang power station
- the Ŏrangch'ŏn power station
- the Paektusan Songun Youth power station
- reclaiming the tideland on Taegye islet
- the construction of houses for 100,000 families in Pyongyang
- the Nyŏngwŏn power station (river Taedong)
- the Taedonggang tile factory that appeared as a comprehensive centre for the production of building materials
- operations were started at new pit at the February 8 Chiktong Youth coal mine
- the belt-conveyer inclined shaft at the Ryŏngdae coal mine
- the heat ray reflection glass production process at the Taean Friendship glass factory
- the North Hwanghae provincial art theatre was built
- the Songdowŏn Youth open-air theatre was built
- many buildings including Mansudae Street, the Majŏn Hotel and the Sŏhŭng gymnasium were built
- the May 11 smeltery was reconstructed on an expansion basis
- the Kujang fish farm put breeding processes on a modern and scientific basis and boosted its capacity
- scientists and technicians launched satellite Kwangmyŏngsŏng-2 by their own efforts and with their own technology, enabling the country to proudly rank itself among the countries capable of launching satellites
- the CNC machine tool-building industry as exemplified by CNC-'Ryŏnha Machine' made its appearance
- the members of the shock brigades of scientists and technicians and technical innovation shock brigades of factories and enterprises across the country made a lot of scientific inventions and realized more than 9,000 technical innovation proposals

Source: KCNA, 25 September 2009.

If the results from Boxes 1 and 2 are summarised, it is clear that heavy industry played a major role, as well as energy production. The latter is shown in the construction of the many power plants, but also the extraction of coal and the building of energy-related equipment. In extractive industries, success has not been big enough to be reported in detail beyond coal production. In addition, the usual efforts at improving agricultural output (rice planting, fish breeding) are evident, as is the already discussed land reclamation; missing, however, was fertiliser production. The improvement in the housing situation is noteworthy, as is the construction of theatres that have a double function as places for entertainment and for ideological education. Finally, we should also note that the missile test is listed as the launch of a domestically built satellite and part of the 150-day battle.

Further confirming the closeness of this campaign to those from the period of orthodox socialism, in addition to 'Pyongyang speed', a new 'speed of Huichon' has been coined by Kim Jong Il during the 150-day battle. On 25 September 2009, *Rodong Shinmun* reported:

> This is a great speed for socialist construction symbolizing and representing the present era of great surge when everyone is making a leaping advance towards a thriving nation, riding on a Songun Chollima ... [it] is an expression of the intense loyalty of the servicepersons and people in the DPRK who unconditionally carry out what Kim Jong Il determines ...

5.2 *The currency reform of November 2009*

The North Korean government initiated a currency reform, to take effect in December 2009, that replaced domestic currency with new bills—50 years after a similar effort in 1959. The exchange rate (100:1) helped to shed two zeros that had become an obvious sign of galloping inflation, one of the negative side-effects of the July 2002 economic liberalisation.

However, this was only a cosmetic action with no immediate economic effect. Of more relevance was the fact that only a very limited amount of old money could be exchanged into the new bills. External reports on the details are not homogeneous, but it seems that those who owned more than about 250,000 old won (black market rate: 2,500 won for US$1, official exchange rate: 180 won to US$1) saw the rest of their savings become worthless. This effectively made the currency reform an attempt at expropriating successful private businesspeople, such as traders in the country's many local markets.

The currency reform was followed by an attempt at closing the markets and by a ban on the use of foreign currency in North Korea; the latter was even extended to foreigners. All these measures taken together are consistent with the return to orthodox and conservative socialism as noted in this overview. The North Korean government has increasing difficulties in curbing a societal transformation that had started taking place with the re-monetisation of North Korea's economy after the famine of 1995-7 and in particular the July 2002 economic reforms. In essence, the state had delegated power to the decentralised markets and relevant forces. After a few less intrusive attempts at retrieving control, the currency reforms constituted a more aggressive move in that direction.[2]

From an economic point of view, the effects of this action promise to be moderate at best. Inflation is caused by an imbalance between high demand and low supply of key goods. By the elimination of the market, inflation can be hidden (again) and transformed into a shortage economy, which was the regular state of affairs in most socialist countries. A simple currency revaluation will have almost no effect whatsoever; the remaining gap between supply and demand will inevitably lead to a new inflationary spiral. The only realistic way to fight inflation is to either reduce demand or increase supply. By restoring full controls over the economy, the state will be able to get nominal inflation under control; however, this will happen at the cost of depriving North Korean money of what little functionality it had earned in the reform years. Prices will become merely expressionless numbers again.

From a political point of view, the currency revaluation was a very telling experience. It showed the desperation of the North Korean state and serves as an indicator of the severity of the current situation. It also shows the DPRK's determination to regain centralised control, rather than riding the tiger and react by liberalising the economy even further. The expropriation of a small but active group of traders and other affluent people, something we could call a middle class, will lay the foundation for the same public discontent that for years was silent

---

[2] For more analysis on the background and effects of the currency reforms, see Rüdiger Frank, 'Money in Socialist Economies: The Case of North Korea', in: *The Asia-Pacific Journal*, 8-2-10, 22 February 2010. Online: http://www.japanfocus.org/-Ruediger-Frank/3307.

and existed mainly below the surface but in the end brought down socialism in Eastern Europe within a historically very short period of time.

The graphic images on the new bills are by far the most spectacular signal from an ideological point of view. Eternal President Kim Il Sung's face and his birthplace at Man'gyŏngdae near Pyongyang remain on the highest denomination, the 5,000-won bill. Unlike on the bills of the year 2002, this time his hair is depicted as grey. For the first time in history, an image of Kim Jong Il has appeared on North Korean money. The 2,000-won bill shows his official birthplace, the log cabin at the 'secret camp' at Mt Paektu beneath Jong Il peak. The 1,000-won bill shows his mother's birthplace in Hoeryŏng in the province of North Hamgyŏng. Thus the 'Three Generals of Mt Paektu' are for the first time depicted together on the three highest North Korean banknotes. A quantitative analysis of both the Korean- and the English-language versions of KCNA shows that coverage of Kim Jong Il's mother Kim Jong Suk has more than tripled between 2002 and 2009.

Interpretation varies. This could be the next step in the process of enshrining the Trinity of Father, Mother and Son for eternity—as a closed system and an eternal source of legitimacy that is not being expanded (and thereby diluted) any further. There are parallels to successful religions such as Christianity and Islam, where current leaders do not base their position on any blood ties. On the other hand, the emphasis on the family instead of Kim Il Sung alone could signal a strengthening of the bloodline as the primary source of leadership legitimacy, which could theoretically be extended limitlessly. The latter could include a grandson of Kim Il Sung, in particular in lieu of any alternative and under the time pressure created by the current leader's life span. It is relatively unlikely that such a model of succession would be sustainable, but it can by no means be excluded that such an attempt will be made.[3]

---

[3] For more details, see Rüdiger Frank, 'Currency Reform and Orthodox Socialism in North Korea', in: *Korea Herald*, 4 December 2009, pp. 1, 4, reprinted in: Nautilus Institute, *Policy Forum Online*, 09-092A, 3 December 2009. Online: http://www.nautilus.org/fora/security/09092Frank.html; and idem, 'Symbolism of the New North Korean Currency: Heralding a Change of Power?', in: Napsnet, *Policy Forum Online*, 09-094A, 10 December 2009. Online: http://www.nautilus.org/fora/security/09094 Frank.html.

6 IDEOLOGY

6.1 *Return to orthodox, conservative socialism*

The year 2009 saw a retraction of previously made points on a number of occasions. On 12 March, during a field guidance trip, Kim Jong Il 'called on officials of the complex to energetically lead the masses by displaying the same work style as the officials did in the 50s and 60s'. This stands in direct contrast to an article written by Kim Jong Il himself in *Rodong Shinmun* of 4 January 2001: 'Things are not what they used to be in the 1960s. So no one should follow the way people used to do things in the past ... We should make constant efforts to renew the landscape to replace the one which was formed in the past, to meet the requirements of the new era.'[4] On 27 March, *Rodong Shinmun* stressed that '[t]he working class is the main player in the DPRK's glorious history of a great surge and acts as a main unit for building an economic power'. This runs counter to a statement that was made in the same newspaper in April 2003: 'In the past, it was recognized as an unbreakable formula in socialist politics to put forth the working class. However, the theory and formula that was generated one and a half centuries ago cannot be applicable to today's reality.'[5]

Orthodox, conservative socialist positions that were stressed in 2009 included collectivism (*chiptanjuŭi*) as the true nature of Korean-style socialism and mode of revolution peculiar to the Korean people. Without collectivism, KCNA wrote, socialism will erode. The spirit of selfless sacrifice is another traditional theme of all socialist ideologies. Reminding readers of the 'arduous march' of the anti-Japanese guerrillas around Kim Il Sung 70 years ago, KCNA pointed at their strong will to fight and win despite harsh conditions and overwhelming enemy strength.

The order of priorities is not entirely clear or consistent. Sometimes ideology is said to be the most important part ('most powerful weapon'); sometimes it is the military: 'The victory on the anti-imperialist

---

[4] Kim Jong Il, '21 seginŭn kŏch'anghan chŏnbyŏnŭi segi, ch'angjoŭi segiida' [The 21st century is a century of great change and creation], in: *Rodong Shinmun*, 4 January 2001, p. 2.

[5] *Rodong Shinmun*, 'Songun chŏngch'inŭn minjokŭi chajusŏngŭl wihan p'ilsŭngŭi pogŏm' [Military-first policy is a precious sword of sure victory for the sovereignty of the nation], 3 April 2003. Online: http://www.kcna.co.jp/calendar/2003/04/04-04/2003-04-04-003.html (accessed 1 May 2003).

military front guarantees the victory on the political and ideological front' (KCNA, 20 June 2009). On the same day, *Rodong Shinmun* dedicated a signed article to the 14th anniversary of Kim Jong Il's work 'Giving Priority to Ideological Work Is Essential for Accomplishing Socialism'. And on 22 June, *Rodong Shinmun* wrote that 'it is the unique revolutionary theory of the Workers' Party of Korea that the people are always sure to triumph when they are awakened and motivated ideologically'.

6.2 *Problems*

A number of very harsh and only partially softened criticisms that appeared in 2009 point at a difficult situation on the domestic ideological front.

A historical article criticised 'the enemies within and without' and the 'renegades to the revolution', referring to the post-1945 period. A strike against pragmatic technocrats could be contained in the following passage: 'What one should guard against in particular in the IT age is the tendency of disregarding the might of ideology, overwhelmed by technology- and science-almighty theory' (KCNA, 8 May 2009).

An indirect criticism of the recently stopped economic reform policy is contained in a KCNA report (20 May 2009) that remembers Kim Il Sung's speech: 'Let Us Repudiate the "Left" Adventurist Line and Follow the Revolutionary Organizational Line'. This could be a hint that a new campaign is being waged against 'sectarian-flunkeys', 'left adventurism', and an unco-ordinated economic reform policy. In a similar tone, *Rodong Shinmun* (12 June 2009), commemorating the 20th anniversary of the publication of Kim Jong Il's work 'Let Us Strengthen the Party and Increase Its Leadership Role', reminded readers that 'Kim Jong Il in his work laid bare the anti-party and counter-revolutionary nature of the revisionists and reformists and clarified the principled matters arising in further strengthening the party and enhancing its leading role as required by the changed environment.'

In an article on the Musan area battle of 1939, KCNA (23 May 2009) wrote:

> On top of this, the enemy continued to spread the lie that the KPRA had perished, whereby some people were losing confidence. The President, with deep grasp of the prevailing situation, launched the Arduous

March unprecedented in history from December 1938 to March 1939 by leading the main unit of the KPRA to keep the Korean revolution in upsurge.

This could be a reference to the present situation and a counter-argument to those who have given up hope and do not believe in the success of North Korea (or the 2012 victory) anymore.

An anecdote from 1936 about Kim Il Sung tells how he criticised young soldiers who had stolen maize from farmers: 'He said the greatest tragedy for a revolutionary was to lose the love of the people' (KCNA, 1 June 2009). This could be a sign that reports about conflicts between the military and farmers are indeed correct, and that there is a real danger of 'losing the love of the people'.

7 OTHER ECONOMIC POLICIES

Traditional positions on socialism were reiterated in economic policy, too. KCNA (4 May 2009) wrote:

> The key to national development is to achieve equality and unity among the members of the nation and channel their interests in one direction. The capitalist society based on mammonism and egoism is an anti-popular society where the interests of the bourgeoisie are defended. It inevitably causes social inequality and antagonism between the exploiter and the exploited classes.

There seems to be a need to explain that capitalism will not be good for development, an indicator that there are forces in North Korea that might think otherwise. The passage on exploitation, moreover, sheds an interesting light on the Kaesŏng Industrial Zone. Last but not least, the classical Marxist notion of a society being divided into two antagonistic classes is revived.

7.1 *Kaesŏng*

The Kaesŏng Industrial Zone (KIZ) has been relatively broadly covered by KCNA. The focal issue has been the allegedly unco-operative position of South Korea, which has been seen as responsible for a slowdown of operations. On 15 May 2009, the Central Special Zone Development Guidance General Bureau informed the South that the North declared null and void the rules and contracts on land rent, land use tax, wages, and all sorts of taxes. The explanation was: (1) the policy so far was an extraordinary and special favour, (2) this favour was now withdrawn because of the South's hostile policy, and (3) North Korea could do what it wanted in Kaesŏng as the area was part of its territory. The latter argument was added on 23 May 2009.

On 11 June, KCNA specified: 'Recalling that many enterprises of the south side are operating in the KIZ at present to gain big profits whereas the north side has not received payments at a proper level ... the north side advanced draft amendments to the contracts ... in the KIZ.' On 19 June, South Korea was accused of wanting deliberately to end work at the zone. The charge was also repeated that the South benefited unilaterally from the zone. On 2 July, KCNA insisted that the South should reciprocate for the North's 'magnanimity' by paying higher land use fees. On 10 July, the South was called an 'ungrateful and impolite counterpart' and was told that '[t]he prospect of the working contact on the KIZ and the zone will entirely depend on the future attitude of the south side.'

7.2 *International economic exchanges*

The 12th Pyongyang Spring International Trade Fair took place in May 2009. Participating nations included China, Russia, Germany, Malaysia, Syria, Sweden, Singapore, Australia, Austria, UK, Italy, Indonesia, Vietnam, Thailand, Poland, Turkey and Taipei of China (i.e. Taiwan). In September, the 5th Pyongyang Autumn International Trade Fair was opened. Kim Mun Jong, director of the Korean International Exhibition Corporation, said in his opening address that 'the DPRK would as ever develop on a wider scale the economic and commercial dealings with all countries which are friendly towards it on the principles of complete equality and reciprocity' (KCNA, 5 September 2009).

North Korean media and representatives have repeatedly stressed that a new international financial and economic order should be established, that the UN's millennium goals for development are regarded as an important yardstick, and that the developed nations have the duty to support developing countries.

An important tool of state-directed execution on international economic policies and co-operation has been the Foreign Trade Bank, which celebrated its 50th anniversary in 2009. In related speeches, the

'rising international prestige and economic potential' of North Korea were proudly mentioned. Vice-Premier O Su Yong 'expressed belief that the bank would boost cooperation and business transaction with banks of foreign countries and thus make steady progress in foreign financial dealings' (KCNA, 24 September 2009).

7.3 *Innovation*

Indigenous development of science and technology is important for any economy that wants to advance beyond a basic level but has limited access to foreign technology. In lieu of private initiative, this field, too, has to be organised by the state with all the known deficiencies of such an approach. For North Korea, international sanctions add to the pressure for the development of its own technologies since access to international patents and licenses is limited. The state's efforts in research and development (R&D) are reflected in a KCNA report of 16 September, when a ceremony for the completion of the first-phase construction of Pyongyang University of Science and Technology was held.

7.4 *Further policies*

In 2009 these have included 'August 3 consumer goods', encompassing ironware, electric appliances, clothing, grass-work, agricultural products and sundry goods produced by industrial establishments, housewives' work-teams, reutilisation production work-teams of direct sales shops, and home welfare service workers across the country. 'August 3 goods' refer to sideline production of consumer goods upon an initiative of Kim Jong Il launched on 3 August 1984.

Another popular theme in North Korean economic policy has been the solution of the food shortage by extending the acreage of arable land. As the effects of deforestation have been devastating (including regular floods), land reclamation has become a core strategy. On 17 August, KCNA reported on a number of tideland reclamation projects. In addition to the economic benefits, KCNA added a hint at nationalist gains: 'As a result, the Korean map has changed beyond recognition.'

8 STRUCTURAL CHANGES AND PERSONNEL POLICY

During 2009, a new ministry and a new commission came into being. On 22 July, the Presidium of the DPRK Supreme People's Assembly issued a decree setting up the Ministry of Foodstuff and Daily Necessities Industry. The obvious conclusion is that more efforts are to be directed at central administration of the production and distribution of food. This reflects the scarcity of this product, but also the desire to dismantle the decentralised market mechanism.

On 19 September, by decree of the SPA, the State Science and Technology Commission of the DPRK was founded. This, too, is in line with tendencies as they could be observed in Eastern European states in the 1980s. As the economies of these countries became more sophisticated, and at the same time the technological gap between socialist and Western countries widened, governments tried to make up for this weakness by starting costly R&D efforts of their own.

KCNA reporting of personnel changes seems to have been somewhat arbitrary. On 3 September, it reported that Ri Hwa Gun had been appointed DPRK ambassador to Brazil, by decree of the SPA Presidium. One day later, Pak Myong Son was appointed vice-premier of the DPRK cabinet. Potentially more significant was a report on 18 September, when a decree of the SPA Presidium was promulgated, relieving Kim Wan Su, the Minister of Finance, of his post and appointing Pak Su Gil as a new vice-premier and Minister of Finance. No reasons were provided, so we can only speculate. In the context of the retracting of the market-oriented economic reforms, it is possible that some officials have been forced to take responsibility for what is regarded, at least at the moment, as a severe threat to the stability of the system by leading figures in the DPRK. It is unclear who these are, and whether we are now seeing either a change of mind by the top leader, or a struggle for power behind the scenes that has now resulted in the purging of the reform faction.

APPENDIX

Table 2 The new cabinet of the DPRK, 2009

Name	Function
Kim Yong Il	Premier of the Cabinet of the DPRK (*naegak ch'ongni*)
Kwak Pom Gi, Thae Jong Su, Ro Tu Chol, O Su Yong	Vice-premiers (*puch'ongni*)
Ro Tu Chol	Chairman of the State Planning Commission
Pak Ui Chun	Minister of Foreign Affairs
Ju Sang Song	Minister of People's Security
Ho Thaek	Minister of Electric Power Industry
Kim Hyong Sik	Minister of Coal Industry
Kang Min Chol	Minister of Mining Industry
Kim Hui Yong	Minister of Oil Industry
Kim Thae Bong	Minister of Metal Industry
Jo Pyong Ju	Minister of Machine-Building Industry
Han Kwang Bok	Minister of Electronics Industry
Tong Jong Ho	Minister of Construction and Building-Materials Industry
Jon Kil Su	Minister of Railways
Ra Tong Hui	Minister of Land and Marine Transport
Kim Chang Sik	Minister of Agriculture
Ri Mu Yong	Minister of Chemical Industry
Ri Ju O	Minister of Light Industry
Ri Ryong Nam	Minister of Foreign Trade
Kim Kwang Yong	Minister of Forestry
Pak Thae Won	Minister of Fisheries
Hwang Hak Won	Minister of Urban Management
Pak Song Nam	Minister of Land and Environmental Conservation
Pae Tal Jun	Minister of State Construction Control
Kim Pong Chol	Minister of Commerce
Mun Ung Jo	Minister of Food Procurement and Administration
Kim Yong Jin	Minister of Education
Ryu Yong Sop	Minister of Posts and Telecommunications
Kang Nung Su	Minister of Culture
Kim Wan Su	Minister of Finance

Jong Yong Su	Minister of Labour
Choe Chang Sik	Minister of Public Health
Kim Ui Sun	Minister of State Inspection
Pyon Yong Rip	President of the State Academy of Sciences
Pak Hak Son	Chairman of the Physical Culture and Sports Guidance Commission
Ri Kwang Gon	President of the Central Bank
Kim Chang Su	Director of the Central Statistical Board
Kim Yong Ho	Director of the Secretariat of the Cabinet
Kim Ung Gwan	Minister of Capital City Construction
Ri Kil Song	Director of the Central Public Prosecutors Office
Kim Pyong Ryul	President of the Central Court

Source: Author's own compilation, based on KCNA.

RELATIONS BETWEEN THE TWO KOREAS IN 2009

Sabine Burghart and James E. Hoare

INTRODUCTION

In 2009, relations between the Republic of Korea (ROK—South Korea) and the Democratic People's Republic of Korea (DPRK—North Korea) continued to be frosty. Hopes that the 'pragmatic and result-oriented' policy of the Lee administration would lead to a shift in the DPRK's position on denuclearisation quickly faded away. In addition to strong rhetoric denouncing the South Korean leadership, military provocations by the DPRK continued: the test-firing of a long-range missile, a second nuclear test, and the launch of seven short-range ballistic missiles. Problems at the last remaining joint inter-Korean economic project, the Kaesŏng Industrial Complex (KIC), intensified in the first half of 2009 but were eventually resolved, at least for the time being. Among the rare positive developments was the 17th round of family reunions held at Mt Kŭmgang during the Ch'usŏk holidays.

1 A PERIOD OF ADJUSTMENT?

Few observers expected that inter-Korean relations would develop more smoothly during the second year of Lee Myung-bak's presidency than they had during the first. Despite several provocative steps such as the 1 December 2008 measures that were unilaterally taken by the North Korean authorities to restrict business activities at the KIC, the detention of a South Korean engineer and the North's threat to nullify all inter-Korean contracts, the ROK government remained firm in its position. Political tensions between the two Koreas primarily affected Hyundai Asan and the small and middle-sized companies of the KIC. The ROK ministry of unification (MOU) played down the difficulties and problems: inter-Korean relations would go through an 'adjustment period' and Lee's policy of 'creative pragmatism' would eventually benefit both Koreas in building an economic community. To many, it appears that the Lee administration is not much interested in improved inter-Korean relations.

The standstill in these relations was overshadowed by the death of two former South Korean presidents, Roh Moo-hyun (23 May) and Kim Dae-jung (18 August), whose engagement policies had led—in the eyes of many Koreans and other observers—to a period of rapprochement and détente on the Korean peninsula. There were hopes that the visit of the high-ranking DPRK delegation to the state funeral for Kim would open a new chapter in stalled relations. Reflecting this mood, South Korean newspapers chose headlines such as 'Even in death, Kim reconciles' (*JoongAng Daily*, 25 August 2009), 'N. Korean visit marks a new stage in relations' (*Chosun Ilbo*, 20 August 2009), 'Funeral of harmony' (*Korea Times*, 22-23 August 2009), and 'Kim Dae-jung unites Koreas, even in death' (*Korea Times*, 25 August 2009). During their three-day stay in Seoul the delegation of six DPRK officials led by Kim Ki Nam, secretary of the North Korean Workers' Party (KWP) Central Committee, met with Lee Myung-bak. Talks were also held between Hyun In-taek, ROK minister of unification, and Kim Yang Gon, head of the unification front department of the KWP.

2 LEE'S 'CREATIVE PRAGMATISM': A SOLUTION TO THE NORTH'S SABRE-RATTLING?

The 'denuclearisation, openness and 3000 plan' (*pihaek kaebang 3000 kusang*) that Lee Myung-bak had announced during his presidential election campaign in 2007, which, on condition of denuclearisation, promised to raise the DPRK GDP per capita to US$3,000, proved inadequate to achieve progress in inter-Korean relations. In September 2009, Lee repeated his offer with a different title: the 'grand bargain' (*kŭraendŭ pagaen*) proposal would comprise a package deal of security guarantees and assistance for the DPRK in return for denuclearisation. The DPRK rejected the proposal, an unsurprising decision to most observers given the DPRK's security concerns and the somewhat condescending tone of the offer.

The economic dimension of inter-Korean co-operation remained a priority in the ROK's North Korea policy of 'mutual benefit and common prosperity'. The emphasis on conditional and reciprocal engagement resulted in a clear shift towards more economic exchanges via the KIC and a strong decrease in the government's approval of social and cultural exchanges. After the DPRK fired a long-range missile in April 2009, inter-Korean economic co-operation and social exchanges were almost entirely halted. According to statistics provided by the MOU, with the exception of business operations taking place at the KIC, only one private joint venture between South and North was approved in 2009 compared to nine in 2008 and six in 2007. Despite rising political tensions, the KIC continued to grow, and 24 new companies moved to the industrial zone in 2009.

The DPRK's verbal provocations against the South continued during 2009. At the end of January, the North Korean Committee for the Peaceful Reunification of the Fatherland released a statement threatening that 'all agreements preventing confrontation between North and South would be nullified' and that the 'inter-Korean sea border would be regarded as void' (Yonhap News Agency, 30 January 2009). In March, the first general-level talks in six years were held at P'anmunjŏm. During the meeting the DPRK condemned the annual joint military exercises of the ROK and United States (US).

The day after the DPRK conducted its second nuclear test, the ROK announced that it would become a full member of the Proliferation Security Initiative (PSI). South Korea's full membership in the PSI had constituted an issue of political debate in the months before. Critics of the ROK's decision pointed at the possible short- and long-term consequences, and warned about increasing military tensions on the Korean peninsula. The DPRK reacted immediately to the ROK's decision, which it defined as a 'declaration of war' (*sŏnjŏn p'ogo*). Furthermore, it declared that it would not abide by the Armistice Agreement signed in 1953, and threatened to retaliate if the South attempted to control its vessels.

Despite such provocations, the intrusion of fishing boats into the other side's territorial waters was usually handled as a routine matter. North Korean nationals who expressed their wish to return to the DPRK were sent back by the South via P'anmunjŏm. The South Korean crew of a fishing boat that was seized in DPRK waters was released after 30 days in detention at the end of August. Military tensions heightened in November when a naval clash involving two vessels between the ROK and DPRK—the first in seven years—occurred in the Yellow Sea, shortly before US President Barack Obama's visit to Seoul. Despite considerable material damage to the vessels, no casualties were reported.

3 KAESŎNG INDUSTRIAL COMPLEX: A PAWN IN THE DPRK'S HANDS?

With the suspension of tourist tours to the Mt Kŭmgang area and the city of Kaesŏng, the KIC is the last surviving joint economic project between the two Koreas. Although the Lee administration approved ten tenant companies in 2009 (a sharp decrease from 53 approvals in 2008), grievances regarding the KIC's vulnerability to political tensions and the '3C issue' (crossings, communication and customs' clearance) remained. From 1 December 2008, the DPRK had implemented several measures that would further constrain business activities at the KIC, and as a consequence trade between the two Koreas declined by more than 8 percent (from US$1.82 billion to US$1.68 billion). The restrictions included the suspension of the cross-border cargo train service, the reduction of the border gate openings from 19 to six daily, the reduction of ROK staff working at KIC by more than half, and a ban on the use of mobile phones, South Korean newspapers and CDs (see *Korea Yearbook 2009*, pp. 62-64). In March 2009, the DPRK authorities completely closed the border gates to KIC to both personnel and goods for three brief periods. These restrictions led to a sharp decline in cross-border traffic: the number of vehicles dropped from 184,072 (2008) to 145,802 in 2009, the number of people crossing the border decreased from 186,775 (2008) to 120,862 in 2009. South Koreans, most of them related to KIC business, represent the majority (120,616) of cross-border visitors. Under the Lee administration, the number of North Koreans visiting the ROK reacted dropped sharply from 1,044 in 2007 to 332 in 2008 and to 246 in 2009.

Relations further deteriorated when a Hyundai Asan engineer and South Korean national, Yu Sŏng-jin, was arrested and detained by the DPRK authorities in March, for allegedly having criticised the DPRK's political system and for trying to persuade a North Korean female employee to defect. Yu was released after four and a half months in North Korean custody.

In April, the DPRK authorities increased pressure on the South over Kaesŏng. During the first official inter-Korean governmental meeting in Kaesŏng for over a year, the North Korean side announced that it intended to review the special benefits for ROK companies, including cheap labour and land fees. In June, the DPRK unilaterally declared invalid all contracts and agreements reached on the KIC between the two Koreas in the past. It demanded a four-fold rise in wages (from the current US$70-US$80 to US$300 per month), and a 30-fold increase in land fees. Working-level meetings in June and July 2009 failed to reach an agreement on wages and rents. In September, however, the two sides managed to agree on a wage increase of 5 percent for North Korean employees.

Among clients, mainly South Korean department stores, these developments caused concerns about growing instability at KIC. Further influenced by the global economic crisis, orders of KIC products dropped by 30 percent in 2009 (Yonhap News Agency, 3 September 2009). According to the Yonhap News Agency, although some small and medium-sized companies had considered temporarily downscaling or even suspending production, only one company, the fur and leather clothes producer Skin Net, had so far withdrawn from the complex. Concerns that the unfavourable business environment would cause other companies to leave the complex have so far remained unfounded.

Amid rising political tensions and stalled inter-Korean projects, Hyun Jung-eun, Hyundai Group chairwoman, left for an eight-day trip to the DPRK on 10 August. Her delegation met with Kim Jong Il and signed a five-point agreement with the DPRK's Asia Pacific Peace Committee on the resumption of joint projects including tours to the city of Kaesŏng and to Mt Kŭmgang. Although the ROK government officially welcomed the accord as a 'positive' sign, it stressed that this agreement had been made on a private level and that its implementation would depend on consensus between the governments.

It is difficult to assess the impact of Hyun's agreement with the DPRK leadership, but in September, the ban on cross-border traffic for South Korean workers and cargo trains was lifted by the DPRK, and the number of crossings allowed went back to the level prior to 1 December 2008. The number of ROK employees who are allowed to stay at KIC was also restored. The KIC's inter-Korean Exchange and Cooperation Consultation Office reopened and resumed its work.[1]

---

[1] After the inter-Korean Exchange and Cooperation Consultation Office was closed in December 2008, paperwork relating to the KIC was exchanged through Chinese officials until the office reopened.

After the inter-Korean Exchange and Cooperation Consultation Office was closed in December 2008, paperwork relating to the KIC was exchanged through Chinese officials until the office reopened. At the end of 2009, 42,561 North Korean (mainly female) workers were employed in 117 South Korean small and medium-sized enterprises. In 2009, firms paid about US$30 million in wages to the North Korean government.

In an attempt to 'improve the international competitiveness' of the KIC, a delegation of South and North Korean officials visited industrial parks in China and Vietnam in December 2009. The study tour's objective was to find an international model that could help to develop the KIC. There have been similar study tours in the past and reports revealed, not surprisingly, that priorities differed between the ROK and DPRK delegation members. Whereas the South Korean officials focused on issues related to infrastructure, safety, tax benefits and customs, their North Korean counterparts showed particular interest in wage regimes and insurance systems.

Business trips to the North not related to KIC activities were further restricted by the ROK after the DPRK test-fired a long-range missile in April 2009. Imports of items in which firms belonging to the North Korean military are allegedly involved were banned. These include imports of natural resources, particularly sand (representing the largest share of imports) and anthracite, as well as pine mushrooms. South Korean import companies need approval from the MOU. This step is seen as an attempt to monitor and control cash flows to the North.

4 HUMANITARIAN ASSISTANCE: OVER TO PRIVATE ORGANISATIONS

The shift in the handling of inter-Korean relations in general, and humanitarian issues in particular, is reflected in steps taken by the Lee administration, such as the restructuring of the MOU and the decrease in food and fertiliser aid to the DPRK. Although earlier plans to abolish the MOU seemed no longer a politically appropriate option, the restructuring of the ministry and the outsourcing of humanitarian aid projects to private organisations went ahead. In May 2009, the MOU announced the closure of its humanitarian co-operation bureau that had been established in 1996. The bureau had been in charge of sending humanitarian aid to North Korea, the arrangement of family reunions, and assistance with the settlement of North Korean defectors.

Instead, the South Korean authorities announced the creation of a new bureau focusing on the analysis of DPRK internal politics. The decision to close the bureau had a highly symbolic significance. In a similar move, the DPRK government abolished its cabinet-level committee for economic co-operation with South Korea that had been established in 2004.

Since the Lee government took office, both official and private assistance to North Korea decreased significantly. In the period between January and May 2009, aid decreased by 60 percent compared to the same period in 2008. The MOU repeatedly emphasised that without prior consultation between the two governments it had no plans to resume massive food and fertiliser aid to North Korea as had been provided by the previous governments. Between 2000 and 2007, the ROK government sent 300,000 to 500,000 tons of rice to the DPRK almost every year within the framework of its engagement policy. Shipments even continued after the first nuclear test conducted in October 2006, although at a lower level. The Lee administration suspended governmental direct food aid to the North but continued providing donations for humanitarian assistance to South Korean and international aid agencies such as the World Health Organisation (WHO) and the United Nations Children's Fund (UNICEF). It selectively outsourced the implementation (and monitoring) of humanitarian projects to local aid organisations and allocated US$29.9 million (a decrease by 2.5 times compared to 2008) to private aid groups. The number of aid organisations receiving state funding fell from 40 in 2008 to ten in 2009. In mid-2009, humanitarian aid that had been suspended after the second nuclear test was resumed to a limited extent through South Korean private aid agencies. In December 2009, the ROK government decided to donate US$22.2 million to WHO, UNICEF and private aid organisations. Official humanitarian aid totalled US$36.42 million in 2009, a 10 percent decrease from US$40.73 million in 2008 (compared to US$376.7 million in 2007, the Roh administration's last year in office).[2]

As in 2008, the North did not choose to actively seek humanitarian aid nor fertilizer from the ROK government until October 2009. In the first half of 2009, the DPRK authorities rejected food aid and medi-

---

[2] In South Korean won, total aid was 46.1 billion won (2009) and 43.8 billion won (2008), suggesting a rise. For conversion to US dollars, the annual median exchange rate of one South Korea won=0.00079 US dollar (2009) and 0.00093 US dollar (2008) has been applied (www.oanda.com).

cine offered by the South Korean Red Cross but they accepted food aid sent by South Korean private organisations. After the first confirmed cases of H1N1 influenza were detected in the DPRK, the North also accepted the South's offer to provide anti-viral medication for 500,000 people worth US$15 million. However, during the Red Cross talks over inter-Korean family reunions held in October the DPRK requested—for the first time since Lee Myung-bak took office—humanitarian aid from the ROK. The ROK government offered a limited volume of corn (10,000 tons worth US$33.38 million) and other humanitarian aid (20 tons of milk powder worth US$126,870 and medicine) to the DPRK. Three months later (January 2010) the offer was accepted by the DPRK. In addition, the MOU provided about US$800,000 for several local humanitarian organisations. According to reports, the DPRK increasingly receives free aid from China and Russia, which apparently replaces the assistance provided by the previous South Korean governments.

In 2009, non-economic, i.e. social and cultural, exchanges between South and North were further restricted by the ROK government. According to MOU statistics, no joint social or cultural exchange projects were approved by the ROK government, compared to three projects in 2008. After the DPRK's second nuclear test on 25 May 2009, South Korean authorities imposed a travel ban on South Korean citizens to North Korea. Business-related travel involving the KIC and the tourist resort at Mt Kŭmgang was exempted from the ban. Despite the implementation of further restrictions on civic visits, the South Korean authorities made some exceptions. For example, aid workers of the South Korean branch of World Vision were allowed to visit the DPRK. The ROK government has been trying to curb social exchanges between the two Koreas. The latest example is its rejection of a request by the country's largest Buddhist order (Chogye) to allow a group of 4,000 adherents to visit North Korea in February 2010.

5 OTHER DEVELOPMENTS

Since the death of a South Korean tourist shot by a North Korean guard for allegedly leaving the Mt Kŭmgang tourist complex territory in July 2008, all tours have been suspended at the ROK government's request. Although the Hyundai Group chairwoman, Hyun Jung-eun, and Kim Jong Il agreed to resume inter-Korean tourism projects during her visit to Pyongyang in August, the situation remained unchanged at the end of the year. The Lee administration has repeatedly rejected calls by the DPRK and South Korean investors to resume the tours, seeing the project as a 'cash cow' for the North Korean leadership. Although investors have suffered heavy financial losses because of the suspension, the ROK MOU signalled that it would not shift from its position as long as the killing of the tourist is not fully explained by the DPRK authorities. It also demands the implementation of specific safety measures to guarantee that a similar incident would not occur in the future.

After several rounds of negotiation between the national Red Cross delegations of the ROK and DPRK, the 17th session of family reunions was held at Mt Kŭmgang from 26 September to 1 October. This reunion, of 195 separated families (888 persons), was the first in two years; about 550 persons came from the ROK and some 330 from the DPRK. Since the 1980s, 16 face-to-face reunions have taken place, and in 2005 life-time video reunions were introduced. More than 128,000 persons are registered at the ROK Separated Family Information Centre. Of those registered almost 43,000 have died, leaving more than 85,000 South Koreans who hope to see their relatives and partners in the North again.

Facing an increasing number of North Korean defectors in the ROK, the South Korean authorities decided to expand the Hana Centre programme. In March, additional community centres for the 15,000 'new settlers' were opened in Seoul, Puj'ŏn and Taegu. These centres are aimed at supporting North Korean defectors after they have completed the three-month resettlement programme at Hanawon, which celebrated its tenth anniversary in July. In September, eleven North Koreans defected from North Hamgyŏng province to the ROK on a fishing boat. Repeated calls from the DPRK authorities to return them to the North were rejected by the South Korean government.

On 6 September 2009, the unannounced discharge of the Hwanggang dam by the DPRK authorities caused rapidly rising water levels on the Imjin river and drowned six South Korean nationals. In a first reaction, the ROK minister of unification, Hyun In-taek, called this incident a 'deliberate action' in a speech to the National Assembly Committee on Unification, Foreign Affairs and Trade. During inter-Korean talks on the 'prevention of flooding from cross-border rivers' held in October 2009, the DPRK side expressed regret at the deaths. This wording was interpreted as an apology and welcomed by the presidential office as a 'considerably positive signal' (Yonhap News Agency, 14 October 2009).

In September 2009, a 20-member ROK delegation attended the celebrations of the official opening of the Pyongyang University of Science and Technology built in Pyongyang with donations from South Korea, US, China, Canada and Australia. Christian groups are the main sponsors of this project. The university's objective is to train North Korean students in advanced technology such as information-communication technology, agricultural and food engineering as well as industrial engineering. According to Yonhap News Agency, the South Korean authorities have been hindering faculty exchanges and withholding the shipment of computers to the DPRK (Yonhap News Agency, 17 September 2009). The ROK has long had a policy of restricting the supply of advanced computers to the DPRK, and now has the additional justification of UN sanctions to do so. But the ROK authorities were less strict with regard to the provision of communication equipment to the DPRK in order to modernise telephone and fax lines in October 2009. The new technology is expected to improve and accelerate procedures related to border crossings at the Demilitarised Zone (DMZ). The military communication lines reopened in both the west and the east sectors of the DMZ at the end of 2009.

6 OUTLOOK

The Lee administration reaffirmed that it would uphold its policy position based on denuclearisation, reform, opening and human rights, while emphasising that it would be flexible in persuading the North to accept these goals. One may question how flexible the ROK can be in its reactions if the DPRK sets the tone. Considering the Lee administration's firm stance, no major shifts and changes in its policy are to be expected. Inter-Korean businesses will continue to be highly vulnerable to political tensions on the Korean peninsula, and it has to be seen if the KIC is sufficiently well developed to withstand future political 'storms'. The last two years under the Lee administration have shown that it has become increasingly difficult for North Korea to receive economic benefits and assistance from the ROK government. Apparently it is able to substitute a great part of this 'lost income' by aid provided by China and Russia. Apart from increasing Chinese and Russian investments, there are also reports about increasing numbers of (Chinese) tourists visiting the DPRK. Taking these and recent developments on the Korean peninsula into account, it must be doubtful if the ROK government's return to a traditional Cold War policy will pay off in the years to come.

FOREIGN RELATIONS OF THE TWO KOREAS IN 2009

James E. Hoare

INTRODUCTION

The Republic of Korea (ROK—South Korea) found it possible to work with the new United States' administration and with a new government in Japan, despite initial apprehension about both. The Democratic People's Republic of Korea (DPRK—North Korea) did not. As usual, much diplomatic activity concerned matters involving the DPRK, with both human rights issues and the ongoing nuclear problem featuring prominently. The health of the North Korean leader, Kim Jong Il, and the question of his successor, continued to attract international attention and speculation.

1 REPUBLIC OF KOREA

1.1 *Relations with the United States*

The return of the Democrats to power in the United States (US) caused some concern in the ROK. President Lee Myung-bak perhaps felt more instinctively at home with fellow conservative President George W. Bush than with the president-elect, Barack Obama, even though US policy initiatives towards the DPRK in the last year of the Bush presidency had raised worries. The Democrats were thought to be in favour of a softer line on the DPRK, and there were many Clinton-era figures associated with the new American administration. In addition, Obama had expressed doubts over the ROK-US free trade agreement (FTA).

In the event, such concerns proved unfounded. As the DPRK, whether for domestic reasons or because of perceived lack of interest from the Obama administration, adopted an increasingly more provocative stance towards both countries, the ROK and US administrations found no difficulty in working together. Secretary of State Hillary Clinton visited Seoul in February. A Lee-Obama summit in June produced a reassurance about a continued US nuclear umbrella to protect the ROK, a commitment reaffirmed by Secretary of Defence Gates when he visited in October. The US welcomed Lee's foreign policy initiatives, which included sending the first-ever ship to join anti-piracy patrols in the Gulf of Aden in March, a commitment to join the Proliferation Security Initiative (PSI) in May, and a pledge to re-deploy some 350 troops to Afghanistan in 2010. The last two were controversial. The previous government had declined to sign up to the PSI because of the consequences of trying to stop a DPRK vessel; the DPRK said that it would treat such a manoeuvre as an act of war. The Afghan decision would break a 2007 pledge to withdraw ROK forces to secure the release of kidnapped ROK missionaries. Although the government brushed aside opposition both from the public and the National Assembly, concern remained, especially after a warning from the Taliban in December that there would be unspecified 'consequences' if the ROK government went back on the 2007 agreement.

Negotiations on the relocation of the US military command from Seoul took place in an apparently positive atmosphere. The move was originally secured in principle in 2003, with a formal agreement in 2004 providing for the transfer of most personnel and facilities by 2009. The timetable has slipped, partly because of local protests but mainly because of the sheer complexity of the process, and the relocation is now expected in 2014-16. By then US military installations in the ROK, which totalled 104 in 2002, should be down to about 47 from the current 70. Most US troops will be deployed in two hubs, one centred on P'yŏngt'aek, south of Seoul, the other in the southeast of the country between Taegu and Chinhae. There were the usual joint military exercises, resulting in the equally usual DPRK objections. The only detraction from the generally good relations with the new administration was the continued US reluctance to ratify the ROK-USA free trade agreement, despite the conciliatory approach that the Lee Myung-bak government had assumed in 2008.[1] This issue and the ongoing nuclear tensions with North Korea were the main topics when President Obama visited Seoul as part of a four-nation tour in November.

---

[1] For background, see Patrick Köllner, 'South Korea in 2008: Domestic Developments and the Economy', in *Korea Yearbook 2009*, pp. 18-20.

1.2 Relations with China

After the upheavals of 2008, relations with China moved into a calmer phase in 2009. But there were still issues to be addressed. Concern over the DPRK, especially after the missile launch—although the Chinese followed the North Korean position that it was a legitimate satellite launch—and the nuclear test in May, coupled with the belief that only China could exert pressure on the DPRK, led to numerous contacts, including a growing number between the military of the two countries. The visits began with a visit by the ROK foreign minister to Beijing in February, where he met his Chinese counterpart and Premier Wen Jiabao. A month later, the chief of staff of the Chinese People's Liberation Army (PLA), Chen Bingde, visited the ROK. He met his ROK counterpart, Kim Tae-young, and toured military bases. In April, President Lee and Chinese President Hu Jintao met in the margins of the G20 in London, and Lee apparently raised the issue of DPRK missiles, without getting much satisfaction. That same month, the ROK navy joined ships from the US, Russia, Mexico and other countries taking part in the multilateral naval review at Qingdao to mark the 60th anniversary of the PLA navy. Following the DPRK nuclear test, Defence Minister Lee Sang-hee went to China for discussions with his Chinese counterpart and with Vice-Premier Xi Jinping. But while there were signs that the Chinese were unhappy about the DPRK's nuclear programme, they were unwilling to go as far as the ROK and other countries wanted in adopting measures to bring pressure on the DPRK, whether at the United Nations (UN) or in a bilateral context.

As the year progressed, the meetings continued, but they all seemed equally frustrating for the South Koreans. The Chinese did not publically endorse President Lee's proposed 'Grand Bargain', by which the DPRK would receive political and economic benefits for abandoning its nuclear programme; this despite Lee's attempts to persuade them to do so on occasions such as his meeting with Hu Jintao in the margins of the UN General Assembly in September, or at the trilateral meeting in Beijing in October. Even the visit of Chinese Vice-Premier Xi Jinping to Seoul in December, during which the Koreans treated Xi and his entourage as though they were on the level of a head of state visit, failed to bring forth the hoped-for endorsement of the ROK approach to the DPRK, however successful the visit was in other ways. Xi's large group of party and government officials indicates just how important Sino-ROK relations have become since the establishment of diplomatic relations in 1992. During the visit, Xi proposed an increase in all levels of contact, including a doubling of trade between the two countries by 2015.

Two-way trade had reached US$180 billion in 2008, making China the ROK's largest trade partner. The balance was in the ROK's favour, with a trade surplus of over US$32 million. The impact of the world financial crisis produced a clear fall in the first half of 2009. The second half of the year saw a revival, and in the end the overall figures, at US$156.2 billion, showed a fall of 16 percent, lower than had been expected. China remained the ROK's main trading partner. Chinese exports to the ROK were some $53.7 billion, down 27.4 percent, while Chinese imports of ROK goods reached $102.8 billion, down 8.5 percent. The prospects for 2010 are good, however. The ROK was China's fourth largest exports recipient, and its second largest source of imports. China was also the largest recipient of ROK overseas investment, with a number of major ROK companies establishing new plants. Hyundai is now China's biggest car manufacturer, for example, and most big ROK companies have a presence in China. The financial crisis was another incentive for the regular contacts between the ROK, Japan and China, which some commentators see as the beginning of an 'East Asian Community', comparable to the European Community. It might also be a substitute for the ROK's stalled FTA talks with China, which have made little progress since 2007 (FTA negotiations with Japan are likewise in abeyance).

The ROK relaxed its rules for visas for Chinese tourists, who now make up a significant percentage of the ROK tourist trade, and whose spending levels are rising. For the second year running, Seoul was the most popular international destination for Chinese travellers. South Korean goods remain popular in China, but some reports say that the 'Korea Wave' of South Korean cultural exports is beginning to wane, with much less interest in South Korean-produced television dramas. Perhaps there is the beginning of a 'China Wave' in the ROK; in March, the first major Chinese drama production since the establishment of relations took place at Seoul's Sejong Cultural Centre.

Some tensions remain. The Lee government has expressed concern over the Chinese treatment of North Koreans in China, especially the policy of returning those caught to the DPRK. There is also worry about China's long-term goals in the DPRK. China has steadily become the North's main trading partner, as well as the main supplier of aid and these trends have increased since the change of government in the ROK in 2008. South Koreans have seen this, and the Chinese reluctance to engage in full sanctions against the DPRK, as part of a plan to assume control over the country and even to absorb it into China. Such a development seems unlikely but the concerns reflect long-standing worries about China's attitude to the Korean peninsula.

In addition, both countries compete internationally for energy resources, a potential flashpoint in years to come. More mundane economic worries include such issues as contaminated foodstuffs from China and patent infringements, which surface from time to time. However, the Chinese and the ROK government have designated 2010 as 'Visit China Year', and both hope that this will further strengthen the relationship.

1.3 Relations with Japan

Relations with Japan continued along the relatively smoother path of 2008, with President Lee and Japanese Prime Minister Asō Tarō, who met twice during the year in Seoul, finding common ground on approaches to the DPRK and the need for a strong relationship with the US. Although Asō lost the general election in September and was replaced as prime minister by the more liberal Hatoyama Yukio, the relationship remained good. Despite some expectation that he might pursue a different policy on North Korea, Hatoyama, as trapped as his predecessors by public opinion on the abduction issue, continued to follow a hard line. Hatoyama and Lee met at the UN General Assembly in New York soon after the former took office, and Hatoyama and his wife visited the ROK in October. Co-operation over dealing with the international economic crisis also brought the ROK, Japan and China together during the year.

The old controversies did not entirely sink from view, though there was less tension over them. April saw a protest about a Japanese history textbook that justified Japanese colonial rule, an issue of particular sensitivity with the approach in 2010 of the 100th anniversary of the annexation of Korea. The conflicting claims over the rocky outcrop known as Tokto in Korea and Takeshima in Japan simmered on. One cause of potential conflict faded at the beginning of the year, when Japan announced that it had no plans to conduct surveys around the islands. This proved an unreliable omen, however, and there were

Korean protests in September over the references to the islands in the annual Japanese defence white paper, and again in December over guidelines to Japanese middle-school teachers that apparently did not mention the islands by name but indicated that Japan's territorial claims should be maintained if discussion arose. The initial reaction was a low-key comment by a Ministry of Foreign Affairs and Trade spokesman, but shifted within the course of a day to a formal protest by the ROK foreign minister to the Japanese ambassador.

Textbooks and Tokto are to some extent theatre that can be turned on or off depending on the state of relations. A more fundamental problem is the economic relationship between the two, exemplified by the stalled negotiations on an FTA. Talks on such an agreement began in 2003 but stopped in 2004 and were not resumed under the Roh Moo-hyun government. President Lee came into office determined to improve relations with Japan, and in theory the negotiations resumed in 2008. In reality, nothing happened. The difficulty lies in the nature of the economic relationship, which leads to a massive trade deficit, estimated at US$174.9 billion in the period 1999-2008 and US$32.2 billion in 2009, for the ROK. The ROK depends on Japan for most of its capital goods and for intermediate goods that support its own manufacturing industry. The fear in the ROK is that if the country's economy was fully opened up to Japan, it would be swamped by an influx of Japanese goods, with consequent damage to the economy (Funabashi 2010). These concerns have led the ROK towards the idea of an East Asian Economic Community of China, Japan and the ROK, an idea that was discussed at a three-way summit held in Beijing in October 2009. All three countries have expressed interest in carrying the idea forward, but it remains very much at the tentative stage for now.

1.4 *Other relations*

Trade, energy needs, and the ROK's growing international economic role were prominent features of 2009. An FTA with the Association of South East Asian Nations (ASEAN) on services came into force in May, while a further ASEAN FTA on investment was initialled in June. India and the ROK signed a comprehensive economic partnership agreement (similar to an FTA) in July, which came into force in November. FTA negotiations continued with Australia, New Zealand,

Canada and the Gulf Co-operation Committee. The ROK initialled an FTA with the European Union (EU) in October; it is expected to enter into force in the second half of 2010. In several cases, negotiations were pushed forward during visits by President Lee or other senior political figures.

A similar pattern emerged in relation to the need to secure energy resources, with Lee and his colleagues regularly visiting areas important to the ROK for oil. The speaker of the National Assembly was in Jordan, Turkey and the United Arab Emirates in January, while Lee visited Indonesia in March and Uzbekistan and Kazakhstan in May. In the case of the latter two countries, ROK interests also include the Korean communities deported from the Soviet Far East to Central Asia on Stalin's orders in the 1930s. These have received much attention from the ROK since the collapse of the Soviet Union and the emergence of independent states in the 1990s. The visit of the Iraqi President Jalal Talabani in February saw the signing of an oil-for-development agreement, while energy co-operation was also a feature of a visit by Russian Deputy Prime Minister Igor Sechin the same month. The second ROK-Africa Forum, held in Seoul in November, was also widely seen as resource related, as was the ROK's pledge to double aid to Africa from the current US$107 million by 2012.

President Lee was one of the co-chairs in April at the Group of 20 (G20) meeting held in London to discuss the ongoing economic crisis. It was agreed at the G20 summit in September that the ROK will host a G20 summit in November 2010. Lee was back in Europe for a visit to Poland, Italy and Sweden in July, when he also met the Pope. In November, the ROK joined the OECD Development Assistance Committee, the first former recipient of OECD aid to do so.

Concern over the DPRK's growing links with Myanmar (Burma) since diplomatic relations were restored between the two countries in 2007 may have been one reason behind a vice-foreign ministerial visit to that country in January. Refugees may have been another concern since some North Korean refugees have begun to arrive in Myanmar; a group of 19 who arrived at the end of 2008 were allowed to go to Thailand in early January. The Thai authorities have been willing to allow such groups to go on to the ROK, after a suitable interval. In July, Defence Minister Lee Sang-hee visited Russia and Mongolia. The opening of a ROK consulate-general in Irkutsk was a sign of the continued development of relations with Russia.

Finally, there was much domestic and international interest, or bemusement, over the news that the Cia-Cia tribe, a small group living around the town of Bau-Bau on Buton island off the southwest coast of Sulawesi in Indonesia, had decided to adopt the Korean alphabet, *han'gŭl*, to record their written language (Wikipedia 2010; *Hankyoreh* 2009). All Koreans are proud of their alphabet and there was much rejoicing at this sign of international recognition.

2 THE DEMOCRATIC PEOPLE'S REPUBLIC OF KOREA

2.1 *The Six Party Talks, the nuclear issue and relations with the United States*

The nuclear issue remained the dominant theme in the DPRK's international relations. The last months of the Bush administration saw an impasse in the Six Party Talks that remained unresolved as the Obama administration came into office in January 2009. Uncertainties over what was happening in the DPRK were a complication, as was the deterioration in relations between the two Koreas, but there were widespread expectations that the DPRK would find the Democrats more congenial interlocutors, especially since a number of those who had been prominent in Korean affairs during the Clinton presidency (1993-2001) were expected to be part of the foreign policy apparatus of the new government. The appointment in February of Stephen Bosworth, a diplomat turned academic with long experience of Korean matters, as the US special representative for North Korea policy was seen as a sign of the Obama administration's wish to engage. The arrival of US food aid, to be closely monitored in accordance with arrangements reached in the Six Party Talks, also seemed a positive omen.

Any high expectations proved short lived. The DPRK apparently indicated that it wanted to send a delegation to the Obama inauguration but was rebuffed. Both the incoming president and Hillary Clinton, the secretary of state, emphasised that a resumption of the Six Party Talks was the way forward and that there could be no compromise on denuclearisation. They also made it clear that there was no question of the US accepting the DPRK as a nuclear power. Other countries followed a similar line. Having set out its stall, the new administration had apparently many more pressing matters on its agenda and made little attempt at cultivating the DPRK. Although a group of US experts, including Stephen Bosworth, went to the DPRK in February, there was no meeting of minds.

The DPRK response to the US position was that the normalisation of relations, including the removal of sanctions, should precede discussions on the nuclear issue. New sources of tension emerged in the spring. As usual, the US State Department report on human rights worldwide, which appeared on 25 February, was highly critical of the DPRK's record. Then the DPRK began preparations for what it described as a satellite launch, asserting that it had the right to pursue peaceful space development under the terms of the 'Treaty on the Principles Governing the Activities of States in the Exploration and Use of Outer Space', to which it is a party. The US response, echoed by several other countries, was that any such move would be in breach of UN Security Council 1718, passed after the DPRK's 2006 nuclear test. The DPRK brushed aside these objections, informing the relevant international bodies on 12 March that a satellite launch was planned. The start of an annual US-ROK military exercise added a further complication, since the DPRK always treats such events as though they were war preparations. A rare meeting at general level of the Military Armistice Commission at P'anmunjŏm, the first for seven years, produced no results.

On 17 March, the DPRK informed the US that it did not want any more food aid and closed the US-manned distribution centres. The same day, in a probably unrelated incident, the DPRK detained two American journalists who, it was alleged, had crossed the Tumen River between China and the DPRK into DPRK territory. A cameraman and a guide who were with the journalists both managed to get back to China. The journalists, Chinese-American Laura Ling and Korean-American Euna Lee from San Francisco-based Current TV (which is linked to US former Vice-President Al Gore), were working on a story about North Korean refugees. The DPRK admitted that they had been detained, accusing them of having illegally crossed the border river and of unspecified 'hostile acts'. From the start of their detention, the US authorities mounted a major effort to have them released. While there was much international condemnation of the DPRK action, many fellow journalists argued that the two had been foolish and irresponsible in their actions, since they may have put refugees and those who assist them at risk. Others noted that illegal border crossings tended to be frowned upon in most countries.

On 5 April, the DPRK, having threatened to respond with force at any attempt to stop it, launched what KCNA described as 'the satellite Kwangmyongsong-2, a shining product of self-reliance, [carried] into space by carrier rocket Unha-2', which was 'smoothly and accurately put into its orbit 9 minutes and 2 seconds after being completely separated from the carrier rocket' (KCNA 2009a). Kim Jong Il watched the launch, and the DPRK media claimed that the satellite was broadcasting revolutionary songs. Although the reality was that while the rocket took off successfully, it broke up soon after, there was an international outcry at the breach of Resolution 1718, together with the usual inaccurate claims about the DPRK's ability to hit parts of the US. China and Russia held back somewhat, apparently accepting the DPRK argument that it had a right to launch a satellite. This unwillingness to condemn the DPRK's actions meant that it was difficult to reach agreement on a further UN Security Council resolution, as Japan and the ROK wanted, and a unanimous statement, brokered by China and the US, was adopted instead. This condemned the launch and called for the tightening of the existing sanctions' regime.

In response, the DPRK announced that it would have nothing further to do with the Six Party Talks and that it was restarting its nuclear programme; the international monitors who had remained in place despite the increasing tension were forced to leave. Some six weeks after the rocket launch, and despite international pleas not to do so, the DPRK conducted its second nuclear test, larger than the one in 2006. This proved too much even for its supporters and, though it took a little time to organise, the UN Security Council unanimously passed Resolution 1874, which strengthened the existing arms embargo and called for inspection of cargo vessels if there were 'reasonable grounds' to believe that they contained prohibited items. As usual, the DPRK reaction was phrased in highly belligerent terms. The DPRK had no choice but to develop its nuclear weapons, and would now proceed to do so, because of the presence of thousands of US nuclear weapons in the ROK.[2] Additional sanctions would be a declaration of war, as would any attempt at a blockade. For good measure, there was also an attack on additional sanctions that were said to be imposed by the US and Japan on alleged money counterfeiting and drug trafficking.

---

[2] This claim was promptly denied by the US, which pointed out that all nuclear weapons had been withdrawn from the ROK in 1991.

The US immediately swung into action. On 24 June, President Obama extended a ban on commerce with the DPRK for twelve months, while the Pentagon announced that it would be monitoring the movement of North Korean ships. For the rest of the year, suspected ships were shadowed and harassed. One, the *Kang Nam*, which was reportedly bound for Myanmar, which it had visited several times before, turned back after being followed by US and Singapore warships. Others were detained, with mixed results. It was not clear whether movements by air were restricted by the UN sanctions, but the US tried to persuade China in particular to check on aircraft flying between the DPRK and Iran, apparently without success. In December, the authorities in Thailand seized a Georgian-registered aircraft that had stopped for refuelling. The crew, four Kazakhs and one from Belarus, were detained when the aircraft was found to be carrying DPRK-made weapons apparently destined for Iraq.

Soon after the UN Resolution on the nuclear issue, the two US journalists were formally put on trial and sentenced to 12 years 'reform through labour' for 'crimes against the Korean nation'. More rocket tests in early July were seen as yet a further challenge to the US. The omens for DPRK-US relations did not look promising. Yet, as with the ROK, even as relations seemed to reach rock bottom, signs indicated a possible drawing back by both sides. The DPRK did not go onto a war footing, and did not implement its threat to withdraw from the 1953 armistice arrangements. It continued to take part in UN activities, with delegations attending UN-convened meetings on the world financial crisis and a special committee on terrorism issues. While the US stressed that it was prepared for all contingencies with regard to the DPRK, Bosworth said on 10 June that the US had no intention either to invade the DPRK or to overthrow the regime. Pleas for clemency for the two journalists came from their families, who maintained that they had never intended to break DPRK law. The fact that they were not transferred to a labour camp, despite the sentence, indicated that the DPRK was willing to do a deal.

So it proved. Although the DPRK and Secretary of State Hillary Clinton hardly hit it off—she describing them as like spoilt children, they responding somewhat ungallantly by describing her variously as a schoolgirl and a pensioner—her husband, former President Bill Clinton, was a different matter. During his presidency relations between the two countries had been at their best, and it was Clinton who flew to the DPRK on 4 August to secure the release of the detained journalists. This he did in meetings with Kim Jong Il, who appeared smiling and animated with a solemn-faced Clinton. The visit was described as private and humanitarian, but it was difficult to believe that Clinton did not carry some form of message on wider issues, or that these were not discussed over dinner.

The DPRK's hostile tone softened somewhat, and it began to row back from its denunciations of the Six Party Talks, which the US still insisted was the way forward. But while the US insisted that there had to be denuclearisation and continued to press on human rights, counterfeiting and other issues, there were signs that it too wanted to get away from the hostility of the first half of the year. In October, Vice-Foreign Minister Ri Gun, the DPRK's number two on nuclear issues, was given a visa to attend an academic conference in California; he also met State Department officials. Some US think tanks began to call for engagement rather than confrontation. There were hints that the US might open a liaison office in the DPRK. Bosworth went to the DPRK in December, the first such visit at that level since October 2008, carrying a personal letter from President Obama to Kim Jong Il. He said that he had found the atmosphere positive. A rare group of visiting US businessmen reported DPRK interest in US trade and investment, but also that their interlocutors seemed unaware that UN sanctions would prevent such trade from developing. But at the end of the year, another problem arose, when a Korean-American Christian activist, Robert Park, crossed the frozen river border from China, carrying a letter calling on Kim Jong Il to free political prisoners, shut prison camps, improve human rights and step down, and was detained by border guards.

Foreign commentators struggled to find an explanation for the DPRK's behaviour. Most saw it, like Hillary Clinton, as a bid for US attention. Kim Jong Il was 'throwing the toys out of the pram' to persuade the US to take the DPRK seriously. If that was the intention, it succeeded, although hardly to the DPRK's advantage. The DPRK's behaviour may partly reflect frustration arising from the change of government and policies in the ROK, continued Japanese hostility, and what they see as US unwillingness to engage seriously with them, for example in removing sanctions with one hand and restoring them with the other. But it may also be that we are seeing a consequence of domestic agendas that are as important as or even more important than what the outside world thinks or does. Kim Jong Il's illness and the question of what happens if he dies or is incapacitated matter in the

DPRK and shows of military might may be a way of saying 'leave us alone to sort out our own problems and if you try to intervene, we can hit back.' There also may be an element of satisfying the generals' demands for more and better weapons, and a desire to complete programmes already begun. Without better insights into the DPRK leadership, the North's motives will remain hard to fathom.

2.2 Relations with China

China remained the DPRK's main international supporter and trading partner, although many suspected that what appeared as trade in Chinese statistics was really disguised aid. The Chinese were ambiguous over the missile tests, arguing that the DPRK had the right to engage in space exploration. However, as we have seen, they eventually agreed to condemn the missile and nuclear tests, but like the Russians, they argued that incentives were better than punishment. It was also widely supposed that, whatever they had signed up to at the Security Council and however angry they were with the DPRK, the Chinese would not be assiduous in their implementing of sanctions.

Numerous two-way visits indicated that relations were still important. They began in January with Wang Jiarui, director of the International Liaison Department of the Chinese Communist Party's Central Committee. Wang met Kim Jong Il, who assured him that the DPRK wanted denuclearisation on the Korean peninsula and peaceful coexistence with the rest of the world. In March, the DPRK Premier Kim Yong Il went to China on the occasion of the 60th anniversary of diplomatic relations between the two countries, to mark the 'DPRK-China Friendship Year' with Chinese Premier Wen Jiabao.

There was no DPRK reference to China's support for Resolution 1874. China's trade and aid to the DPRK continued as before; figures indicate that some 70 percent of DPRK trade is with China, which is also supposed to account for the bulk of international assistance to the country. China also supported the DPRK (and Myanmar) over human rights' criticism at the UN at various times during the year. Trade with the DPRK is especially important for China's northeastern provinces, which have declined economically since the beginning of China's own economic reforms in the 1970s. Perhaps in connection with this trade, the DPRK opened a consular office in Dandong, the main transit point for goods, in August.

China maintained that it was working to bring the DPRK back to the Six Party Talks; these after all, had been convened by China, which acted as the chair at plenary meetings. In September, Chinese State Councillor Dai Bingguo visited Pyongyang with a party and government delegation, bringing with him a letter from President Hu Jintao. The main purpose of the visit may have been the organisation of a reciprocal visit by Premier Wen for the end of the 'Year of Friendship', but the nuclear issue also featured on the agenda. The New China News Agency reported that Kim Jong Il told Dai that the DPRK would continue to work for denuclearisation through bilateral and multilateral channels.

Wen duly went to Pyongyang for the closing ceremony for 'Friendship Year'. He got a bear hug from Kim Jong Il and both attended a performance of 'Arirang'. KCNA reported that Kim Jong Il told Wen that Kim Il Sung had wanted the denuclearisation of the Korean peninsula. Kim also said that if the US would agree to bilateral talks, then there was a possibility that the DPRK would join in multilateral talks, adding that the 'six-party talks are also included in the multilateral talk' (KCNA 2009b).

Two visits towards the end of the year showed the continued importance of the relationship to both countries. In November, the Chinese defence minister, Colonel General Liang Guanglie, visited the DPRK, the first visit by a defence minister since April 2006. He met Kim Jong Il and pledged to improve military relations, that had been 'sealed in blood'—a reference to the 1950-53 Korean War. In mid-December, the DPRK Minister of People's Security Ju Sang Song visited China for talks with his Chinese counterpart. The Chinese side agreed to supply unspecified aid materials.

2.3 Relations with Japan

On 13 January, the DPRK released Yoshiaki Sawada, a suspected drugs dealer held since 2003, on humanitarian grounds.[3] If this was a gesture of conciliation towards Japan, it failed completely. The state of relations was perhaps better indicated by the governor of Tokyo, Ishihara Shintarō, speaking at the Foreign Correspondent's Club on

---

[3] Sawada admitted on his return to Japan that he was a *yakuza*, that is a member of a criminal organisation, and that he had been engaged in a drugs' deal in Pyongyang.

the day that Sawada was released. After attacking other countries for not doing enough to solve the issue of Japanese abducted by the DPRK and for failing to force denuclearisation, he said that it would be best if China took over the DPRK.

Ishihara is something of a maverick, known for his extreme views, but his comments probably struck a chord with many Japanese. Japan's attitude to the DPRK remained hostile, even when the autumn election brought the more liberal Hatoyama government to power. Japan, which sees itself particularly threatened by DPRK missiles, toughened up its existing sanctions regime after the April satellite launch, banning all trade with the DPRK until April 2010. Japan also imposed visa controls on North Koreans and has limited remittances from Koreans in Japan. The trade restrictions are more symbolic than anything else, since most DPRK trade goes through China, and Japanese ministers have lamented that Japanese companies are willing to circumvent the restrictions.

The Japanese government has continued to put pressure on Chōsen Sōren, the pro-DPRK association of Koreans in Japan. The latest development has been an attempt to exclude the children at the 12 schools that the organisation runs from new rules that provide for the payment of fees from public funds for children attending private schools. This has aroused concern, since the children's parents are taxpayers, and other schools catering for minority groups have not been excluded.

2.4 *Relations with Russia*

According to one Russian commentator, this was the year that the Russians finally became exasperated with the DPRK. Georgy Toloraya, writing in the online *Asia-Pacific Journal,* said that until 2009, Russia felt that the DPRK had a genuine grievance against the US, which had not played fair over the removal of sanctions and other promises. However, the decision to test a second nuclear device was a step too far, and the Russian government accepted that the DPRK nuclear programme had to be stopped. This led President Medvedev to sign a decree putting into force the UN sanctions agreed at the Security Council in June (Toloraya 2010). However, the fact that it took Medvedev until 30 October to do this showed that concerns in Russia over isolating the DPRK had not evaporated.

The sanctions issue apart, relations seemed much as usual. The Russian foreign minister visited in April, soon after the missile tests, and reported that the DPRK had no intention of returning to the Six Party Talks. In September, Russia made a gift of food aid. In November, Sergei Mikhailovich Mironov, chair of the Russian Federation Council, visited at the invitation of the Supreme People's Assembly; the two assemblies pledged to improve their links.

2.5 *Other relations*

It is easy to forget that missiles, nuclear tests and abductions, which catch so much of the world's media attention, are not the only distinguishing marks of the DPRK's international relations. As noted above, the DPRK sent delegations to UN meetings on the financial crisis and on terrorism. Although it rejected UN criticism of its human rights record as usual, maintaining that they were the result of bias, the DPRK engaged in discussions on the rights of women and children. In another UN-related issue, the United Nations Development Programme (UNDP) quietly reopened its office in Pyongyang. UNDP closed the office after allegations of mismanagement of funds but was cleared of the charge in 2009, although right-wing media and think tanks in the US continue to attack it.

The DPRK foreign minister was in Cuba, Brazil and Peru in April, partly to attend the non-aligned meeting in Havana. That same month, Kim Yong Nam, president of the Presidium of the DPRK Supreme People's Assembly, visited Singapore, South Africa, where he attended the inauguration of President Zuma, and Zimbabwe. Kim also attended the 15th non-aligned summit in Egypt in July, where he said that there was no question of the DPRK returning to the Six Party Talks. The foreign minister was in Myanmar, Laos and Cambodia in October.

Alleged links between Myanmar and the DPRK led to much speculation but not many facts. The stories relate to claims that the DPRK has helped the Myanmar regime to build some form of underground complex whose exact purpose is not known, that it has supplied weapons to the regime, and that it is helping Myanmar acquire a nuclear weapons' capability. News that the US navy was tracking a DPRK ship, the *Kang Nam*, which was suspected of carrying weapons to Myanmar in breach of UN Resolution 1874, intensified the speculation; but since the ship returned to the DPRK without reaching Myanmar, the incident did not add to the facts, although that did not stop the speculation.

European contacts with the DPRK remained limited. A British parliamentary delegation led by Lord Alton of Liverpool went in February, and a delegation of EU socialist parties visited in March. Perhaps the most surprising visit was that by the former French minister, Jack Lang, who went as President Sarkozy's special representative in November. Although France has no diplomatic relations with the DPRK, and has said that it will not until there is an improvement in the country's human rights' record, there are contacts, and some DPRK students have studied in France. Lang, who met the nominal head of state, Kim Yong Nam, and Foreign Minister Pak Ui Chun, said that he had received an undertaking to engage in a dialogue on the issue. KCNA reported that France would open a 'Cooperation and Cultural Action Office' in Pyongyang as the first phase for normalising the relations between the two countries. There were rumours that the US and the ROK had indicated that such a move would send the wrong signal to Pyongyang for so long as the nuclear issue remains unresolved.

Finally, the DPRK football team's qualification for the finals of the 2010 World Cup to be held in South Africa awakened memories of the country's performance in the 1966 World Cup. And there is also the possibility that the two Koreas might end up playing each other, which adds to the interest.

REFERENCES

Funabashi, Yoichi (2010), 'Japan-Korea FTA Cornerstone of the East Asia Community'. Online: http://www.eastasiaforum.org/2010/04/20/japan-korea-fta-cornerstone-of-the-east-asian-community/ (accessed 21 April 2010)

Hankyoreh (2009), 'Cia'Cia adopts Hangul to preserve spoken language', in: *Hankyoreh* online edition, 10 August 2009. Online: http://english.hani.co.kr/arti/english_edition/e_international/369998.html (accessed 26 April 2010)

KCNA (2009a), 5 April 2009, 'Kim Jong Il Observes Launch of Satellite Kwangmyongsong-2'. Online: http://www.kcna.co.jp/item/2009/200904/news05/20090405-12ee.html (accessed 2 May 2010)

KCNA (2009b), 5 October 2009, 'Kim Jong Il Visits Wen Jiabao at State Guest House'. Online: http://www.kcna.co.jp/item/2009/200910/news05/20091005-19ee.html (accessed 4 May 2010)

Toloraya, Georgy (2010), 'Russia and the Korean Knot', in: *Asia-Pacific Journal* 16-2-10, 19 April 2010. Online: www.japanfocus.org/-Georgy.Toloraya/3345 (accessed 27 April 2010)

Wikipedia (2010), 'Cia-Cia Language'. Online: http://en.wikipedia.org/wiki/Cia-Cia_language (accessed 26 April 2010)

CONFLICT MANAGEMENT IN URBAN PLANNING: THE RESTORATION OF THE CH'ŎNGGYECH'ŎN RIVER IN SEOUL

Annette J. Erpenstein

ABSTRACT

After 40 years of accelerated economic growth, South Korea and its capital Seoul have performed a basic shift towards quality in urban planning. A 5.7 km-long, chronically congested, elevated freeway at the core of Seoul was removed to restore the Ch'ŏnggyech'ŏn, a stream that had been buried underground in the 1970s. This ambitious project was started in 2002 and completed in 2005. The Ch'ŏnggyech'ŏn restoration can be viewed as a rare achievement in urban revitalisation policy in South Korea, but the urban planning process, the criteria for evaluation, and the management of conflict during the restoration may not be viewed as equally successful as the project itself, leaving room for improvement and further consideration.

1 INTRODUCTION

The Ch'ŏnggyech'ŏn project represents the decisive project management skills and leadership of Lee Myung-bak, mayor of Seoul from 1 July 2002 to 30 June 2006, as well as the successful implementation of the project that paved his way to becoming the president of South Korea in February 2008. As the project contains all the aspects of urban mega-project management of a metropolitan urban area, it can be considered a contemporary example of urban planning conflict management in South Korea. Specifically, it highlights the interaction of various stakeholders, including numerous affected groups such as the media, politicians and individual protagonists, within a democratic process of urban planning and conflict management. Furthermore, it brings out the main points and preconditions under which city development is carried out. It is an interesting question for urban planning professionals how such a big project could be so quickly completed in the downtown area of a megacity, when in significantly smaller cities in other democratic countries, legal hurdles prolong projects, cause them to become cost prohibitive, or hinder any city development at all.

After examining the historical importance of the Ch'ŏnggyech'ŏn river in the urban fabric as well as the restoration process, this paper analyses the political, economic, cognitive, and implementation aspects of the project. It illustrates how the restoration of the 5.7 km river in the city centre of a metropolitan population of more than 20 million was completed in just over three years despite large-scale public confrontation. The author discusses the structures and motivations that led the main protagonists and the instruments of power and resources that either supported or hindered the decision process.

The paper is based on consultation of Ch'ŏnggyech'ŏn-related literature and publications, as well as a comprehensive analysis of print media published in English and in three Korean newspapers (*Chosun Ilbo*, *Donga Ilbo* and *Hankyoreh*) from January 2002 to December 2005, during which period the project was introduced, planned and accomplished. Furthermore, between 2004 and 2009, the author interviewed 76 people who were involved in the project. All interviews have been transcribed and are used in anonymised form.[1]

The conflict management experience of the Ch'ŏnggyech'ŏn project gives insights into the strengths and weaknesses of the Korean urban planning system and its capabilities for political conflict management. Furthermore, it exemplifies the behaviour and patterns of action of the current political leadership on the local and national level. The successes of this project may contribute to creating more transparent processes for those involved in similar projects and enable a more effective conflict management for future projects both in Korea and elsewhere.

2 Historical Background of the Ch'ŏnggyech'ŏn River

The Ch'ŏnggyech'ŏn, which was known as the 'Kaech'ŏn' (open riverlet) in the Chosŏn dynasty (1392-1910), has been part of Seoul's historical and cultural centre for the last 600 years. Although the his-

---

[1] The transcripts can be inspected as components of the author's doctorate at the Faculty of Geography, Westfaelische Wilhelms-University in Muenster, 2010.

tory of early settlements in the Seoul area can be traced far back, when the Paekche dynasty (traditional dates 18 BC-AD 663) set up its first capital in the region, the city began to flourish when the Chosŏn dynasty designated it as its capital under the name of Hanyang, in 1394 (Kim 2003: 3).

This location was chosen because of the disposition of the surrounding mountains and the Ch'ŏnggyech'ŏn river in the middle, making the city easier to defend and allowing it to be laid out in a perfect geomantic shape (i.e., according to the knowledge of earth energies and in harmony between man and nature). When Seoul became the Chosŏn capital, the fortress walls were built, enclosing an administrative area of five districts with a radius of ten *ri* (some four kilometres) (Lee Ki-suk 2003: 23). The sources of the inner-city Ch'ŏnggyech'ŏn were Mt Inwang, located in the northwest of Seoul, the southern foot of Mt Pukhan, and the northern foot of Mt Nam. According to ancient documents, 23 tributaries flowed into the Ch'ŏnggyech'ŏn.

Its total length extends 10.92 km. The Kyŏngbok and Ch'angdŏk palaces and the quarters of the upper class and high-ranking officials, the *yangban*, were located in the area north of the river, while merchants and craftsmen were concentrated along Chongno Street, and the lower class traditionally lived in the area south of the Ch'ŏnggyech'ŏn (Lee Ki-suk 2003: 28). The river has therefore not only divided the capital geographically, but has also played a symbolic role as the boundary in politics, society and culture. Centrally located within the capital, the Ch'ŏnggyech'ŏn served many important functions, such as a source of water, a washing place, and a natural sewerage system.

2.1 *Function and maintenance*

As an intermittent stream, the Ch'ŏnggyech'ŏn was originally a dry, seasonally flowing brook. Flooding was thus a major problem until the water management authority called for large-scale construction work on the urban stream. In 1407, construction was first carried out by digging out the bottom of the stream and expanding its width as well as building an embankment with stone and wood (Lah 2005: 2). Though there was controversy over the use of urban streams in the early days of the Chosŏn dynasty, King Sejong decided it was to be used as a sewer. Ever since that time, dredging work became an unavoidable option in maintaining the stream's function of flood prevention and stopping the spread of illness. Despite the government's financial difficulties dredging was persistently conducted every two to three years until 1908.

From 1394—when approximately 100,000 people were living in the capital—up until the end of the 19th century, the population of Seoul grew slowly and the city never expanded its administrative boundary. According to a survey conducted at the time, the number of citizens in the five main districts was only 196,898 people in 1900 (SDI 2003: 25). In contrast, at that time Tokyo had a population of 3.69 million and Berlin was home to two million.

2.2 Coverage work and negligence

With an increasing population and more intense use, the most serious problem in the Ch'ŏnggyech'ŏn area was sanitation. During the rainy season of July and August, many houses near the stream were repeatedly flooded, and contagious diseases swept over the whole city. Because of this, the mortality rate in the area of the river was the highest in Seoul (SMG 2005: 23). In the early 1900s, the government started covering the stream for military, sanitary and flood control purposes. However, this was not connected with the full-scale covering construction work.

With the occupation of the Korean peninsula in 1910 by Japan, the country lost not only its dynasty, but also its independence, and until 1945 was subjected to Japanese colonial domination. To further the economic exploitation of Korea and to demonstrate supremacy, the Japanese colonial government deliberately interrupted the geomantic urban structure by placing various colonial government buildings at central points in the geomantic, or *fengshui* (Korean: *p'ungsu*) structure, and by extending the road system, building according to modern housing patterns, and introducing variegated industrial facilities both inside and outside the city. During that time, squatter areas appeared and grew near railroad tracks, on embankments, along streams and under bridges because farmers had lost their holdings and moved to the city, or were relocated through city planning projects. In addition to the spread of poorer quarters and slums along the Ch'ŏnggyech'ŏn and other streams, the Japanese colonial government neglected the required dredging and cleaning maintenance. During this period, the river was renamed several times and was completely altered in every respect. As the city grew and developed, the old structure and sights disappeared. In a complete reversal of the residential environment of the areas north and south of the Ch'ŏnggyech'ŏn, the north, which was once the residential area of the yangban, turned into a poor Korean neighbourhood. The south of the river, previously inhabited by labouring people, became a clean and upmarket Japanese area.

With the end of World War II, Korea regained liberation from colonial rule, but was divided into North and South. The city of Seoul suddenly had to deal with a huge number of Koreans returning from Japan and China, and saw an even greater increase in the growth of shanty homes throughout the city. After independence, the political chaos of the situation almost brought the construction of a covering over the Ch'ŏnggyech'ŏn to a halt. Furthermore, the drainage system in Seoul was left unattended, repair and maintenance work was not adequately carried out as a result of financial hardship, and the accumulation of soil and sand became extremely critical.

Shortly thereafter, as a result of the Korean War, the entire country, but especially Seoul, which had been twice abandoned and recaptured by UN troops from North Korean, then Chinese forces, experienced total destruction. When the 1953 Korean armistice agreement was signed, many refugees from North Korea poured in to Seoul, which was located just south of the new de-militarised zone. The Ch'ŏnggyech'ŏn in the city centre became a symbol of poverty and squalor as shanty homes rapidly spread along the streams and on hillsides. The ever-fluctuating population of Seoul decreased sharply from 1.7 million in 1950 to 0.6 million in 1951, but then jumped in 1953 to one million and ultimately reached two million in 1959 (SDI 2005: 8, 9). At the end of the war, the South Korean economy was similar to that of Sudan or other developing countries, and millions starved.

2.3 *Modern times*

Much effort went into repairing war damage, but it was not possible to carry out drainage maintenance or reconstruction immediately. Nevertheless, in 1954, US$52 million was provided for repair work on drainage systems including the Ch'ŏnggyech'ŏn (SMG 2005: 37). Furthermore, in 1955, construction of a close conduit extending

135.8 m was carried out upstream of Kwangt'ong bridge, the first covering since the Japanese colonial period. Larger-scale covering construction work, 2,358.5 m in length and 16-54 m in width, was put in hand between 25 May 1958 and December 1961, in the central downtown area between Kwangt'ong bridge and Ogansu gate/bridge.

During the military dictatorship of General Park Chung-hee (1961-79), development was even faster. From 1965 to 1966, the area to the east between the Ogansu bridge, Tongdaemun and Ch'ŏnggyegyo 2 was covered over. Work on the first overpass, the Ch'ŏnggyech'ŏn expressway, began on 15 August 1967 and ended on 15 August 1971. The building of the expressway marked a historic moment in Korean construction in terms of its length and the scale of operation. The road itself became a symbol of the development of Seoul and the pride of a dynamically emerging country. To improve the sanitary conditions of the covered Ch'ŏnggyech'ŏn, waste pipes were constructed in 1984, and in 1992 a basic management plan for the drainage system was established and a reorganisation project for the system was conducted. By 2000, about 168,000 vehicles would daily use this main urban traffic artery (Park 2005).

In the meantime, Seoul became a city with 10.3 million citizens living within the city boundaries and 22 million living in the greater metropolitan area. This means that almost 50 percent of all 48 million South Koreans are living on 1 percent of the total land area of South Korea. An 80 percent degree of urbanisation puts Korea at the top of all industrial nations in the world. Seoul itself is the undisputed administrative, economic, financial and educational centre of South Korea.

3 EXCAVATING A LAYERED REALITY

In 2002 the new mayor of Seoul, Lee Myung-bak, directly elected by the citizens of Seoul, proposed the restoration of the Ch'ŏnggyech'ŏn river as his main campaign promise. The project, which appealed to the imagination of many of his electors, could yield considerable economic benefit for downtown Seoul and could look to business for support in addition to improving the environment and quality of life in the capital. In his aim to create a city that was environmentally friendly and livable-in, and also to improve the economic and financial position of Seoul, Lee aimed to move urban policy from development to the sustainable.

Even though the Ch'ŏnggyech'ŏn river was in the past more likely to be associated with negative attributes such as sewerage, traffic, noise and dirt, many people became enthusiastic about its restoration. The idea appealed even to many members of the opposition parties, such as the late president Roh Moo-hyun, and many non-governmental organisations. Within the context of various political, economic, social and environmental objectives to be achieved, the goals of the differently involved stakeholders varied considerably, from total ecological and historical restoration to modern, technical landscape architecture within the urban setting. Depending on personal motivation and power resources, action groups could hope more or less to convince the public and move the political system in their direction. Important factors in facilitating the social-political negotiation processes emerged in the formal planning system and democratic arrangements at the local level, in practices of social-cultural conflict, and in sociopolitical priorities (e.g. economic, environmental, historical) in the weighting of planning decisions in respect of the public.

In order to excavate the layered reality of this project, this paper endeavours to highlight in a concentrated and analytical fashion the main aspects of success and failure from an action-oriented, geographical research perspective grounded in urban planning. It will focus on the strengths and weaknesses of the current democratic process of urban planning, stakeholder and conflict management in the Ch'ŏnggyech'ŏn project, and the power of geographical imagination in planning decisions.

4 STRENGTHS AND WEAKNESSES OF THE CURRENT DEMOCRATIC PROCESS OF URBAN PLANNING

Although the first self-governing form of administration was introduced in 1960 with elected local parliaments and mayors, successive military governments suspended it from 1961 to 1995. When local elections were held in 1995, the first parliament and first mayor of Seoul, Cho Soon, were directly elected by the citizens. Self-government is laid down in Article 117 of the Korean Constitution of 1997 as follows: 'Local autonomy: local government shall deal with administrative matters pertaining to the welfare of local residents, manage properties, and may enact provisions relating to local autonomy, within the limit of acts and subordinate statutes.' Korean local government may be considered young, having existed for only 15 years, with only four mayors of Seoul elected directly by the citizens within that period.

The practice of self-government as a form of grassroots democracy provides information about the local anchoring and actual functioning of democracy and about practical interaction between government, institutions and citizens. It is of even greater interest since Korean history until the 20th century offers no experience in transferring power from the ruling class to the common people. The monarchy and the highly concentrated central government did not leave room to pass on power to local government (Choi 2000). Hence, a closer look at the urban planning process in Seoul shows how democracy works at the local level and how the historical, social and political background may have a positive or negative impact upon the outcome of urban development.

The local political system in urban planning decisions provides for relatively strong powers for the mayor and weaker powers for the city council. As the head of the city administration, the mayor gives the guidelines and themes for urban development during his term and manages the distribution of information and the budget. The city council is also charged with approving the budget, but 'because of the local council's low expertise and resources, political initiatives are likely to come from the local bureaucracy headed by the mayor' (Park 2006: 19). The real challenge for a mayor lies in convincing and coping with those public officials who still tend to develop functional loyalties based upon professional expertise as defined by the central bureaucracy, in a reflection of past authoritarian government.

Since the time that the right of self-government took effect, civil rights such as participation in urban planning projects have been practiced regularly. These are cornerstones for democracy, as free and independent media contribute to a well-informed public in such urban planning processes. Active and involved citizens, moreover, are needed who are well informed, know their rights, and participate in any way; in addition, organised and vibrant non-governmental organisations have to be part of the process so that all aspects of urban planning can be heard and taken into consideration. Although the process of democratisation in South Korea was strongly pushed forward by workers' and students' movements, non-governmental organisations concerned with ecological, civil, women's or consumers' rights and the protection of monuments now reflect a short but growing history.

Looking at a concrete urban planning process in comparison with Western, for example, German, procedure, one can find some smaller differences in planning procedure and powers of decision that must be addressed because of the huge impact these differences have upon the capacity to act of certain groups and stakeholders and upon the possibility of influencing the outcome of the urban development project.

First of all, the initiation of proceedings in Korea is conducted by the mayor. The city council can indirectly influence an urban planning project by approval or disapproval of the budget. The political power and urban planning initiative lies with the mayor unless the city is financially dependent upon subsidies from the central government, which is not the case with Seoul (Park 2006: 19).[2] The democratic instrument of public participation is, according to Korean law, a single-stage process, where public hearing and the participation of public representatives and residents take place. In the case of major changes after public participation, the procedure has to be repeated. This stands in contrast to the German planning process which is, in general, conducted as a double-stage process where the blueprint plan is discussed with citizens and public representatives in an early planning stage, then later on in an 'Offenlegung' (literally 'disclosure'), before the concrete and detailed final plan is publicly discussed. As in Korea, this public hearing has to be repeated if major changes induce the revision of the plan.

After full deliberation in the City Planning Commission, the blueprint plan in Korea can proceed to the next stage for application for permission. While the City Planning Commission in Germany is an independent advisory body consisting of politicians according to political majorities, the members of the City Planning Commission in Korea are professional consultants, experts, and politicians appointed by the city government for two years. In both cases the City Planning Commission works as an advisory body: in Germany to the city council, in Korea to the mayor. Last but not least, the final act of considering and balancing the suggestions and objections made by stakeholders, citizens and public bodies in Korea is made by the mayor. In

---

[2] According to a study of the Ministry of Government Administration and Home Affairs (MOGAHA) 70 percent of all cities in South Korea depend on subsidies from central government for up to 50 percent of their budgets (MOGAHA 2006).

Germany, this process usually takes place in a public discussion held by the city council.

Even though the urban planning process from the outside appears similar, since large parts are inspired by German planning law and the German system, the practical implementation shows strong emphasis on the position and power of the mayor. What is the reason for this and what impact does this have upon urban planning procedures and urban development itself?

After World War II, South Korea was integrated under the growing influence of Anglo-American and European legal systems. Knowledge of German law had already been introduced by the Japanese colonial government, Japan having itself adopted the German concept of a constitution in the late 19th century in an attempt to modernise its own constitution (Hyun 1990). The current South Korean legal system can be seen as a hybrid system of traditional East Asian law, new continental European law and Anglo-American law. Within the context of 2000 years of the Asian-Korean legal tradition, one issue has been if and how positive, correct and traditional Confucian principles merge with this hybrid system (Lee Yeong-heui 2003). A sign of the still ongoing assimilation process between Eastern and Western values in everyday life can be experienced in the widespread culture of dispute prevention commonly practiced in Korea. This is exemplified by the Korean habit of attempting to choose a golden mean in situations of conflict according to the principle of maintaining harmony. This habit makes it easier for Koreans to accept compromises and partial successes.

The long Confucian tradition has had an effect on the democratic system and on local planning practice, in the form of a strong bureaucratic hierarchy that in particular empowers the mayor in dealing with civil rights in urban planning. Citizens in South Korea still have a tendency to make less use of their civil rights compared to citizens in older Western democracies. This pronounced behaviour leads back to a tradition that supports strong leadership and dutiful citizens.

From such perspectives, it can be postulated that the legal reception of social change in Korea is an ongoing process which proceeds nonetheless in the background because the subjects of such reception are the individuals who must approve and follow these rights in their pattern of behaviour. In the process of the Ch'ŏnggyech'ŏn restoration project, one sees the full range of conflicts that arise in the legal process of urban planning and in exercising urban planning rights in Korean society. We will therefore take a closer look at the actual restoration process from 2002 to 2005.

5 STAKEHOLDER AND CONFLICT MANAGEMENT IN THE CH'ŎNGGYECH'ŎN PROJECT

A determined effort to restore the buried river in downtown Seoul first emerged in 2000 among scholars. Support was garnered by Ms Park Kyung-ni, the respected and well-known novelist and environmentalist, among researchers and universities and with the public. She gave a first key interview on 1 January 2002 in *Hankyoreh* newspaper on how important the Ch'ŏnggyech'ŏn restoration was for the citizens of Seoul (*Hankyoreh*, 1 January 2002; SMG 2004b; Interviews 1_03, 1_09, 2_51). In the run-up to the 2002 election, the topic was picked by Lee Myung-bak, a mayoral candidate and former CEO of Hyundai Construction (the job earned him the nickname of 'Bulldozer'), who was searching for something to win the sympathy of the voters. After consulting with many professionals and carefully weighing the opportunities and risks of this cutting-edge, fashionable urban planning project, he finally announced it as his number one official promise, to be finished in his term of office if he were elected (*Chosun Ilbo*, 14 June 2002). Even though the public was doubtful about the feasibility of the project, the majority voted for him and chose him as the fourth directly elected mayor of Seoul.

5.1 *Political strategy: participation, utilisation, complicity*

Equipped as mayor of Seoul with decision-making powers, the support of the majority of the city council, and financial independence from the central government, Lee first aimed for the endorsement of the founding members of the Ch'ŏnggyech'ŏn restoration project. These scholars and opinion leaders with outstanding positions in Korea brought valuable knowledge and research data to the project to make it work in practice and additionally to convince the public that it was supported by experts from different backgrounds. In order to commit these scholars to the course of the restoration project to be undertaken by the city of Seoul, the mayor invited them to become influential members of the Citizens' Committee (SMG 2004b; Interviews 1_03, 1_09, 2_22, 2_40, 3_63).

At the request of the founding scholars, this Citizens' Committee was equipped by a special city ordinance number 4032 from Seoul city council with extended rights which enabled the committee to approve the Ch'ŏnggyech'ŏn blueprint plan before further procedure. Then 127 members were appointed for various areas such as science, culture, religion, politics, and non-government organisations along with other representatives in a well-intended procedure undertaken by independent scholars coupled with the goal-oriented thinking of the city of Seoul (SMG 2004b). Parts of the Citizens' Committee became centres for nurturing the restoration idea, while the huge bodies of the Seoul Development Institute (SDI) and the Seoul Metropolitan Government (SMG) came to be seen as the obedient agents of mayoral power and tools to secure personal claims to power and even higher political aims (Cho 2005: 238; Interviews 2_28, 2_40).

As an experienced businessman, the mayor demonstrated his strong intention to keep his promise and sold his idea to the citizens of Seoul, to the Koreans, and, later on, internationally, claiming that Seoul was undergoing a paradigm shift from dynamic development that lacked environmental and social aspects to a liveable and sustainable city (*Time Magazine* 2006: 19). He promised the citizens of Seoul in many interviews that Kangbuk, the northern part of Seoul, which had been falling behind in the last 20 years, would be balanced with Kangnam in the south, which continued to grow in importance and land value (MBN Chodaeseok 2002). This would ensure that Seoul would bloom and thrive in all parts of the city and therefore become the future financial hub of Asia (*Chosun Ilbo*, 18 October 2002). On the reverse side, he and the city administration described in dangerous terms the conditions of the Ch'ŏnggyech'ŏn elevated highway and the poisoned water and air in the underground (*Korea Times*, 11 June 2003). The SDI and the SMG launched this multi-faceted research to the public, while the media, most of which are politically conservative and happen to be located in the northern part of Seoul close to the Ch'ŏnggyech'ŏn, showed themselves to be willing and uncritical partners in the project. Since the whole project, at an estimated US$360 million, could be paid from the current 2002-2005 budget (SMG 2004b; *Donga Ilbo*, 12 August 2002), the public bought into the idea of this environmentally friendly financial hub of Asia.

The number and evaluation of the media reports mirror the tendency of public opinion on the restoration project. Out of 350 articles that were published from July 2002, when the mayor was elected, until April 2003, right before the demolition of the highway started, more than 70 percent were neutral, positive or very positive (Lah 2003).

Table 1   Attitude of print media coverage

Attitude	very negative	negative	neutral	positive	very positive	total
Frequency	40	58	129	66	57	350
Percentage	11.43%	16.57%	36.86%	18.86%	16.29%	100%

Source: Lah 2003: 161.

After demolition had started and the 'point of no return' had passed, coverage in all conservative papers became more and more positive as the end of the restoration project neared.

5.2   Traffic issues

In the beginning, the biggest concern of the public was traffic related. Before the Ch'ŏnggyech'ŏn elevated highway (a four-lane, two-way highway) and the Ch'ŏnggyech'ŏn road (two to four lanes on each side) were dismantled, daily traffic volume was 168,556 vehicles (Park 2005: 10). On the basis of the 1991-92 report of the Korean Society of Civil Engineering that had detected several serious instances of damage on piers, beams and top plates of the construction, major repair work took place from 1994 to 1999. Access to the elevated highway by all vehicles except passenger cars was prohibited from mid-1997. Follow-up research on the road conditions made further repair work necessary in different sections. It was scheduled to start in 2003 for three years with a budget of US$100 million each year. Even though some organisations like the Korean Society of Transportation opposed the demolition of this arterial road, traffic experts were convinced that it would have only limited impact on downtown traffic speed. This prognosis of the SDI was based on its experience when in 1999 a major tunnel had to be closed without replacement and the expected traffic chaos did not occur, leading researchers to the possibility of the scientific mathematical explanation of the Braess Paradox.[3] The experiences from the past combined with theoretical knowledge were applied to the Ch'ŏnggyech'ŏn project. In an effort to reduce inconvenience, the city of Seoul increased public transportation services in conjunction with widespread public information about the upcoming project. In order to reduce public inconvenience during the construction, the city preserved two lanes on each side of the Ch'ŏnggyech'ŏn for access to buildings and countless shops; as a result, chaos was prevented.

In comparison with the Western world, the modal split, especially in Seoul, remains with two-thirds in favour of public and non-motorised transportation. This was a major contribution in reducing the negative impact on the downtown traffic situation (SMG 2008). In July 2004, the city of Seoul introduced bus-only lanes and implemented an easier, more efficient and effective combined subway and bus system that allows payment by rechargeable cards and combines use of all public transportation systems in the Seoul metropolitan area. Seoul has currently one of the best examples of easy, inexpensive, safe and fast transportation systems in the world.

5.3 Co-operation and participation

At the outset, the institutionalised co-operation between the Seoul Metropolitan Government, the Seoul Development Institute and the Citizens' Committee worked quite efficiently and successfully and generally in a spirit of mutual trust despite all the substantive differences. A notable example is the fact that the Citizens' Committee approved the blueprint plan in January 2003 under preconditions because the metropolitan government was under time pressure and promised to incorporate the request for changes in the plan primarily

---

[3] The phenomenon of the Braess Paradox, named after the mathematician Dietrich Braess, states that adding extra capacity to a network (e.g. adding roads to a transportation network) can sometimes damage performance at equilibrium. When the moving entities selfishly choose their route, it can reduce overall performance. Vice versa, less capacity does not necessarily cause chaos.

in regard to ecological and cultural aspects (Interviews 1_09, 2_40, 3_62).[4]

The six subdivisions of the Citizens' Committee—history and culture, natural environment, public work, transportation, urban planning, and public opinion—each researched, worked and discussed within their fields, giving recommendations to the steering committee, which would make the final decision and forward it to the corresponding department in the metropolitan government. Each subdivision consisted of 13 to 15 people, half of them independent experts and representatives and half public officials from the SDI, the SMG and their contractor; the steering committee comprised 29 members headed by the mayor.

Decisive public controversies over the Ch'ŏnggyech'ŏn restoration among the involved experts arose in connection with ecological aspects, merchants, cultural preservation, and future city planning. In illustration of the ecological aspect, some of the experts interviewed hoped to restore the full length of 10 km of the Ch'ŏnggyech'ŏn stream and wanted to restore it as near to nature as possible, including receiving water from the upper reaches (Interviews 1_03, 1_09, 2_36, 2_40). Since the mayor was determined to finish the project on his terms and within budget, the upper reaches, where several tributaries of the stream wind through neighbourhoods, were soon excluded from the project to avoid time-consuming and costly procedures with landowners. Furthermore, it was decided that the river should carry water at any time of the year and should not be restored to the state of intermittent stream it once had. Since a connection to the upper stream was not possible and the groundwater level had fallen on average by 25 m, the water supplying the restored Ch'ŏnggyech'ŏn is pumped from the Han river and from several subway stations that pump the groundwater to the starting point where it is released though a fountain into the new river bed. Currently, 120,000 tons of purified water at biological oxygen demand (BOD) level per day run through the Ch'ŏnggyech'ŏn. The river bed is waterproof sealed so that the water cannot seep away, and additional combined stormwater and sewage pipelines were constructed next to and under it (SMG 2004b).

---

[4] All quoted interviews were part of the qualitative research undertaken by the author from 2004 to 2009 within her doctoral thesis. Interviews were undertaken in three phases. The first number in each reference, from 1 to 3, indicates the particular phase when an interview was recorded. The second number represents the consecutive numbering of the interview within the total number of interviews. See also footnote 1.

5.4 Downtown business issues

The surrounding area along the Ch'ŏnggyech'ŏn stretches 5.7 km from east to west and covers 13 *dong* (the smallest municipal administrative unit) in four different *ku* (district office). About 6,000 buildings are involved: 29 percent offices, 49 percent commercial premises, 13 percent residential buildings, and 9 percent for miscellaneous purposes (Park 2005: 11). Two hundred thousand merchants in this area are engaged in wholesale and retail trades selling tools, electronic goods, electric appliances, lights, clothes, shoes, costume jewellery, decorations, toys and accessories and form a vital part of the economy of the capital. Some experts define the area as the only cluster for cloth production in Korea (Kim 2002: 8).

Despite the fact that all of the merchants were concerned that the construction work would affect their businesses in one way or another, the assessment of this group differs substantially over two issues: increase of rental prices and increase in sales. While the landowners appreciated the enhancement in values, the commercial tenants either were concerned that their businesses might not be competitive enough to pay for higher rents or hoped for more and better business opportunities in a refurbished urban environment. Depending upon these individual assessments, they became correspondingly engaged in opposing unions that tried to fight for their rights. The tenants who expected positive effects for their businesses were less engaged or not engaged at all in protest activities. Others feared that the restoration project would have adverse effects and therefore opposed it. Out of about 60 different existing business unions in that area, two developed negotiations with the city of Seoul: the Ch'ŏnggyech'ŏn Business Area Defenders Union (CBADU), and the Clothes Stores Association (CSA). Their main goal was to obtain as much direct or indirect compensation from the city of Seoul as possible (Lah 2005: 7; Interviews 1_07, 1_10, 2_493_66).

Recognising that the two unions had stronger and weaker ties, the city started to negotiate just with the weaker group in an attempt to split the merchants' coalition or at least to alienate the two groups from each other. Significant public relations efforts by the city persuaded the majority of the public to favour the project and the mayor. The members of the CBADU were dissatisfied with the weak position of their leadership and the organisation collapsed (Lah 2005: 7; Interview 2_66).

From the beginning of the negotiations the city made it clear that there was no legal ground for any compensation because the blueprint plan and the construction were carried out on city-owned public ground. Furthermore, they pointed out that no direct financial compensation would be paid. Nevertheless, the city took measures to reduce the inconvenience to businesses in the area, such as maintaining two lanes on each side of the construction, providing a free parking lot and shuttle bus services for customers, and reducing the noise and dust caused by the demolition. In addition, the metropolitan government offered measures to revitalise the activities of stores in the area in the forms of loans for the renewal of existing buildings (up to US$800,000 for each store) and of up to US$10 million for modernising the markets. The city promised to purchase goods needed by the city in the stores alongside the Ch'ŏnggyech'ŏn (SMG 2004b).

For storeowners wishing to move away from the area, the city provided some sites (Munjŏng-dong in southern Seoul, of which construction finished in 2009) and provided financial support. After countless meetings, several demonstrations and mutual threats, the CSA finally agreed on 21 June, nine days before the beginning of the scheduled demolition of the Ch'ŏnggyech'ŏn elevated highway, on these compensation measures. After the demolition work had started, the merchants voiced opposition to the project but had no further resources left to enforce their demands, so they eventually gave up (Interviews 1_10, 2_23, 3_66).

The city never became engaged in any negotiation with the group of about 3,000 street vendors in the Ch'ŏnggyech'ŏn area, arguing that their businesses were illegal and that the city therefore had no legal responsibility to offer compensation. After protests, the suicide of at least one street vendor (*Hankyoreh*, 26 August 2002), and a final violent demonstration on 30 November 2003, the day before the street vendors were forced to leave for ongoing construction work, the city offered temporary space in the closed-down Tongdaemun baseball stadium. This was eventually torn down in 2008, right after Lee Myung-bak was elected president.

5.5 *Historical issues*

It was known that ancient bridges from the 15th century and other remains were tossed into the Ch'ŏnggyech'ŏn and might still be there under the road structure. The city accordingly planned to restore at least Kwangt'ong bridge and to relocate Sup'yo bridge from a park near to the river. Research and excavation of ancient cultural and historical remains such as stones, piers, abutments and frame stones from six bridges and 467 metres of stone embankments on both sides of the stream were carried out parallel to the demolition work of the Ch'ŏnggyech'ŏn road (SMG 2004b).

Historians and experts insisted on stopping demolition work for a proper survey and excavation of the objects found and to discuss the consequences for future development. But without the strong support of the cultural heritage administration of the Ministry of Culture and Tourism, which did not wish to become involved in the Ch'ŏnggyech'ŏn project in any way, the experts could not stop the ongoing construction. Because the mayor was in the opposition party to the president, cultural heritage experts were hesitant to enter into open confrontation on the continuing construction even at the expense of culture heritage (Interview: 1_39, 2_40).

While cultural experts had been unable to agree whether it would be better to replace the real bridges to their original locations or to restore them upstream, the city of Seoul, in order to keep to the scheduled timeline and budget, decided to relocate one bridge (Kwangt'ong, dating to 1411) 120 m upstream to avoid traffic disruption and property challenges at its original location. The relocation of another bridge (Sup'yo bridge, dating to 1420, listed as tangible cultural property no. 18), which was brought to another location before the Ch'ŏnggyech'ŏn road was built, was delayed. Professionals and experts mainly from the city were concerned that the relocation of the bridge could damage the stones and that furthermore, the differences in dimensions with the site could interrupt the water flow on rainy days during periods of intense monsoon. They suggested building a wooden replica at the original place and delaying the replacement of the original bridge until a proper solution could be found. At present, the replica is still at the original location on the restored Ch'ŏnggyech'ŏn and the original Sup'yo bridge is at Changchung park in Seoul. Most of the other excavated stones such as the embankments have been stored and not re-erected at their original or at any other location (SMG 2005).

5.6 Conflict management and outcome

The co-operation between the Citizens' Committee and the Seoul Metropolitan Government fell apart mainly over disputes about the cultural heritage. After the Committee helped and approved the blueprint, co-operation with the public administration became more and more difficult until members of the city of Seoul publicly sought to discredit the work of the Citizens' Committee to show their political power (*Donga Ilbo*, 9 March 2004). As a result, most of the independent members of the Citizens' Committee launched a determined opposition to the Ch'ŏnggyech'ŏn restoration to the extent of suing the mayor of Seoul and officially resigned on 15 September 2004 (*Donga Ilbo*, 14 June 2004, 12 July 2004; *Hankyoreh*, 2 August 2004; Citizens' Committee, 15 September 2004).

Right from the start of the Ch'ŏnggyech'ŏn project, experts and public media were polarised over the general direction of urban development in the Ch'ŏnggyech'ŏn area. Supporters of development argued that the northern part of Seoul, Kangbuk, especially the business areas along the river, had long been neglected and therefore had fallen behind Kangnam, the modern, luxurious and favoured southern part of Seoul. In order to balance development between north and south Seoul and to make the city more economically competitive, public and private investment was encouraged. Besides improvement measures to distribute more streets for pedestrians throughout downtown Seoul, an urban redevelopment plan was applied for all neighbouring areas along the Ch'ŏnggyech'ŏn to upgrade the inner city. In order to encourage new investment and to ensure profits in many areas, building heights, which were mainly fixed at 12 storeys, were raised up to 90 m, easing off construction regulations. As an immediate result, several new public and private development projects started up during the construction work on the Ch'ŏnggyech'ŏn restoration, such as the Lotte castle apartment complex and the competition and negotiation for the Se'un Sang'a shopping district.

The supporters of restoration contended on the other hand that the Ch'ŏnggyech'ŏn area is a vibrant part of the city and the backbone of the economy, especially for industrial businesses, tertiary industries and manufacturing establishments, most of which are located in the north of Seoul (SDI 2002: 69, 71, 73, 75; SDI 2007: 83, 85, 87, 89). They argued that urban development should be carried out based on long-term research and careful study of the existing structures and as a socially acceptable refurbishment to secure the historical grown structure and social pattern of this part of the city. Most of the adherents of the restoration argument therefore opposed the idea for gentrification and to raise heights in order to lower speculation (*Hankyoreh*, 24 May 2002, 14 November 2002, 8 May 2005; *Donga Ilbo*, 27 October 2002; *Chosun Ilbo*, 1 November 2002, 25 February 2004). At the time of the opening of the Ch'ŏnggyech'ŏn stream on 1 October 2005, land prices near the river for some residential and commercial buildings were already rising, and by 2005 prices had caught up with Kangnam, as Table 2 shows.

Table 2   Residential and commercial trends of prices between 2000 and 2005

KRW / sqm	Residential		Commercial	
	2000	2005	2000	2005
Kangbuk				
Sŏdaemun-gu	600,000	1,200,000	3,900,000	7,200,000
Chongno-gu	900,000	1,500,000	4,900,000	7,200,000
Chung-gu	1,500,000	1,800,000	6,100,000	9,000,000
Tongdaemun-gu	1,100,000	1,400,000	2,800,000	3,900,000
Sŏngdong-gu	900,000	1,400,000	2,100,000	3,300,000
Kangnam				
Sŏch'o-gu	1,600,000	3,100,000	4,100,000	7,500,000
Kangnam-gu	1,900,000	3,500,000	5,900,000	9,400,000

Source: SDI 2002: 101; SDI 2007: 114.

Apartment prices with views of the Ch'ŏnggyech'ŏn rose from US$240,000-US$280,000 per p'yŏng in July 2003 to US$310,000-US$350,000 per p'yŏng in October 2005 (1 p'yŏng=3.3 square metres) (*Donga Ilbo*, 3 October 2005).[5] Furthermore, the influx of financially strong chain stores supplying tourist needs, such as coffee shops, convenience stores and restaurants, resulted in competition for small businesses, cheap labour and traditional craftsmanship.

---

[5] The fact that the vice-mayor was convicted for taking bribes from construction companies in May 2005 leaves a bitter aftertaste to the priorities in urban planning related to the Ch'ŏnggyech'ŏn.

6 THE POWER OF GEOGRAPHICAL IMAGINATION IN PLANNING DECISIONS

The Ch'ŏnggyech'ŏn project has many indisputable benefits, such as more open public space, green areas and water, more fresh air and less pollution and noise along the restored stream in downtown Seoul. However, without a vision and the media that bought into it to convince the public, it would not have been possible.

The media were favourable to the Ch'ŏnggyech'ŏn restoration project, and most of them published facts and stories provided by the Seoul Metropolitan Government and the Seoul Development Institute, such as estimates about the impact on traffic, economic benefit effects or cooling effects (*Chosun Ilbo*, 4 July 2002, 2 March 2003, 22 May 2003; *Donga Ilbo*, 13 April 2003, 22 May 2003; Lah 2005: 9, 10, 12). The visualisation of the benefits was successfully sold to citizens, shifting the people's memories and perceptions away from an old polluted sewer lined with shanty homes to a vision of a clear, open water stream with a green landscape with birds and fish where stressed citizens of Seoul could relax. They linked it even more successfully with the idea of economic growth for Seoul and the idea of becoming the 'financial hub of Asia'.

Although some of the visualizations were not accurate, the city continues to use them, and the media and the public have not questioned them. The city, for example, proudly presents images with slightly inclined green river banks so that citizens are able to reach the water everywhere. However, the technical demands for flood control make it impossible to reach the stream, the level of which has been lowered by 7-15 m, without using stairs. These idealistic images were reinforced in numerous empirical and research studies conducted mainly by the SDI and underscored ecological, natural and cultural advantages, for example, the improvement of air, temperature and noise quality along the new river. In order to highlight the vision of Seoul as the international financial and IT centre of Asia, city experts provided benefit-cost analyses predicting 180,000 new jobs in ten years and US$200 million-US$3.3 billion in economic value and benefit (*Hankyoreh*, 23 April 2002; SMG 2002; SMG 2005). Yang Yun-jae, assistant mayor of Seoul, had this to say when interviewed on 1 June 2004: 'The city of Seoul creating this idea of [Ch'ŏnggyech'ŏn] is bound to trigger a major paradigm shift in urban planning; depending upon redevelopment initiated in the surrounding areas of the stream, the project could spawn an economic ripple effect ranging anywhere between 8 to 23 trillion Won [US$23 billion]' (SMG 2004a). After the Ch'ŏnggyech'ŏn project was completed, more and more questions and data arose saying the SMG had played down and glossed over the cost of US$360 million for the restoration and that the actual cost was US$900 million (Cho 2005: 236, PSPD 2005; Choi and Greenfield 2009).

Ch'ŏnggyech'ŏn is a big attraction in Seoul for citizens and tourists alike. Every weekday about 53,000 visitors and on weekend days 125,000 people on average show up to see and walk along the stream. The city has therefore to spend US$1.7 million in pumping and labour costs to maintain the waterflow and the quality of the water, which has been in danger of eutrophication due to the artificial waterbed (SMG 2005: 2; *Money Today* 2009).

7 CONCLUSION

So what is the lesson to be learned from the Ch'ŏnggyech'ŏn restoration project?

First of all, that urban planning in South Korea gets things done even in a megacity and in a very short period of time.

Thanks to an abbreviated planning procedure and the strengthened position of the mayor, decision-making can be compressed and shortened. The Korean urban planning system empowers the mayor to select the urban planning project and gives him political and democratic authority that comes equipped with a lot of manpower (allocatable resources) to accomplish the task. The Confucian ethical and moral principles of obedience to and respect of leaders and striving to be a good part of the community continue to influence human relations, although to an increasingly smaller extent. Therefore urban planning procedures in South Korea are more likely to be supported by the public, or at least accepted by them, than those in Western democracies where individuals tend to put personal interest over what is considered to be public interest. In contrast to Western countries, where hierarchy tends to have a negative connotation and is often viewed critically, in Asian societies like South Korea it is more likely to be considered as positive, since a strong political or business leader has the obligation to act for the benefit of the community or his employees like a caring father.

The Ch'ŏnggyech'ŏn example shows that this collectivist orientation fosters the habit and success of strong leaders and their projects and, furthermore, that different stakeholders tend to be satisfied with partial success, as many experts who have actively worked on the Ch'ŏnggyech'ŏn project confirm (Interviews 1_03, 1_07, 1_09, 2_38, 2_41). The continuing strong, broad public approval and support for the project shows that the public values the accomplishment even though it might not yet be 100 percent satisfactory. Instead, critics follow a careful development and a step-by-step strategy (Cho 2005: 238). They hope that this graduated action will maintain and add to common public values and to the final success of the urban planning project in the future (Lah 2005; Interviews 3_62, 3_73).

This approach offers some special advantages: urban planning projects can be done much faster and are more time- and cost- efficient than many of the lengthy, conflict-laden projects in other democratic countries (Lah 2005: 229). Furthermore, it is the aim of politicians in South Korea to accomplish things and to create 'facts'. Once a project has been completed, everyone has to deal with the findings and from that point the projects can be improved little by little (Interviews 1_09, 3_73).

Disadvantages of this strategy include inadequacies in the planning procedure. These can mean deficiencies or procedural flaws in the course of consideration, for example a lack of conflict awareness because problems have not always been properly addressed; other weaknesses can be misconceptions in balancing the interests of stakeholders, poor decisions, and errors in vision (Interviews 2_40, 2_53, 2_54, 3_63). Such problems can set up a bad example. A critical examination of the pros and cons shows that the establishment of criteria for development in urban planning processes is left to a few people and is not necessarily the result of a social dialogue or consensus. Furthermore, the processes and the negotiations with stakeholders in the urban planning approach cannot be judged open-ended in the Ch'ŏnggyech'ŏn case because of the strict preconditions set by the mayor. 'We had this God-given time frame' (Interview 2_35).

Leaving aside the priorities of urban development, the following must be noted concerning the democratic process of urban development: although the city presents, discusses and collects suggestions and concerns from the public, the public hearing satisfied merely the procedural requirement (Lah 2005: 15). It is doubtful how far public opinion was reflected, since the actual decision and the reasons for specific decisions eventually concentrate upon one person's 'Black Box' decision (Interviews 2_54, 2_56, 3_63; Lah 2005: 12). In hindsight, it is quite obvious that in this case study the strong leadership of the mayor was politically motivated and the Ch'ŏnggyech'ŏn project had to be accomplished at whatever price in his term to pave his way to the presidency (*Hankyoreh*, 26 August 2002, 2 June 2003; Interviews 1_09, 2_54, 3_68 2_56).

It can be argued that the Ch'ŏnggyech'ŏn restoration should be more than a three-year project to revitalise and landscape an artificial stream. Indeed, it should serve as the impetus to move forward with a sustainable and long-term plan to revive Seoul's historical and current centre in a socially acceptable manner that makes a serious attempt to include citizen participation in the urban planning process and meet the interest in a transparent democratic process. Strengthening management in the areas of public dispute resolution and consensus-building methods changes the way of managing differences in society. A large-scale urban project like the Ch'ŏnggyech'ŏn restoration could have used a more collaborative approach in which participatory decisions could be made.

In the view of some, it requires proper information for the public, and critical citizens and journalists are needed to question and control political decision-making in their function as the fourth power in the state. The existing Citizens' Committee could be a good and helpful tool for empowered public participation, but needs to grow from a paper tiger into a watchdog of democracy in the arena of urban planning procedure (Interviews 2_54, 3_62). The selection of its members should therefore follow a transparent and independent selection process that covers a broad cross-section of civil society. The Citizens' Committee needs to be financially and functionally independent with its own office, money and staff working full-time on behalf of the Citizens' Committee members. Such independence would have a direct effect in helping to strengthen their rights, and would have to be flanked by strong rights so that members might reject or validate the urban planning project at different stages of the project (Lah 2005). Finally, all courses of action under consideration should be open to the public and transparent so that everyone can comprehend the implications. This would benefit the transparency of the urban planning process and its criteria in weighing views and would also control personally or politically motivated decisions by powerful individuals.

From a simplified Western perspective, it is noteworthy that the overall priorities in the urban planning process of the Ch'ŏnggyech'ŏn project were, in addition to observing the time and budget frames, oriented towards technical and developmental issues. The Ch'ŏnggyech'ŏn urban policy places greater value on flood control and economic development than on long-term solutions, ecological sustainability and social acceptability, or refurbishment and preservation of monuments. Taking into consideration that the most benefited and favoured group in the project are land and building owners, developers and construction companies, the less powerful and less organised lower classes would appear to have been left to the hands of the free market, and gentrification was intentionally and knowingly accepted (Cho 2005: 237). This weighting takes into account the importance that decision-makers attach to urban planning projects and, most likely, what South Korean society accepts.

Nevertheless, South Korea has undertaken a dynamic change from monarchy and colonialism to become an internationally respected democracy within approximately 50 years. The signs of an inclusive democracy and the self-confident participation of citizens in the urban planning process can be read as indicators that collaborative government and powerful participation are on their way. The Citizens' Committee as an instrument to get stakeholders directly involved in the urban planning process and in decision-making seems to be a useful tool to institutionalise public participation and one that Western city planners might find interesting as a model. The future will tell whether the Ch'ŏnggyech'ŏn project has been an historic paradigm shift in urban development, and it will be interesting to see how the democratic urban planning process in South Korea continues to develop and which criteria will emerge as its future cornerstones.

REFERENCES

Cho Myung-rae (2005), 'Cheonggyecheon, an Imitation of Nature', in: *Space Magazine*, 11, pp. 236-9
Choi Bong-seok (2000), 'Direct democratic participation by citizens in local-level decision-making', dissertation, Faculty of Jurisprudence, University of Hannover, Hannover: Freie Universität Hannover
Choi, Jaz Hee-jeong and Adam Greenfield (2009), 'To Connect and Flow in Seoul: Ubiquitous Technologies, Urban Infrastructure and Everyday Life in the Contemporary Korean City', in: Marcus Foth (ed.), *Handbook of Research on Urban Informatics: the Practice and Promise of the Real-time City*, Hershey PA: IGI Global, pp. 21-36
Chosŏn Ilbo (Korean edition), 14 June 2002; 4 July 2002; 1 November 2002; 2 March 2003; 22 May 2003; 25 February 2004. Online: http://www.chosun.com
Chosun Ilbo (English edition) (2002), 'Not Just Development', 18 October 2002. Online: http://english.sisul.or.kr/grobal/cheonggye/eng/WebContent/index.html (accessed 11 March 2004)
Citizens' Committee (2004), 'Ch'ŏnggyech'ŏn Pokwŏn Simin' [Ch'ŏnggyech'ŏn Restoration Citizens' Committee], 15 September 2004, internal document from the resigning members of the Ch'ŏnggyech'ŏn Restoration Citizens' Committee to the mayor of Seoul
Donga Ilbo (Korean edition), 12 August 2002, p. 13; 27 October 2002; 13 April 2003; 22 May 2003; 9 March 2004; 14 June 2004; 12 July 2004. Online: http://www.donga.com
Donga Ilbo (English edition) (2005), 'A Cheonggyecheon View Is Worth 70 Million Won', 3 October 2005. Online: http://english.donga.com/srv/service.php3?biid=2005100397028 (accessed 23 December 2009)
Hankyŏreh (Korean edition), 1 January 2002, p. 25; 23 April 2002, p. 2; 24 May 2002, p. 25; 26 August 2002, p. 6; 14 November 2002, p. 25; 2 June 2003; 2 August 2004. Online: http://www.hani.co.kr
Hankyoreh (English edition) (2004), 'Controversy over the Rushed Development in Cheonggyecheon Area', 2 August 2004. Online: http://english.hani.co.kr/kisa/section-014000000/home01.html (accessed 12 November 2007)
Hankyoreh (English edition) (2005), 'Rumors around Seoul City Height Limitation Ease', 8 May 2005. Online: http://english.hani.co.kr/kisa/section-014000000/home01.html (accessed 12 November 2007)
Hyun Soong-jong (1990), 'Das traditionelle koreanische und das moderne westliche Recht' [Traditional Korean and modern Western law], in: Manfred Rehbinder and Ju-chan Sonn (eds), *Zur Rezeption des deutschen Rechts in Korea* [On the reception of German law in Korea], Baden-Baden: Nomos Verlagsgesellschaft, pp. 17-28
Kim Dong-ju (2002), 'Regional Industrial Cluster in Korea in a Knowledge and Information Area', in: *Space and Environment*, 17, pp. 7-10
Kim Kwang-joong (2003), 'Growth and Change of the 20th Century Seoul', in: Seoul Development Institute (eds), *Seoul: 20th Century Growth & Change of the Last 100 Years*. Seoul: Seoul Development Institute, pp. 1-21
Korea Times (2003), 'Mayor Shaping City as Global Business Hub', 11 June 2003. Online: http://english.sisul.or.kr/grobal/cheonggye/eng/WebContent/index.html (accessed 11th March 2003)

Lah Tae-joon (2003), 'Ch'ŏnggyech'ŏn Pokwŏnsaŏbŭi Ŏllonpodo naeyongbunsŏk' [Analysing the contents of press reports on Cheonggyecheon restoration projects], in: *Chŏngch'aek Punsŏk P'yŏnggahak Hoebo* [Journal of the policy analyzing and evaluation committee], 13 (2), pp. 149-67

Lah Tae-joon (2005), 'The Huge Success of Cheonggyecheon: What is Left?', unpublished manuscript, Yonsei University, Seoul, pp. 1-21

Lee Ki-suk (2003), 'Seoul's Urban Growth in the 20th Century: From a Pre-modern City to a Global Metropolis', in: Seoul Development Institute (eds), *Seoul: 20th Century Growth & Change of the Last 100 Years*, Seoul: Seoul Development Institute, pp. 21-91

Lee Yeong-heui (2003), 'Normative Rahmenbedingungen' [Normative framework], interdisciplinary research paper undertaken within the departments of business, environment and settlement of the Technical University of Berlin, Berlin: Technical University of Berlin

MBN Chodaeseok (2002), Interview with Seoul Mayor Lee Myung-bak, 16 October 2002. Online: http://english.sisul.or.kr/grobal/cheonggye/eng/WebContent/index.html (accessed 13 February 2005)

MOGAHA (Ministry of Government Administration of Home Affairs South Korea) (2006), *Financial Report on Central Government Subsidies*, Seoul. Online: http://www.mopas.go.kr/gpms/ns/mogaha/user/userlayout/english/bulletin/userBtView.action?userBtBean.bbsSeq=1006174&userBtBean.ctxCd=1030&userBtBean.ctxType=21010009&currentPage= (accessed 15 March 2010)

Money Today (2009), 'Cheonggyecheon water-bloom'. Online: http://www.mt.co.kr/index.html (accessed 19 December 2009)

Park Chong-min (2006), 'Local Government and Community Power in Korea', paper delivered at the International Political Science Association World Congress, Fukuoka. Online: http://www.ekoreajournal.net/archive/detail.jsp?BACKFLAG=Y&VOLUMENO=46&BOOKNUM=4&PAPERNUM=2&SEASON=Winter&YEAR=2006 (accessed 15 March 2010)

Park Kil-dong (2005), 'Cheonggyecheon Restoration Project'. Online: http://www.wfeo.org/documents/download/Cheonggeycheon%20Restoration%20Project_%20Korea.pdf (accessed 15 March 2010)

PSPD (People's Solidarity for Participatory Democracy) (2005). Online: http://blog.peoplepower21.org.PSPD/14796 (accessed 24 February 2009)

SDI (Seoul Development Institute) (2002), *Thematic Maps of Seoul 2002*. Seoul: Seoul Development Institute

SDI (2003), *Seoul: 20th Century*, Seoul: Seoul Development Institute

SDI (2005), *Major Statistics and Trends*, Seoul: Seoul Development Institute

SDI (2007), *Thematic Maps of Seoul 2007*, Seoul: Seoul Development Institute

SMG (Seoul Metropolitan Government) (2002), interview with the mayor of Seoul, Lee Myung-bak, 3 July 2002. Online: http://english.seoul.go.kr/cheonggye/media_home/1225995_13579.html

SMG (2004a), interview with the assistant mayor of Seoul, Yang Yun-jae, 1 June 2004. Online: http://www.metro.seoul.kr/kor2000/chungaehome/en/seoul/sub_htm/2sub_02.htm (accessed 15 March 2010)

SMG (2004b), 'Cheonggyecheon Restoration Project'. Online: http://english.sisul.or.kr/grobal/cheonggye/eng/WebContent/index.html (accessed 30 November 2005)

SMG (2005), 'Back to A Future: Cheonggyecheon Restoration Project', Seoul: Seoul Metropolitan Government

SMG (2008), 'Dynamic Business Hub'. Online: http://74.125.155.132/search?q=cache:NJU2GWmJGMAJ:english.seoul.go.kr/db/kcp/vision2.php+Seoul+and+economic+and+business+hub&cd=2&hl=en&ct=clnk&gl=us&client=safari (accessed 15 March 2010)

Time Magazine (2006), 'Saving Seoul'. Online: http://www.time.com/time/asia/covers/501060515/story.html (accessed 1 February 2006)

THE ROLE OF THINK TANKS IN THE SOUTH KOREAN DISCOURSE ON EAST ASIA

Thomas Kern and Alexander Ruser

Abstract

This article examines the influence of think tanks on South Korean political discourse pertaining to East Asia. The growing importance of regionalisation in Northeast Asia is related to intra-regional economic developments, the emergence of transnational political institutions and cultural interdependencies. In recent years, think tank publications dealing with this topic have increased considerably. In this paper, we investigate the hypotheses that (1) think tanks are privileged participants in the public discourse, and (2) that they operate in South Korea as intermediary agents between the scientific community and lawmakers. On this basis, they contribute considerably to the construction of regional identity in East Asia. Biographical data of South Korean lawmakers and think tank personnel indicate that the growing attention to regional issues in South Korea can be explained at least in part by institutional isomorphism and close network ties between think tanks and political institutions.

1 Introduction

The political discourse in the Republic of Korea (ROK—South Korea) and other Northeast Asian countries is increasingly shaped by voices stressing the need for a higher degree of cultural, political, and economic integration. Despite considerable instabilities in the relationships between South Korea, Japan, China, Taiwan and—of course—the People's Democratic Republic of Korea (DPRK—North Korea) over the past decade, academic circles increasingly debate (North)East Asia's capacity to emerge as an equal political and economic counterpart to the European Union (EU) and the United States (US). In this context, think tanks play a central role because they initiate public discussions and shape political agendas. Think tanks are often described as privileged participants of public discourse because they operate as 'switchboards' (Stone 1996: 95) between the scientific community[1] and the political establishment. Many observers agree that think tanks exert a tremendous influence on political decision-making by translating academic knowledge into the language of politics. Thus, in order to assess the political relevance of academic discourses, it is necessary to cultivate a broader understanding of how think tanks operate in the intermediate space between science and politics.

Against this background, this study has two purposes. First, it will provide an outline of recent academic discussions concerning the process of regional integration in Northeast Asia. Second, it will scrutinise the involvement of think tanks in this discussion by examining the case of South Korea in particular. It will also investigate various hypotheses on ways in which this engagement might affect the political process. The cultural homogeneity of the educational backgrounds of think tank personnel and political decision-makers considerably facilitates the transfer of academic 'ideas' and 'concepts' into political agendas. Think tanks are able to shape the political discourse because they are closely interrelated with political actors in dense professional and personal networks. Following the concept of 'normative isomorphism' elaborated by DiMaggio and Powell (1983) (see Section 4.2 below), the article seeks to develop a more detailed understanding regarding the influence of a shared educational socialisation, common vocabulary, and similar professional standards.

In light of recent historical and political tensions in Northeast Asia, the legacy of past (violent) confrontations between neighbours in the region is often conceived as a major obstacle to regionalisation and regional integration. However, from a sociological point of view, conflict and integration are not a contradiction in terms; rather, they are two sides of the same coin. Against this background, the rise of a stimulating discourse on Northeast Asia has been particularly visible in South Korea. A first line of argument stresses the necessity of re-

---

[1] In the following the term 'scientific community' refers to all persons professionally engaged in scientific research. Additionally the concept implies the acceptance of 'scientific standards' by the members of the community during academic education. Membership depends (at least partially) on this consent and can not be derived from any actual position in the academic field alone: 'The socialization of scientists tends to produce persons who are strongly committed to the central values of science that they unthinkingly accept them' (Hagstrom 1965: 9).

solving the legacies of Japanese colonial rule (Kern and Nam 2009). Under the government of Japanese Prime Minister Koizumi, South Korea (and China) were submerged several times by waves of fierce protests against his visits to the Yasukuni shrine, where war criminals of World War II have been consecrated. Another contentious issue involves the conflict related to the isle of Tokto, which, as yet, remains unresolved.[2] A second line of argument refers to shared experiences and stories of economic success in the Northeast Asian region (which, most recently, also includes China). In this context, the political discourse in South Korea increasingly refers to Northeast Asia as an important frame of reference for legitimising the increasing liberalisation of economic relations and the development of intra-regional political institutions.

This study begins with a discussion of the analytical relevance of concepts such as world region, regionalisation, regionalism, and regional identity. In the fields of international relations and globalisation studies, these concepts have become increasingly important in recent years. Next, it will thoroughly examine the role think tanks play in shaping the discourse on regionalisation in South Korea. Basing itself on concepts from neo-institutionalism in organisational theory, the paper will develop various hypotheses to guide an empirical analysis of think tank personnel and political decision-makers in South Korea.

2 ANALYTICAL RELEVANCE OF REGIONALISATION

Concepts like 'region', 'regionalisation', and 'regionalism' are not as simple and unproblematic as they may appear in everyday language. In empirical reality, regions are neither naturally nor geographically given. Rather, they are social constructions (within material geographical contexts) with far-reaching political consequences. This fact is particularly true for the so-called 'world regions',[3] which can be defined in very different ways according to cultural, political, or economic criteria (Arnason et al. 2005; Ben-Rafael and Sternberg 2005; Huntington 1996; Katzenstein 2005; Miller 2005). In considering world regions as constructed on the basis of shared historical and cul-

---

[2] Tensions between the two countries intensified in 2005 when the Korean territorial claim to the island of Tokto was challenged by Japanese legislative projects.

[3] In this paper, the terms 'region' and 'world region' are used synonymously.

tural experiences, for example, Lewis and Wigen (1997: 157) define these regions as 'large sociospatial groupings delimited largely on the grounds of shared history and culture'.[4] Arnason (2003), however, stresses that the cultural dimension must not be separated from political and economic factors. Accordingly, world regions are characterised by a comparatively high degree of internal—cultural, economic and political—integration. This conceptualisation thus remains unsatisfactory, as it should also involve the formation of an at least rudimentary collective identity that is shared by the inhabitants of the region.[5] In other words, the delineation of world regions is largely based on a process of discursive boundary construction and identity formation (Eder 2006).

Meanwhile, the concept of *regionalisation* is related to processes of cultural, political and economic integration and exchange within a world region. The structural outcome of these interactions is usually unintentional and is instead determined by the momentum of cultural and economic markets. The concept of *regional identity* depends on 'the shared perception of belonging to a particular community' (Hurrell 1997: 39). In this sense, a region must be conceived of—like the nation state—as an 'imagined community' (Anderson 1983) with possibly great political and economic potential. Although the concepts of regionalisation and regional identity are closely connected—the formation of regional identities often accelerates the process of regionalisation, and, conversely, the process of regionalisation facilitates the construction of regional identities—the relationship between both phenomena is not necessarily linear. In contrast to both concepts, we define *regionalism* as the 'conscious policy of states or sub-state regions to coordinate activities and arrangements in a greater region' (Wyatt-Walter 1997: 77). Accordingly, regionalism refers to the intentional efforts made by nation states and other political actors to intensify intra-regional cooperation. As for the academic relevance of re-

---

[4] 'Although the number of regions, as well as the borders between them, vary somewhat from one map to another, most world regionalisation systems arrive at the same set of macrocultural zones: East Asia, Southeast Asia, South Asia, Southwest Asia and North Africa, Europe, Russia and environs, sub-Saharan Africa, Latin America, Australia and New Zealand, and the United States and Canada. Oceania and Central Asia are sometimes added to this list' (Lewis and Wigen 1997: 157).

[5] 'Some civilizations are more regional than others, and some regions are more civilizational than others, but the task of civilizational theory is to account for the spectrum of variations on both sides, rather than to single out the most congruent cases' (Arnason 2003: 315).

gionalisation, regional identities, and regionalism to the social sciences, Hurrell (2007: 136-144) stresses four important aspects:

- First of all, the very concept of a world region emphasises *cultural interdependencies* among modern societies. The more the focus of analysis shifts from nation states[6] to world regions, the more sensitivity grows for exchanges across borders without neglecting the relevance of cultural boundaries.[7] This issue plays a central role in recent sociological discussions about 'multiple modernities' (Eisenstadt 1982, 2000) .
- Secondly, world regions are distinctive political, economic, and cultural spaces having relatively independent influence (as opposed to nation states) on the network of international relations. An increasing density of intra-regional relations and exchanges not only increases the level of regional integration, but also promotes the formation of a multipolar international order with extensive political and economic consequences (Huntington 1996; Katzenstein 2005).
- Thirdly, world regions are playing an increasingly important role as an intermediate space between global institutions and nation states. For example, many countries seek to enhance economic co-operation with their neighbours in order to improve their position on the global markets. In some cases, such as the EU, they attempt to boost economic growth by deregulating and liberalising intra-regional exchange. In other cases, they seek political co-operation in order to strengthen their negotiating position in the sphere of international relations. In this sense, regionalism is 'governance beyond the state' (Hurrell 2007: 139).
- Finally, many authors discuss whether the formation of world regions might not simply be an intermediary stage on the way to global integration, or whether the rise of regional institutions in the long term leads to the formation of (potential) 'regional states'. Possible outcomes extend from a culturally homogenous 'world society' (Lechner and Boli 2005; Meyer 2007) to a multipolar world order of civilisations, 'each windowless, self-enclosed and

---

[6] According to the sociological tradition, cultural boundaries constitute the framework for the formation of collective identities (Anderson 1983).

[7] Our focus on regions deviates significantly from theoretical concepts, which simply assume that globalisation is accompanied by cultural homogenisation (Boli and Elliott 2008; Meyer 2007; Ritzer 2004, 2007).

with little possibility of mutual understanding' (Hurrell, 2007: 138; see also Huntington 1996). Presently, such discussions are highly speculative. Nevertheless, they delineate the scope of current changes in the field of international relations and highlight the relevancy of regional integration processes to the social sciences.

3 THINK TANKS AND POLITICAL DISCOURSE

Over the last two decades, public discourse pertaining to the political and economic integration of East Asia has increased considerably worldwide. In this sense, the process of regionalisation and the formation of a regional identity must be seen as a discursive project. Concerning the development of this discourse, the central question relates to the leading participants, organisations and individuals who are able to feed the public discourse with relevant topics (*agenda setting*), to spread established concepts and ideas, and to act as 'second hand dealers of ideas' (Stone 1996). Recently, new types of intermediary organisations—so-called think tanks—have established themselves as a central link between the scientific community and the political establishment in the public discourse, alongside classical state, civic and mass media actors.[8] Like management consultancies in the realm of the economy, think tanks are relatively independent consultant agencies 'that generate policy-oriented research, analysis and advice on domestic and international issues that enables policymakers and the public to make informed decisions about public policy issues' (McGann 2007: 4).

Think tanks play increasingly important roles in the legitimisation of political programmes and decisions, by grounding them in scientific research. Currently, their number is estimated at about 5,000 worldwide (McGann 2007: 5). Over 50 percent of existing think tanks were established after 1980. About two-thirds are located in Western Europe and North America, while almost 12 percent operate in East Asia. The research literature distinguishes basically two (ideal) types of thinks tanks (Weaver 1989), with the first type being committed to the principles of impartial and independent scientific analysis ('universities without students'). The second type is concerned with the

---

[8] Think tanks are increasingly the subject of institutional policy studies and research about pressure groups and political decision-making.

promotion and circulation of specific political and ideological ideas ('advocacy think tanks'). Although it is impossible to distinguish strictly between 'indifferent interest' (Bourdieu 1998) and academic lobbying for specific purposes, both dimensions delimit the intellectual field in which think tanks operate. While their reputations are based on scientific expertise, the topics and results of their research usually address a non-scientific audience, political and civic actors in particular. Therefore, in empirical reality, the action orientation of a particular think tank is usually the product of a specific combination of both dimensions, somewhere between 'university without students' and 'advocacy' (Weaver 1989).

However, the heterogeneity of think tanks results not only from different action orientations, but also from the composition of staff members. Think tanks often consist of a mixture of academic researchers, 'spin doctors' (journalists, PR specialists and so forth), and politicians, whose job it is to manage these think tanks professionally and attempt to further the impact of a particular think tank upon the public (Weaver 1989). At least in the US, a heterogeneous staff is often intentionally sought out in hopes of increasing the effectiveness of the exchange between state institutions and the public sphere.[9] From this perspective, the political influence of think tanks appears to be mostly indirect and 'limited to constructing a political agenda, developing policy alternatives and diffusing ideas to shape public understanding of issues' (Stone 1996: 3). Accordingly, scientific analysis must take into account the structural and cultural context of a specific think tank as part of an 'epistemic community' (Stone 1996: 94-95).[10] Thus, precisely because think tanks act as an intellectual avant-garde, propagating solutions to specific political problems in the public discourse, they represent an appropriate starting point for a critical discourse analysis.[11]

---

[9] In contrast, the results below of our study on South Korean think tanks indicate a surprising professional and academic homogeneity among their employees.

[10] As a consequence, think tanks are often perceived as a 'switchboard through which connections are made, rather than being a depository of activity and authority' (Stone 1996: 95). These epistemic communities mainly perform four functions: intellectual innovation, diffusion, policy selection, and policy persistence (Stone 1996).

[11] 'It should be kept in mind that Think Tanks represent only a portion of the epistemic community, not all of it. Critical discourse analysis accounts for this as it assumes that any (pattern of) interpretation has to assert itself. Since public opinion is not colonized 'automatically' by their interpretive frames, Think Tanks should rather be conceptualized as influential voices in public discourse than as manipulative puppeteers as suggested by some researchers' (Dixon 2000; translation by authors).

Hence, as in the case of other public actors, the influence of think tanks is not limited to political decision-making processes. Many studies about the public sphere frequently stress the value of intellectual activities promoting the rise and change of ideologies and collective identities (Snow et al. 1986; Snow and Benford 1988, 1992). Public actors accordingly 'think a lot [...], along with the related activities of reasoning, judging arguments, evaluating evidence, testing predictions, recognizing connections, and developing new knowledge' (Johnston and Oliver 2005: 193). Such activities positively affect identity formation in the public sphere by producing collectively shared meaning and interpretation systems. However, compared with most other public actors, members of think tanks find themselves in a relatively privileged position through the strong scientific legitimacy with which they evaluate arguments and proofs (statements), develop new solutions to various problems, make predictions for the future, and provide the public with new knowledge ('surveys'). In doing so, they are creating an intellectual horizon for collective identity formation.

With respect to the regionalisation of East Asia, think tanks have played a leading role in intensifying intra-regional co-operation (Wanandi 2008: 7). In the process, they have focused on the fields of economic and security policies in particular. For instance, in 1980, the Pacific Economic Cooperation Council (PECC) was established, parallel to the Asia Pacific Economic Cooperation (APEC), as a forum for representatives from the realms of politics, economics and science to come together in support of the integration of the Asia-Pacific region and share their political suggestions. As one example of such sharing, the founding and advancement of the Council for Security Cooperation in the Asia Pacific (CSCAP) illustrates that professional think tanks may exert significant influence on the process of regional integration. The history of the Council can be traced back to a series of informal consultations of regional think tanks in the early 1990s. Ultimately, the fundamental co-operation established there was to spawn the 'most ambitious proposal to date for a regularised, focused and inclusive non-governmental process on Asia Pacific security matters'.[12] CSCAP now includes 23 member organisations.

Think tanks also significantly affected the development of the ASEAN. For instance, in 1988, organisations from Indonesia, Malay-

---

[12] For further information see http://cscap.org.

sia, Singapore and Thailand established the ASEAN Institute of Strategic and International Studies (ASEAN-ISIS), which claims intellectual authorship of the formation of the Asia Regional Forum (ARF) in 1990. In the years that followed, this forum of think tanks was subsequently extended to welcome new members from China, Japan, South Korea and the US. Further transnational think tank networks were established in connection with the ASEAN+3 and the East Asian Summit.

> In East Asia many think tanks are cooperating with each other to fill a gap in this part of the world by organizing regional cooperation arrangements such as the PECC (Pacific Economic Cooperation Council) as the second track of APEC (Asia Pacific Economic Cooperation). PECC has been a pioneer in the development of a tri-partite institution (involving business, academe, and officials in private capacity) to provide policy suggestions to governments. It was also instrumental in the creation of APEC as the formal inter-governmental institution in the wider Asia Pacific region. APEC has become the most important economic regional institution for the Asia Pacific (Wanandi 2008: 7).

Against this background, think tank networks appear to have played a major role in the establishment of political ties in Northeast Asia. The following section will examine this assumption by analysing the impact of South Korean think tanks on the national *discourse* on regionalisation.

4 THE DISCOURSE ON REGIONALISATION IN SOUTH KOREA

4.1 *Growing influence of think tanks*

Think tanks are revealed as key actors in the discourse surrounding regionalisation in East Asia due to their extensive influence on intellectual preparation for and legitimation of political decisions. Owing to their centrality at the intersection between academic, political and public spheres, they are in a favourable position to introduce and promote new ideas in national and transnational political discourses. Over the last few years, South Korean political discourse has been increasingly shaped by think tanks. Although no central directory or database for think tank registration exists, it seems reasonable to assume that their numbers have increased significantly over the last three decades.

The US Foreign Policy Research Institute (FPRI) estimates the total number of think tanks in South Korea to be 35 (McGann 2010: 17). Recently, the FPRI and the Japanese National Institute for Research Advancement (NIRA) have taken the lead in academic discussions about think tanks by conducting large research projects and constructing databases containing comprehensive information about think tanks. For this study, our own research and the online databases of the FPRI and NIRA provided information on a total of 19 think tanks in South Korea.[13] Although this number includes only a portion of the total, it seems likely that these agencies represent the most visible and influential ones. The majority of them were established within the last three decades. In our sample, one think tank was founded in the 1960s, ten in the 1970s, three in the 1980s, four in the 1990s, and two in the 2000s. In terms of annual budgets, the biggest think tank by far is the Korea Development Institute (KDI) (US$35 million), followed by the Korea Institute for Defense Analyses (KIDA) US$22 million) and the Korea Labor Institute (KLI) (US$13.5 million).[14] Nine think tanks—including the three largest institutes—are funded by the state. The other ten are independent but are related to private universities in most cases. Although the influence of think tanks is usually limited to national political and economic issues in South Korea, the global 'Go-To Think Tanks' report of the FPRI (McGann 2010: 40) lists the KDI in 11th place among the top 40 think tanks in Asia.

Concerning the South Korean discourse about regionalisation, Figure 1 displays the total number of publications containing a reference to East Asia (within the title, abstract, or keywords) listed on the Internet websites of 14 think tanks[15] and in the DBPIA[16] (ttokttokhan haksulnonmun chisik beisŭ—*Smart Academic Knowledge Base*) full-text database of Korean journals. The think tank sample includes 214 items, the DBPIA sample 1,847 items. As revealed in Figure 1, the number of think tank publications concerning regional issues and

---

[13] The Consortium of Non-Traditional Security Studies in Asia (NTS—established in 2007) was not listed in these databases. However, we included it in our study because of its large and influential international academic and civic network.

[14] The figures are from 2005. They are taken from the Internet database, NIRA's *World Directory of Think Tanks*. Online: http://niradb.jp/search/nwdtt/ (accessed 24 February 2010).

[15] It should be noted that the number of English-language publications referring to East Asia considerably exceeds the number of Korean-language publications that do so. Therefore, we limited our search to publications in the English language.

[16] For further information see http://www.dbpia.co.kr/.

problems has significantly increased since 1997. Between 1997 and 2009, the total number of publications on East Asian issues increased in two stages from 30 to 214 items. In the first stage (1997–2002), the number grew more than twofold (from 30 to 64), and in the second stage (2002–09), the number more than tripled (from 64 to 214). Although the number of items appears to have decreased sharply in 2009, it is possible that not all relevant publications of this year have been recorded yet in our Internet database sources.

Figure 1   Frequency of publications on East Asia (1990-2009)

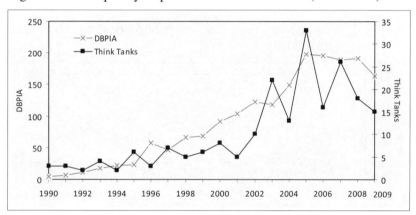

Source: DBPIA (full-text database of Korean journals, articles and proceedings) (accessed 24 February 2010); Internet websites of 14 South Korean think tanks (EAI, IFANS, IFES, IGE, Ilmin, KDI, KEEI, KIEP, KIET, KLI, KREI, KRIHS, NTS, Sejong)[17] (accessed 23 February 2010).

The overwhelming majority of our sample explicitly refers to Northeast Asian issues, with only some articles and books referring to Southeast Asia. Of the various think tanks, four alone contributed nearly 50 percent of the publications: KDI contributed about 20 percent, the Korea Institute for Industrial Economics and Trade (KIET) 12 percent, the Sejong Institute 9 percent, and the Institute of Foreign

---

[17] Abbreviations: EAI = East Asia Institute, IFANS = Institute of Foreign Affairs and National Security, IFES = Institute for Far Eastern Studies, IGE = Institute for Global Economics, KDI = Korea Development Institute, KEEI = Korea Energy Economics Institute, KIEP = Korea Institute for International Economic Policy, KIET = Korea Institute for Industrial Economics and Trade, KLI = Korea Labor Institute, KREI = Korea Rural Economic Institute, KRIHS = Korea Research Institute for Human Settlements, NTS = Consortium of Non-Traditional Security Studies in Asia, Sejong = Sejong Institute.

Affairs and National Security (IFANS) 7 percent. The KDI and the KIET concentrate predominantly on economic issues, while the Sejong Institute and the IFANS tend to focus on political issues. Figure 1 and Figure 2 reveal a highly significant correlation[18] between the distributions of think tank publications and the articles listed in the DBPIA database, the most comprehensive full-text database on academic articles in the Korean language. This finding underscores the strong link between think tanks and the academic world. This connection is an important precondition for their function as an intermediary agent of regionalism between science and politics.

Figure 2   Cumulative frequency of publications on East Asia (1990-2009)

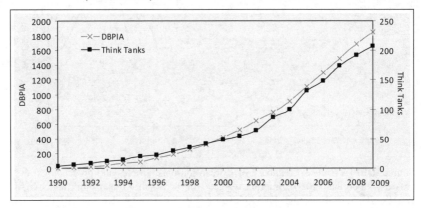

Source: DBPIA (full-text database of Korean journals, articles and proceedings) (accessed 24 February 2010); Internet websites of 14 South Korean think tanks (EAI, IFANS, IFES, IGE, Ilmin, KDI, KEEI, KIEP, KIET, KLI, KREI, KRIHS, NTS, Sejong)[19] (accessed 23 February 2010).

Many different historical, economic and political reasons have contributed to the significant increase in discourse on East Asia in 2002. It should be taken into account that most South Korean think tanks are embedded in international academic networks, particularly in the US and Western Europe. The impressive growth in publications should, therefore, also be regarded as a response to international debates concerning the growing economic and political importance of 'East Asia'

---

[18] The correlation coefficient (Pearson's R) for the distributions displayed in Figure 1 is 0.85. This correlation is significant at the 0.01 level (2-tailed).

[19] Abbreviations: see footnote 17.

in a globalising world after the end of the Cold War. As a consequence, the image of East Asia presented in these publications is strongly influenced by discourses of the scientific community not only in East Asia, but also in North America and Europe. Nevertheless, the specific contribution of South Korean think tanks is not limited to reproducing Western images of East Asia. They often perform a double function: first of all, they 'translate' international debates and concepts into the cultural and political context of South Korea (Kern 2010) and—in so doing—shape the (national) political discourse on this issue. Secondly, through active participation in international discussions, they provide contributions from a specifically Korean perspective. As a comprehensive discussion of the latter would exceed the scope of this article, the following sections concentrate on the ways in which think tanks affect national policies and discourse in South Korea.

4.2 *Institutional isomorphism*

As previously mentioned, think tanks strongly influence the manner in which academic concepts (universities without students) and organised interests (advocacies) are translated into political agendas. Impressively rising numbers of think tanks worldwide and extensive research on the impact of the advice offered by think tanks underscore this assumption (Dixon 2000; Stone 1996). However, the question as to how think tanks perform their function remains. Most researchers stress the importance of financial resources (campaigning) and personal relations (networks) between think tanks and the political establishment.[20] Yet the specific connections between both sides and the mechanisms by which academic ideas and interests translate into political decisions remain open to debate. In light of this information, the following section examines the degree to which the concept of institutional isomorphism explains the intermediary role of think tanks among academia, state institutions and the public sphere. In this context, we will focus in particular on the shared 'cognitive base' (Di-

---

[20] Dixon, for example, offers a detailed reconstruction of personal and financial ties between parts of the British political elite, enterprises and highly influential think tanks (Dixon 2000).

Maggio and Powell 1983: 152) of think tank personnel and the political elite in South Korea.

In their famous article 'The Iron Cage Revisited: Institutional Isomorphism and Collective Rationality in Organizational Fields', DiMaggio and Powell (1983) stress that formal organisations are continually involved in fierce competition for scarce economic, social and cultural resources. As this competition implies serious uncertainties,[21] the need for orientation and promising solutions is insatiable. According to DiMaggio and Powell, the major strategy for coping with this uncertainty and ensuring survival of the organisation is to adopt successful strategies from other units. As a consequence, the structures and discourses within organisational fields are becoming increasingly homogeneous. DiMaggio and Powell describe this process as institutional isomorphism understood as 'a constraining process that forces one unit in a population to resemble other units that face the same set of environmental conditions' (ibid.: 149). They identify three mechanisms by which institutional isomorphic change occurs: '(1) coercive isomorphism that stems from political influence and the problem of legitimacy; (2) mimetic isomorphism, resulting from standard responses to uncertainty; and (3) normative isomorphism, associated with professionalization' (ibid.: 150).

In light of this classification, we believe that the mechanism of normative isomorphism provides a promising model to explain the manner in which connections between think tank expertise and political agenda-setting function. An important mechanism of creating normative change involves the 'filtering of personnel' (DiMaggio and Powell 1983: 152). Accordingly, organisations hire individuals from other units within the same institutional field. This practice promotes structural homogenisation by strengthening professional socialisation and facilitating the diffusion of skills, standard methods, and even organisational vocabularies. Thus, think tank personnel and political representatives may understand each other simply because *they already speak the same language*.[22] Taking DiMaggio and Powell's dis-

---

[21] Concerning goals, strategies and communication, for example.

[22] Similar education may affect the ways in which think tank personnel and politicians view political problems and define the background of economic challenges or cultural and social developments: 'To the extent managers and key staff are drawn from the same universities and filtered in a common set of attributes, they will tend to view problems in a similar fashion, see the same policies, procedures, and structures as normatively sanctioned and legitimated, and approach decisions in much the same way' (DiMaggio and Powell, 1983: 153).

tinction of two possible lines of normative isomorphism into account, it is possible to articulate two distinct hypotheses:

> Two aspects of professionalization are important sources of isomorphism. One is the resting of formal education and of legitimation in a cognitive base produced by university specialists; the second is the growth and elaboration of professional networks that span organizations and across which new models diffuse rapidly. Universities and professional training institutions are important centers for the development of organizational norms among professional managers and their staff. [...] Such mechanisms create a pool of almost interchangeable individuals who occupy similar positions across a range of organizations and possess a similarity of orientation and disposition that may override variations in tradition and control that might otherwise shape organizational behavior (DiMaggio and Powell: 152).

The first hypothesis concerns the shared educational background of think tank personnel and political decision-makers: The more similar the educational socialisation, the greater the influence of think tanks. In this case, similar linguistic patterns and cognitive representations in discourse about regionalisation and the rise of regional identities in East Asia comply with scientific models taught, for example, at leading academic institutions.[23] The second hypothesis is related to the way in which 'almost interchangeable individuals' (ibid.: 152) establish career networks. Close personal ties between consulting personnel and political decision-makers go a long way to explaining the general permeability of the boundary between political and scientific community for think tank expertise.[24]

The concept of a cognitive base is closely related to the idea of 'cognitive legitimacy' (Suchman 1995: 582), which assumes that the legitimacy (of an organisation) depends on its ability to create a 'set of intersubjective givens that submerge the possibility of dissent'[25] (ibid.: 583). This means that professional standards and methods can become

---

[23] Similar studies exist, dealing with the spread of specific economic beliefs and methods, such as the internationalisation of the so-called Chicago Boys (Huneeus 2000).

[24] A well-documented aspect of such career networks can be found in various studies about 'lobbying' and political interest groups, which not only recruit staff from the political elite but may function as stepping stones for political careers as well.

[25] Professionalisation not only prevents deviation from 'givens' but also promotes standardisation of the organisational personal itself: 'The formalization of the cognitive base of a profession has a powerful effect on professional unification because its allows a deeper and a more thorough standardization of the production of producers ...' (Larson 1977: 40).

'taken for granted'. If 'professionals are heavily influenced by ideas generated within their profession', as Roy and Séguin suggest (2000: 456), evidence for a joint cognitive base of think tank personnel and Korean lawmakers would point towards an affinity in the 'way of thinking' and the constitution of a 'cognitive community' (Fleck 1980). Such 'professional networks give salience to emerging phenomena and provide fertile grounds for promoting new successful endeavours, by means such as newsletters, conferences and so forth' (Roy and Séguin 2000: 456). As Strang and Meyer (1993) have shown, scientification and professionalisation are central to the diffusion of institutional models because they 'are devices for turning local and parochial practice into universally applicable principles that can rationally be adopted …' (Strang and Meyer: 502). Thus, the permeability of the boundary between political and scientific community for think tank expertise may be due to the joint cognitive base of think tank personnel and lawmakers resulting from similarities in their academic socialisation.

4.3 *Political relevance*

The following analysis attempts to shed light on career path formation of think tanks and political institutions. Our methodological approach consisted of a series of analyses of descriptive data showing the association between the academic/professional background of members of the South Korean National Assembly and the personnel of leading think tanks. The data were collected from the official web-based curriculum vitae of current members of the National Assembly and employee information for seven think tanks in our sample; together, the data covered 56 percent of the publications about East Asia.[26] The database on political decision-makers contained information about 297 lawmakers. Additional background information about 197 employees of South Korean think tanks was obtained from Internet websites. According to our leading hypotheses described in Section 5.2 above, the data were examined for evidence of related patterns of academic education and career paths between the two groups compared. The se-

---

[26] This group of think tanks includes the Korea Development Institute (KDI), East Asia Institute (EAI), Korea Institute for International Economic Policy (KIEP), Korea Labor Institute (KLI), Sejong Institute, Korea Institute for Industrial Economics and Trade (KIET).

lected data concentrate on details related to the highest academic degrees earned, the universities attended, and previous professional experience. Particular attention was paid to actual and/or past connections of think tank personnel and the political establishment (such as official co-operation, consultancy positions, and so forth).

To assess the similarity of educational socialisation of think tank personnel and political decision-makers, we first examined the background of Korean lawmakers in the national assembly. Our data reveal that Korean lawmakers have a comparatively high degree of formal education. As revealed in Figure 3, among the 297 representatives in the Korean parliament, 268, or 90 percent, graduated from a university, and 25 percent hold a Ph.D. (The corresponding percentages of members from the German Bundestag are 62 percent and 18 percent (Mause 2008: 32).) Fifty-eight percent of the Korean lawmakers graduated from (at least) one of the three leading universities of the country, with 38 percent having graduated from Seoul National University, 13 percent from Yonsei University, and 10 percent from Korea University.[27] Thus, the educational socialisation of the political elite in Korea appears to be quite homogenous. Furthermore, 21 percent of Korean lawmakers studied abroad—18 percent in the US. This finding underscores the strong ties between the US and South Korea.[28]

When compared to the educational background of lawmakers, our results reveal a strikingly similar pattern for think tank members: an overwhelming majority of 33 percent graduated from Seoul National University, 9 percent from Yonsei University, and another 9 percent from Korea University. The combined total percentage of graduates from the three leading universities in South Korea amounts to 49 percent. While this value is slightly less than the percentage of lawmakers who attended leading South Korean universities, it indicates a considerable homogeneity between the two camps. Furthermore, the dominance of US university educational institutions in the educational career of think tank personnel appears to be even greater: More than a third (37 percent) never graduated from a South Korean University. This means that they received their entire academic educational training abroad. Fifty-four percent graduated from US universities and

---

[27] The sum of the single three universities deviates from the compound value of 58 percent because many students transfer between these three universities.

[28] For the educational socialisation of South Korean think tank members, we collected data from the corresponding Internet websites. Almost all of the think tank members (96 percent) hold a Ph.D.

11 percent from European universities. Only 30 percent spent their entire academic career in South Korea.

Figure 3   Academic degrees of think tank personnel and lawmakers (South Korea/Germany)

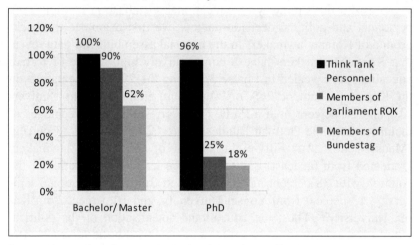

Source: Own calculations on the basis of data from official Internet websites (accessed 2010); Mause (2008).

Our results underscore the high degree of internationalisation that exists in South Korean think tanks. Furthermore, the think tank personnel and political decision-makers are impressively homogenous with respect to their educational backgrounds. This finding supports our hypothesis concerning the political relevance of the current discourse on East Asia. The effect is further enhanced by the dense network of close ties that exist between think tank personnel and political decision-makers. According to the CVs of our sample, 21 percent of the research fellows and consultants perform some type of official function as an advisor or expert in a political institution. Considering that many think tank employees may not have included their political functions in their CVs, the real number is presumably much higher. In addition, remembering that nine out of nineteen think tanks (including the largest ones) are funded by the South Korean government, it is even more reasonable to assume that think tank expertise exerts a relatively strong influence on political decision-making.

5 Conclusion

The discourse on regionalisation is playing an increasingly important role in South Korea. The results of this study seem to confirm our assumptions with regard to the growing importance of regionalisation in general, and to the key role of think tanks as mediators between the scientific community and the political establishment in particular. Our analysis of 207 think tank publications indicates that the interest in regional issues has considerably increased in recent years. The expansion of the various think tank research activities in this field is especially notable given their central position at the intersection between the academic, political and public spheres within Korean society *and* their integration in intra-regional and global academic networks.

On the basis of our examination of the similarities between the academic education and career paths of think tank employees and those of the members of the National Assembly, we discovered indications implying a common 'cognitive base' shared by the two groups when they were compared. Above all, our analysis revealed the importance of academic training. With the vast majority of the elected representatives holding an academic degree, and the fact that having a doctorate is the normal case for think tank personnel, members of both groups seem to speak 'the same language' already. This fact facilitates the 'translation' of scientific discourse into political agendas. Furthermore, in order to provide scientific consultation, many influential thinks tanks in South Korea are funded by the state. Consequently, a large proportion of think tank employees work officially as advisers for various ministries and state authorities.

Two additional results are worth mentioning: first, we found evidence supporting the significance of Korean alumni ties. Three Korean universities (Seoul National, Yonsei, Korea University) together account for considerably more than half (58 percent) of the universities visited by lawmakers. A similar figure applies in regards to think tank personnel. About 50 percent graduated from either Seoul National University, Korea University or Yonsei University. Second, significant numbers of think tank personnel and lawmakers have studied abroad. Many of them accordingly have strong ties to US universities. Consequently, members of both groups may have received a certain 'cosmopolitan socialisation', which possibly fosters ideas of international integration and global co-operation. Our findings therefore correspond with the predictions of neo-institutional theory concerning the mechanism of normative isomorphism. The shared educational background of think tank personnel and members of parliament favours the development of similar orientations and dispositions, which appear to have facilitated the diffusion of concepts such as 'region' and 'regionalisation'.

However, these results also help to identify areas in which further research is necessary. For example, additional research is required in order to evaluate whether the findings presented here are limited to the case of Korea, or whether we can discern similar patterns in other East Asian countries. It is also necessary to examine whether or not the discourse pertaining to East Asia is limited to a cosmopolitan academic and political elite. The influence of civic actors and economic elites must also be taken into account. Comparative analyses could provide further information about the differences between world regions and nation states, and the role of think tanks in shaping international discourse.[29] Finally, the interplay between national, international and transnational institutional levels should be studied from a longitudinal perspective in order to describe the specific dynamics of regional integration in Northeast Asia.

---

[29] The contrast between the heterogeneity of American think tank personnel mentioned above (Weaver 1989: 656) and our findings, which suggest the dominance of professional academic backgrounds and the specific function of think tanks as 'career hubs' in South Korea, is particularly interesting. Weaver explains this heterogeneity as a result of strategic decisions made by think tanks. The question as to whether or not strategic considerations in Korea differ from those of their American counterparts remains unresolved and would make for an interesting subject in future research.

REFERENCES

Anderson, Benedict (1983), *Imagined Communities: Reflections on the Origin and Spread of Nationalism*, London: Verso
Arnason, Johann P. (2003), *Civilizations in Dispute. Historical Questions and Theoretical Traditions*, Leiden: Brill
Arnason, Johann P., Shmuel N. Eisenstadt and Björn Wittrock (2005), *Axial Civilization and World History*, Leiden: Brill
Ben-Rafael, Eliezer and Yitzhak Sternberg (2005), *Comparing Modernities. Pluralism versus Homogenity*, Leiden: Brill
Boli, John and Yitzhak Sternberg (2005), 'Facade Diversity. The Individualization of Cultural Difference', in: *International Sociology*, 23, pp. 540-60
Bourdieu, Pierre (1998), *Praktische Vernunft. Zur Theorie des Handelns*, Frankfurt am Main: Suhrkamp
DiMaggio, Paul J. and Walter W. Powell (1983), 'The Iron Cage Revisited: Institutional Isomorphism and Collective Rationality', in: *American Sociological Review*, 48, pp. 147-60
Dixon, Keith (2000), *Die Evangelisten des Marktes. Die britischen Intellektuellen und der Thatcherismus*, Konstanz: UVK Universitätsverlag Konstanz GmbH
Eder, Klaus (2006), 'Europe's Borders: The Narrative Construction of the Boundaries', in: *European Journal of Social Theory*, 9, pp. 255-71
Eisenstadt, Shmuel N. (1982), 'The Axial Age: The Emergence of Transcendental Visions and the Rise of Clerics', in: *European Journal of Sociology*, 23, pp. 294-314
Eisenstadt, Shmuel N. (2000), *Die Vielfalt der Moderne*, Weilerswist: Velbrueck Wissenschaft
Fleck, Ludwik ([1935] 1980), *Entstehung und Entwicklung einer wissenschaftlichen Tatsache. Einführung in die Lehre von Denkstil und Denkkollektiv*, Basel: Schwabe (1935), reprinted Frankfurt am Main: Suhrkamp (1980)
Hagstrom, W. (1965), *The Scientific Community*, New York and London: Basic Books
Huneeus, Carlos (2000), 'Technocrats and Politicians in an Authoritarian Regime. The "ODEPLAN Boys" and the "Gremialists" in Pinochet's Chile', in: *Journal of Latin American Studies*, 32, pp. 461-501
Huntington, Samuel P. (1996), *The Clash of Civilizations and the Remaking of the World Order*, New York: Simon & Schuster
Hurrell, Andrew (1997), 'Regionalism in Theoretical Perspective', in: Louise Fawcett and Andrew Hurrell (eds), *Regionalism in World Politics: Regional Organization and International Order*, Oxford: Oxford University Press, pp. 37-73
Hurrell, Andrew (2007), 'One World? Many Worlds? The Place of Regions in the Study of International Society', in: *International Affairs*, 83, pp. 127-46
Johnston, Hank and Pamela E. Oliver (2005), 'What a Good Idea! Ideologies and Frames in Social Movement Research', in: Hank Johnston and John A. Noakes (eds), *Frames of Protest: Social Movements and the Framing Perspective*, Lanham MD: Rowman & Littlefield Publishers, pp. 185-204
Katzenstein, Peter J. (2005), *A World of Regions: Asia and Europe in the American Imperium*, Ithaca NY: Cornell University Press
Kern, Thomas (2010), 'Translating Global Values into National Contexts: The Rise of Environmentalism in South Korea', in: *International Sociology*, forthcoming
Kern, Thomas and Sang-hui Nam (2009), 'The Korean Comfort Women Movement and the Formation of a Public Sphere in East Asia', in: Rüdiger Frank, James E. Hoare, Patrick Köllner and Susan Pares (eds), *Korea Yearbook 2009: Politics, Economy and Society*, Leiden: Brill, pp. 227-55

Larson, M. S. (1977). *The Rise of Professionalism*, Berkeley CA: University of California Press
Lechner, Frank J. and John Boli (2005), *World Culture: Origins and Consequences*, Malden MA: Blackwell Publishing
Lewis, Martin W. and Kären Wigen (1997), *The Myth of Continents: A Critique of Metageography*, Berkeley CA: University of California Press
Mause, Karsten (2008), 'Die Nebentätigkeiten der Bundestagsabgeordneten'. Online: http://www.uni-graz.at/socialpolitik/papers/Mause.pdf (accessed 26 February 2010)
McGann, James G. (2007), *The Global 'Go-To Think Tanks': The Leading Public Policy Research Organizations in the World*. Online: http://www.fpri.org/research/thinktanks/mcgann.globalgotothinktanks.pdf (accessed 23 August 2009)
McGann, James G. (2010), *The Global 'Go-To Think Tanks': The Leading Public Policy Research Organizations in the World*. Online: http://www.sas.upenn.edu/irp/documents/2009GlobalGoToReportThinkTankIndex_1.31.2010.0 2.01.pdf (accessed 24 February 2010)
Meyer, John W. (2007), 'Globalization: Theory and Trends', in: *International Journal of Comparative Sociology*, 48, pp. 261-73
Miller, Max (2005), *Worlds of Capitalism: Institutions, Governance, and Economic Change in the Era of Globalization*, London: Routledge
Ritzer, George (2004), *The McDonaldization of Society* (revised edition), Thousand Oaks CA: Pine Forge Press
Ritzer, George (2007), *The Globalization of Nothing 2*, Thousand Oaks CA: Pine Forge Press
Roy, Claude and Francine Séguin (2000), 'The Institutionalization of Efficiency-oriented Approaches for Public Service Improvement', in: *Public Productivity & Management Review*, 23, 4, pp. 449-68
Snow, David A. and Robert D. Benford (1988), 'Ideology, Frame Resonance, and Participant Mobilization', in: Bert Klandermans, Hanspeter Kriesi and Sidney Tarrow (eds), *International Social Movement Research: From Structure to Action*, Greenwich CT: JAI Press, pp. 197-217
Snow, David A. and Robert D. Benford (1992), 'Master Frames and Cycles of Protest', in: Aldon D. Morris and Carol McClurg Mueller (eds), *Frontiers in Social Movement Theory*, New Haven CT: Yale University Press, pp. 133-55
Snow, David A., Steven K. Worden and Robert D. Benford (1986), 'Frame Alignment Processes, Micromobilization and Movement Participation', in: *American Sociological Review*, 51, pp. 464-81
Stone, Diane (1996), *Capturing the Political Imagination. Think Tanks and the Policy Process*, London, Portland: Frank Cass
Strang, David and John W. Meyer (1993), 'Institutional Conditions for Diffusion', in: *Theory and Society*, 22, pp. 487-511
Suchman, Mark C. (1995), 'Managing Legitimacy: Strategic and Institutional Approaches', in: *Academy of Management Review*, 20 (3), pp. 517-610
Wanandi, Jusuf (2008), 'The Importance of Think Tanks in the Twenty-first Century', in: *Asia-Pacific Review*, 15, pp. 6-8
Weaver, R. Kent (1989), 'The Changing World of Think Tanks', in: *PS: Political Science and Politics*, 22, pp. 563-78
Wyatt-Walter, Andrew (1997), 'Regionalism, Globalization, and World Economic Order', in: Louise Fawcett and Andrew Hurrell (eds), *Regionalism in World Politics. Regional Organization in World Politics*, New York: Oxford University Press, pp. 74-121

SOUTH KOREA'S ECONOMIC POLICY RESPONSE TO THE GLOBAL FINANCIAL CRISIS

Werner Pascha

ABSTRACT

For the second time in somewhat more than a decade, the Republic of Korea has been hit by a major economic crisis. While the so-called Asian financial crisis of 1997-8 is history, it is still unclear whether the global financial and economic crisis, which culminated with the collapse of Lehman Brothers in September 2008, is already over. In both cases, South Korea has done remarkably well to overcome quickly what at some stage have appeared as very severe challenges. It is tempting to conjecture whether the South Korean adjustment to the second crisis may have been influenced by memories of the first. Certain lessons may have been assimilated from the 1997-8 crisis, such as the need for speedy and decisive action to meet fiscal and economic difficulties, but also to contain social unrest. Institutional mechanisms, some established since the earlier crisis, have helped, as has the top-down system of administration in South Korea, which allows for swift decisions.

1 INTRODUCING THE ISSUES

The aim of this paper is twofold. First and straightforwardly, it will trace how the Republic of Korea (South Korea—henceforth Korea) has handled the 2008 crisis so far.[1] The first year of the crisis, i.e. September 2008 to September 2009, will be taken as the principal reference period. The appropriateness of economic policy measures will be its major concern.

Second, it will search for some connection between the 1997-8 and the 2008-09 crises. A number of recent contributions to experimental

---

[1] Research on this topic was originally undertaken for the project 'Comparative Crisis Management—Assessing the Policy Responses to the 2008-9 Economic Downturn' of the Bertelsmann Stiftung. The foundation's financial support is gratefully acknowledged.

economics have shown that individuals who face a risk and have to make a decision under risk act differently in the light of their background experiences. Those who have already been exposed to a similar situation act differently from those who have only a theoretical knowledge of different pay-outs.[2] It seems tempting to extrapolate these findings from the methodological level of individuals to the societal level. In the confined space of this paper, this can only be on the basis of a conjecture, possibly motivating further research. Still, the Korean case of crisis adjustment is interesting, because decisions made to face the new crisis may have been influenced by memories of another severe economic crisis just a decade before. One might expect that some of the following subjective lessons have been internalised by decision-makers: swift action to regain market trust is important; involving international players can be burdensome; social consequences have to be accounted for.

The first two parts of the paper will trace Korea's economic situation when it faced the crisis and see how Korea was affected by the global financial crisis, which was to turn into a major global economic crisis. The article will next trace policy responses and see how they resonated with the performance of the Korean economy. As a fourth step, it will look at the political boundary conditions. The paper will conclude by looking for connections between the two major crises.

2 THE SOUTH KOREAN ECONOMY ON THE EVE OF THE GLOBAL FINANCIAL AND ECONOMIC CRISIS

At the outbreak of the financial crisis in September 2008 (taking the Lehman Brothers insolvency as the starting point), the new government under President Lee Myung-bak was not even one year in office. Lee had started as a pro-business president, but even in his first months in office had had to face a number of setbacks. Some of his pet project ideas, with which he wanted to strengthen economic

---

[2] Rakow and Newell (2010) report that decision-makers in an experiment act differently depending on whether options and their outcomes are described to them or when they experience actual draws. In experiments about buying insurance, Kusev et al. (2009) notice that participants may fear exaggerated risks, and this may be caused by the accessibility of certain events in memory. Starbuck (2009) finds that learning from rare events is important and difficult, and may have significant influence not only on individuals but on organisations as well.

growth, were not well received. The vision of building a canal through the mountainous centre of the peninsula, for instance, was facing stiff opposition, and it did not help much that the president tried to overcome opposition like a 'bulldozer'—as he is sometimes called. The biggest macro-economic concern in early 2008, however, while not having been caused by the new government, was inflation due to rising import prices of energy and other resources.

In terms of President Lee's pro-business approach, one important objective was to 'drastically improve the investment environment', through measures like tax-cutting and making the country more attractive for foreign investors. A second economic objective was to 'sharply streamline regulations', a third to 'create new jobs through green growth', and finally to 'promote new growth engines and the service industry' (Cheong Wa Dae 2009). More specifically, following the slogan 'Economy first!', Lee had promised 'Korea 747', implying 7 percent of economic growth, a per capita-income of US$40,000 and a ranking of seventh among the major global economies; this lofty vision was already regarded as unrealistic by many, even by well-disposed, observers, when Lee took office. Nominally, the government also followed some welfare and distribution-oriented goals like better child care, revival of underachieving regions, expansion of social services, etc., but the pro-growth priorities were clear.

Already before the global financial crisis fully erupted during the third quarter of 2008, South Korea had been experiencing macro-economic problems. While the economy still expanded by 5 percent in 2007 and by 5.8 percent in the first quarter of 2008 (year on year basis), it deteriorated subsequently, reaching negative territory in the fourth quarter (ADB 2009: 172-6). Import value had been increasing strongly since late 2007, driven by higher raw material and energy prices, on which South Korea has to rely. Accordingly, inflation had become an issue, consumer prices rising 4.8 percent (year-on-year) in October 2008, well beyond the 2.5 percent to 3.5 percent target zone. Job growth, domestic consumption, investment and corporate profits were also negatively affected by these developments before the financial crisis set in. In addition, the won had begun to devalue before September 2008, further worsening problems.

Given this setting of macro-economic circumstances, what position was South Korea in to weather a global economic storm? Since the 1960s, the South Korean economy as one of the East Asian newly emerging economies has been very much integrated in regional and global trade flows. It is considered one of the premier examples of an outward-oriented development model. Being extremely resource-poor, the country's 'business model' consists of processing imported raw materials and intermediate goods, adding value and exporting the goods. China has become the major trading partner for both exports and imports (21 percent and 16 percent market share respectively in 2006, figures based on Korea International Trade Association data), while other major trading partners are the US and Japan. Korea is thus intimately linked to some of those economies that are also subject to the impact of the financial crisis and its consequences for real demand. In the area of international investment, South Korea is deeply integrated with the world economy. At the end of 2007 (Bank of Korea 2009a), it held US$597 billion in assets abroad, compared to liabilities of US$826 billion. In terms of foreign direct investment (FDI), Korea has recently made strong moves into China in order to tap its market and to use it as an export base to the world market; between 2004 and 2007, FDI assets increased from US$7.5 billion to US$23.7 billion. In this respect too, South Korea has become very dependent on the global market and on China in particular.

Speculative exuberance in the real estate sector has been a considerable issue for Korean governments for many years. During 2005-07, however, the former government, concerned about bubble phenomena and an uneven distribution of wealth, took a number of countermeasures such as price ceilings on new apartments and raising capital gains taxes, etc. As a consequence, residential construction had declined and was actually contributing to the weakness of domestic demand at the outbreak of the crisis (OECD 2008: 22).

Compared to the situation of the late 1990s and in comparison with many other countries, the situation in Korean banking seemed quite healthy at the outbreak of the recent crisis. Because of the preceding real estate boom, Korea had introduced regulations on a loan-to-value ratio of mortgage loans, so it was possible to avoid an excessive financing of blown-up real estate prices (Park 2009). In June 2008, the capital adequacy ratio for Korea's commercial banks was 11.16 percent (based on Basel II), and thus seemed quite safe, again in comparison to other banks in the world (see Figure 1 below). A closer look reveals that some problems began to loom among Korean banks. This was particularly (Bank of Korea 2008: 52) the case with the liquidity ratio, which is defined as the ratio of current assets with three months or less remaining maturity to current liabilities with three months or less remaining maturity. According to Korean financial supervision, this ratio should be above 100 percent for commercial banks. While it had usually surpassed 110 percent for many years, it dropped close to 100 percent in late 2007. Banks are reported to have tried 'quick fixes' to overcome this situation, a move that contributed to severe problems when the financing possibilities seriously deteriorated during 2008.

Figure 1 Capital adequacy ratio trends of Korean, US and major global banks

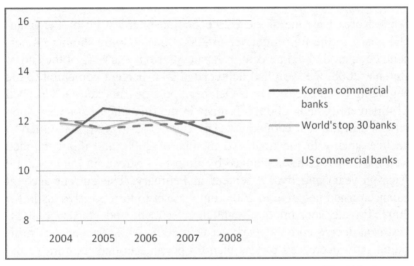

Notes: End of year values; world's top 30 banks: simple average of Bank for International Settlements ratios (based on volume of tier-1 capital); US banks: total assets more then US$10 billion.
Source: Bank of Korea (2008: 73), abbreviated.

In terms of latitude for fiscal policy measures, it should be stressed that traditionally South Korea has followed an extremely prudent policy with respect to government debt. In 2007, the share of central government debt to GDP was only 29 percent, one of the lowest values among OECD economies. The government thus had ample room to make use of a deficit-financed stimulus package.

The pre-crisis main interest rate of the Bank of Korea was 5.25 percent, a seven-and-a-half year high. From this perspective, there was leeway for rate cuts to stimulate the economy, at least at first sight. There were two concerns, however. One was inflationary pressure, which made rate cuts less attractive. Consumer prices indeed continued to rise into the spring of 2009. A second was the exchange rate. Under flexible rates—a major difference to the 1997 crisis—there was concern that a rate cut might lead to an uncontrollable further decline of the won due to foreign investors repatriating their funds.

3 THE CRISIS AND ECONOMIC POLICY REACTIONS

3.1 *Effects of the crisis*

South Korea was one of the G20 economies hardest hit by the financial crisis. In the fourth quarter of 2008, the economy shrank 3.4 percent, compared to 4.3 percent in Japan (year-on-year). As of the end of October 2008, the won had depreciated 24.5 percent compared to the beginning of the year; by 16 October, the stock market had dropped 31.4 percent (Chang 2008). Changes in the financial sector were soon reflected in the real economy (ADB 2009: 172-6). Exports started to decline steeply in the final two months of 2008, and this continued well into 2009. Exports plunged by almost 34 percent in January 2009 (year-on-year) and by 17 percent in February. The current account balance turned negative in 2008, but was set to turn positive again for 2009. Private consumption, capital investment and construction investment decreased on a yearly basis in 2008, while the capacity utilisation ratio decreased to less than 65 percent around the turn of the year. As a consequence, GDP shrank in the final quarter of 2008, but thanks to higher growth in the first quarters, Korea still achieved 2.5 percent of GDP growth in 2008. In terms of employment, it was possible to contain unemployment at 3.2 percent in 2008, mainly a result of a surge in the number of workers dropping out of the labour force during the downturn. The number of temporary workers has increased significantly in recent years, which has offered a seemingly convenient buffer for employment adjustment. On the other side of the coin, this trend meant that the welfare situation of those affected at the bottom of the labour force seriously deteriorated and developed into a major social issue in 2009. Even a pro-market government like President Lee Myung-bak's could not avoid facing and reacting to this problem.

Various interest groups were affected by the financial crisis. The exposure of the Korean financial system to toxic financial assets was small, so this has not become a major issue for policy responses.

Banks and enterprises, however, were seriously affected by the international liquidity crunch and by the steep drop of export markets. While the effects on groups like exporters and stock market investors were cushioned fairly quickly by the eventual rebound of markets from early 2009, low-income households continue to suffer from the pressure on companies to remain competitive under extremely difficult circumstances. This has not been reflected so much in official unemployment figures, which have not moved beyond the 4 percent range during the crisis. Indeed, regular employees of established companies enjoy quite attractive salaries and benefits. However, companies have had to compensate for these costly measures, and many less fortunate workers have had to accept badly paid irregular or temporary work or have left the active work force. Given Korea's still incomplete social security system, suffering and discontent have become quite considerable.

3.2 *Policy reactions*

The central bank had raised interest rates as late as August 2008 to fight inflationary pressure. Only in September 2008, with the bankruptcy of Lehman Brothers, did the government begin to notice the severity of the coming crisis. The first major measure was the announcement by the Ministry of Strategy and Finance on 26 September 2008 that it had injected US$10 billion into the currency swap market to help domestic banks to overcome their US dollar funding shortages; a ban on short-selling stocks followed on 30 September (*New York Times* 2008). In this context, the Bank of Korea extended its existing swap agreements with the United States (US), China and Japan beyond its normal limits, also in excess of those arranged through the Chiang Mai Initiative. A ceiling of US$30 billion with the US was announced on 30 October 2008, with an expiry date of one year later. In addition, foreign currency liquidity was provided to financial institutions. The total volume amounted to US$50 billion, mainly for short-term borrowings and trade finance. There was also some easing on regulations concerning foreign currency loans. Below the surface, the Ministry of Strategy and Finance is believed to have engaged in urging foreign-exchange players 'to curb their dollar purchases' (*Economist* 2009); this was not done under an emergency order, as has been claimed.

The strong decline of the Korean won in late 2008, associated with a significant withdrawal of funds held in Korea by foreign investors, impelled the government to defend the won. It did so not only by using its own foreign reserves (which were reduced by a tenth in October 2008 alone), but also by making use of the extended swap agreements with the US, China and Japan mentioned above. The memory of the 1997-8 crisis, during which the Korean won had come under strong pressure, igniting the painful rescue and recovery process, probably persuaded the government to back the won temporarily. This time, the intervention was more successful, and it was possible to weather the most critical months of global risk aversion without a breakdown of Korea's financial system. However, the effectiveness of support in favour of the won remained unstable, as the won came under some renewed sharp pressure in February to March 2009 (ADB 2009: 174).

Decisions about fiscal measures started only a little later and were also significant. A fiscal stimulus programme was announced in early November 2008 (Wassener 2008). This package encompassed a volume of some 3.6 percent in 2009; the effect in 2010 will still be 1.2 percent (see Table 1). The package includes measures for self-employed and low-income households, which make up about a third of the total and thus cannot be considered negligible. Tax measures account for another percentage point; some part of this measure also includes a social component, as explained elsewhere (Lybecker and Lueth 2009: 10).

Most fiscal measures were earmarked for 2009. The most important expenditure measure however, the 'Green New Deal', which was announced in January 2009, covers a four-year period. According to an estimate from HSBC Global Research (HSBC 2009), the whole programme amounts to 3.5 percent of GDP for 2009. HSBC expected the cost for 2009 to be less than 1 percent of Korea's GDP. Some fiscal stimulus had already been achieved in 2008 as a result of the various measures; the OECD reckoned it to be in the range of around 1 percent of GDP for 2008 (OECD 2009).

Somewhat more than a quarter of the fiscal measures consists of tax measures. They refer to changes in the personal income tax and the corporate income tax rates. The personal income tax changes include some distributive element, through a bigger percentage reduction for lower-income classes and an absolute per-person deduction element. Among the remaining 72 percent (for 2009), namely expenditure-related items, income support for low-income households, labour market-related measures, support for small and medium enterprises (SMEs), and investment measures may be noted.

Table 1   Fiscal stimulus packages (in percent of GDP)

	2009	2010
Revenue measures	-1.0	-1.2
Permanent tax cuts	-0.7	-1.0
Temporary measures	-0.3	-0.2
Expenditure measures	2.6	
2009 revised budget	1.0	...
SOC expansion in regional areas	0.4	...
Support for SMEs and self-employed	0.3	...
Support for low-income households	0.1	...
Local government support	0.1	...
Other	0.1	...
2009 supplementary budget	1.7	...
Support for low-income households	0.4	...
Support for SMEs and self-employed	0.4	...
Support for employment	0.3	...
Local government support	0.3	...
Green growth and other investment spending	0.2	...
Total	3.6	1.2

Source: Lybecker and Lueth 2009: 10, based on Korean authorities and IMF staff estimates.

Support for the financial sector is not included in the measures listed above. The major finance-related measure (Bank of Korea 2009b) was a number of base rate reductions from 5.25 percent to 2.0 percent between October 2008 and February 2009. Another important area of action was the encouragement of funds to support the financial markets in overcoming a credit crunch, for instance through the broadening of eligible collateral. The Bank of Korea also used quantitative easing: the aggregate credit ceiling was raised from 6.5 trillion to 9.0 trillion won to increase the credit supply capacity of banks. An additional measure is a support scheme for bank recapitalisation, encompassing up to 20 trillion won.

Unconventional measures in the sense of quantitative easing to encourage the supply of capital from the banks to the ailing corporate sector have thus been used. The danger of an excessive lengthening of the balance sheet has been limited, however, because the measure was to some extent cancelled out by the lending out of currency reserves. Moreover, as the base rate is still well above zero, conventional monetary policy still works quite well and the International Monetary Fund (IMF) assumes that the unwinding of the unconventional measures, already under way in mid-2009, will proceed quite smoothly (IMF 2009a: 19).

The manoeuvring in late 2008 to avoid a serious lack of US dollars in the banks, necessary to refinance their exposure, involved some rather informal calibration with other financial players, probably somewhat beyond the established rules, although this is difficult to substantiate. These considerations notwithstanding, the financial programmes do spell out conditions for support and are not arbitrary in their execution (Bank of Korea, undated).

While South Korea was not bound in its national monetary policy, the necessary reduction of interest rates meant that the depreciation of the won through an outflow of funds that were used to fill gaps in balance sheets elsewhere, was able to gain even more speed. From this perspective, it is comprehensible that the Bank of Korea engaged in some major, costly defence of the won. While the Asian Development Bank (ADB) joins in the usual doubt whether this support of a currency was truly effective, it does not blame the Bank of Korea (and Korean government authorities) for having tried this measure under difficult circumstances, but reasons that Korea may have gone too far with its capital account liberalisation in recent years (ADB 2009: 174).

Both on the monetary and on the fiscal side, funding needs have not posed serious problems for the Korean government authorities. The most critical period lay in the weeks immediately following the Lehman collapse in September 2008, but financial market conditions soon relaxed. Already in early 2009, risk premiums on government bonds and prime corporate as well as bank bonds relaxed (Financial Services Commission 2009a). This has also been reflected in the positive outlook of leading international rating agencies during 2009. Moody's announced on 16 September 2009 that it would retain its A2 rating for Korea's long-term foreign currency debt, a rating that it has kept throughout the recent financial crisis (Channels 2009). Background factors for this more or less stable appraisal include the relatively low level of public debt in Korea, the significant foreign reserves and the comparatively sound situation of the Korean banking system, with capital-adequacy ratios above 12 and thus well beyond the recommended bottom level of seven.

Several measures can be understood as horizontal industrial support, the most prominent among them being the already mentioned corporate tax cut. Other measures can better be understood as vertical industrial policies, supporting earmarked parts of industry (Ministry of Strategy and Finance 2009a). This holds for the support of SMEs, for example: because of the dominance of the big conglomerate groups, the weakness of smaller companies, aggravated through the financial crisis, has been a persistent problem for Korean governments over the years. One feature of a tax deduction for investments is a bigger rate offered to investment in provincial areas, which is also indirectly a support for SMEs. Assistance for specific industries as it relates to the automobile industry, for instance, includes a tax deduction of 30 percent, offered for a limited period to support domestic sales of Korean automobiles. Under the 'Green New Deal', a special tax deduction is given to solar cell manufacturing plants. Finally, under the same programme, the cleaning of Korea's four biggest rivers and the erection of flood defences mean a substantial boost for the construction sector.

3.3 'Green New Deal'

The major programmatic scheme among the stimulus package is indeed the 'Green New Deal'. It includes nine major projects (see Table 2). Among the total of US$36 billion (spread over four years), almost US$6 billion are earmarked to improve energy conservation in villages and schools, US$7 billion on mass transit and railroads and almost US$11 billion on river restoration (see figures below in Table 2). Major elements of this package had already been contemplated before the crisis, and had been criticised as a support scheme for the construction industry, for which Lee Myung-bak had worked for many years. After the crisis had set in, a major argument for the scheme became job creation: 960,000 are to be created within four years, 140,000 of them in 2009 (Ministry of Strategy and Finance 2009b). Most of these jobs will be for manual labour, so the project can also be considered social policy on behalf of the weak and potentially underemployed. This emphasis on low-quality labour has received considerable criticism, though, as many of those likely to benefit may be foreigners working in Korea.[3]

Many observers doubt the sincerity of the whole project and some even talk of a 'green bubble'. In terms of CO_2 reduction potential, however, scholars of the Kiel Institute for World Economics argue that the volume of 7.37 million tons to be saved is comparable in size to the much larger German economic stimulus programme (Klepper et al. 2009: 19).

Table 2 South Korea's Green New Deal

Project	Employment	USD mill.
Energy efficiency		
Energy conservation (villages and schools)	170,702	5,841
Fuel-efficient vehicles	9,348	1,800
Environmentally friendly living space	10,789	351
Mass transit and railroads	138,067	7,005
Energy efficiency sub-total	*328,906*	*14,997*
Low carbon power (clean energy)	4,674	1,800
Water and waste management		
River restoration	199,960	10,505
Forest restoration	133,630	1,754
Water resource-management (small and medium-sized dams)	16,132	684
Resource recycling (including fuel from waste)	16,196	675
National green information (GIS) infrastructure	3,120	270
Water sub-total	*369,038*	*13,888*
Total for the nine major projects	702,618	30,685
Total for the Green New Deal	960,000	36,280

Source: HSBC 2009: 21, based on South Korea Ministry of Strategy and Finance and HSBC data.

The policies introduced in favour of business make a reasonable effort not to support the 'laggards', but to address substantial short- and longer-term issues in the Korean economy. The weakness of the SME sector, for instance, is well known, and crisis support is a necessary means to safeguard its survival. The Green New Deal has been legitimated as a major instrument in support of manual labour jobs, i.e. jobs for those most affected by the crisis. The government argues that 96 percent of the 960,000 jobs to be created through the four-year pro-

---

[3] I am grateful to an anonymous referee for this valuable addition.

gramme are of this type (while high-tech and R&D jobs in the green sector are promoted rather through a longer-term government project on developing future core technologies and new growth engines) (Ministry of Strategy and Finance 2009b: 14). However, it is frequently argued that from a cost-benefit perspective, the significant funds spent on the programme could more effectively be used elsewhere; the strong emphasis on construction work with dubious socio-economic benefits is seen as a problematic bias of the programme. Moreover, there are ecological concerns about the physical repercussions of the sheer size of the projects.

The Green New Deal is the most imaginative part of the crisis rescue package. It is not totally new, though, but an upgraded version of previous projects and plans (Ministry of Strategy and Finance 2009b: 8). Almost parallel to the announcement of the Green New Deal in January 2009, the government announced its intention to support 'new growth engines', namely 17 industries such as sustainable energy, information technologies, healthcare and tourism. Like the Green New Deal, this programme is also designed for four years, with 17 percent of 6.3 trillion won to be spent in 2009 (Chung 2009). While this programme is sometimes included in summaries of governmental responses to the global crisis (e.g., OECD 2009: 16), it seems more sensible to interpret it as part of long-term concerns of Korean governments to engage in sector-specific industrial policies, with the timing being coincidental.

One might ask more explicitly whether the policy measures were only driven by short-term concerns, or whether other conditions played a role. From a welfare perspective, these may have been longer-term developmental issues, from a public choice perspective, the vested interests of strong socio-economic players. To a considerable extent, the crisis response was of course driven by short-term necessities. This holds in particular for the finance-related parts of the programme, which had to provide an answer to the severe decline of the won, the capital outflows, and the lack of dollar funds for refinancing.

The Green New Deal is the most interesting part of the crisis response, because it combines a strong bias towards construction work, shrewdly advocated for with the creation of manual labour-type job opportunities, and a lofty vision of a 'Green Korea', which addresses one of the accepted long-term challenges of Korea as an advanced, maturing economy (see David Shim's paper in this volume for a critical approach). The Korean government was quite successful in stressing this latter aspect with the international community (see, for instance, UN News Service 2009). Indeed, Korea incorporates the third-biggest green stimulus among major economies, with US$31 billion, though it is far behind China with US$221 billion and the US with US$112 billion. In relative terms (in percent of total stimulus), it has the largest volume with 81 percent, compared to the EU with 59 percent in second place and China with 38 percent in third place (HSBC 2009: 3). In the domestic political arena, however, more critical voices are raised. According to this version, while the Lee Myung-bak government received severe criticism during the first few months of the presidency with its (over-)ambitious proposal to build a 'Grand Canal' right through mountainous South Korea, it has used the 'opportunity' of the financial turmoil to repackage its construction plans as an anti-depression New Deal, painted with a green colour.

The stimulus policies, particularly the Green New Deal, which accounts for 81 percent of the total, do indeed consider some of the major developmental bottlenecks of the future Korean economy. The SME-related parts address a severe structural problem of the current economic framework. They do not, however, in supporting vulnerable SMEs, help to create a competitive economy, but preserve arguably unsustainable business models. As noted above, the Green New Deal has been criticised on ecological grounds, and the opposition parties argue that the river projects may even lead to water shortages in some parts of the country.

3.4 *How the measures are viewed*

Have the measures been protectionist? The stimulus package has not included explicit 'buy national' clauses. The independent Global Trade Alert (http://www.globaltradealert.org) has listed a number of measures by South Korea that possibly restrict trade, but with one exception they hardly relate to the stimulus measures undertaken in response to the global crisis. The biggest measure mentioned refers to a US$3 billion sale-and-leaseback scheme for ships on behalf of Korean shipping companies, run by the Korea Asset Management Corporation. This measure is accompanied by other instruments to help shipbuilders; these include loans and guarantees of the Export-Import Bank of Korea and the Korea Export Insurance Corporation (Germany

Trade and Invest 2009). Apart from that, the temporary tax reduction for purchasing a new car has a clearly domestic angle. Moreover, the Green New Deal with its focus on the construction business has an obvious bias in favour of domestic construction companies. Korean construction companies enjoy a position of significant international competitiveness and have been hurt by the impact of the global crisis on new major construction projects all over the world. While only Korean companies will be able to act as general contractors for Green New Deal projects, Western companies seem to be optimistic that they will be able to attract business as sub-contractors in public work programmes.[4] Summing up, there is no particularly strong bias in favour of export industries in the programmes. However, the automobile industry and the construction industry, both objects of support, are two of the strongest Korean export sectors.

The government was aware of potential implementation problems and had earmarked 60 percent of the fiscal stimulus measures for 2009 for the first half of the fiscal year. Korean actors are often considered fast in executing decisions—sometimes at the cost of careful reflection of possible side-effects. The implementation of programmes has moved along quite swiftly. To substantiate this claim, some 17 percent of the whole stimulus measures were already executed in 2008, one of the highest percentages in the OECD area, according to an OECD appraisal in June 2009 (OECD 2009: 7).

The IMF has estimated the multiplier effects in Korea, using a general equilibrium model based on a multi-country setting and calibrated for Korean circumstances (Lybecker and Lueth 2009). According to calculations with this model, multipliers in Korea are generally smaller compared to many other countries. For instance, first-year effects of a 1 percent increase in GDP through government investment and consumption are 0.8 percentage points, those of a temporary cut of personal income tax only 0.1 to 0.15 percent. The relatively small size of these effects can be related to the openness of the economy and international leakage effects. If multipliers are calculated on the assumption of international co-ordination, they are significantly higher (for instance, around 1.3 percent in the first year in the case of consumption and investment). The IMF authors view positively Korea's choice of a rather large stimulus package, to which may be added the

---

[4] Personal communication from a senior representative of a Western chamber of commerce in Korea, October 2009.

fact that the low government debt offers considerable leeway and that the Korean fiscal system has quite small automatic stabilisers.

In the Korean economics profession at large, views are of course more divided (for instance, see Yoo 2009). Many observers support the government, though some complain that the fiscal measures have been taken somewhat late, after an initial period of insecurity in late 2008. Apart from that, the stimulus measures have been criticised often not so much on the basis of doubts about their macro-economic effectiveness, but rather for wider concerns, including debt servicing, and for considerations of efficiency in terms of serving the longer needs of the country (ecological considerations, human capital issues, overcoming social imbalances).

3.5 *Labour and social policy measures*

An essential part of any anti-crisis programme lies in labour and social policy measures. In Korea's case, the former include the following (Ministry of Strategy and Finance 2008): instituting and expanding an internship programme for young adults to avoid youth unemployment, increasing employment maintenance support, support for the reduction of working hours as a contribution to job-sharing, wage support for job-sharing including paid training leave.

The following social policy measures are included in the Korean government's crisis response (Ministry of Strategy and Finance 2008): increasing support for those who have become 'newly poor' and for low-income households suffering from the slowdown, emergency relief aid and permanent rental housing support for low-income households, expanding the range of the livelihood support programme to reduce gaps in this programme, increased school expenses support for low-income university students, support for the educational environment in elementary, secondary and preschool education, support for farmers and fishermen (working capital, guarantees, tariff rate quotas).

As has been mentioned before (see Section 3.2), such measures roughly encompass a third of the total stimulus package and thus so go well beyond a minor supplement. Nevertheless, the political opposition has criticised the government for not doing enough about social issues. Particularly during 2009, the Lee administration has done a lot in proof of its compassionate credentials. For instance, in August 2009 the government announced that it would cut the tax incentives for large firms and wealthy individuals again (Kim 2009).

In this struggle, the government faces several restrictions. One issue centres around the weaknesses in Korea's social security system, a consequence of the fact that Korea has reached advanced-economy status only recently. Any kind of socially motivated measure taken by the government under such circumstances may look insufficient, because the challenges are so huge. The second critical restriction is the impact of any measure on the price competitiveness of Korean industry. Korea has reached a critical wage level, and its position is endangered by cheaper suppliers elsewhere (as well as by more advanced suppliers from the West). Following social policies that eventually make labour more costly could soon lead to a major upheaval in Korea's competitiveness and cut off the swift recovery. From this perspective, the Lee government has done surprisingly well so far to find flexible responses to the shifting economic, political and social challenges it has been facing throughout the crisis.

Consumption support measures can also be considered as socially oriented in a wider sense. The major item included in the anti-crisis measures to support consumption is a permanent personal income tax cut, to be executed in two tranches in 2009 and 2010. It encompasses a reduction of two percentage points, i.e. from the range of 8 percent-35 percent to 6 percent-33 percent. Already in 2009 the lowest tax bracket was able to enjoy relief from the full two percentage points. The per-person deduction has been raised (Lybecker and 2009: 10). In comparison to other OECD countries, Korea is ranked in fifth place with respect to the size of personal income tax reduction in relation to GDP (OECD 2009: 9). The social policy measures mentioned above contain a de facto consumer 'cheque' element inasmuch as low-income households can easily receive 'cash back' to relieve them from soaring energy prices, a result of the won depreciation.

Generally speaking, the government uses formulas to identify the beneficiaries of its programmes. With its support schemes for low-income households, the usual demarcation point is defined with respect to income in relation to the minimum cost of living (Ministry of Strategy and Finance 2009c).

3.6 *Organisational aspects*

On an institutional level, there has been no major organisational change to the set-up in financial supervision in the wake of the recent crisis. The 'emergency economic meetings' chaired by the president (see Section 5 below) are an ad hoc device with probably no longer-term relevance. The IMF has recently suggested considering better co-ordination between financial supervision, monetary policy and lender-of-last-resort facilities in Korea, possibly in the framework of a 'financial stability council'. However, the Korean side has argued in favour of a clear delineation of supervisory responsibilities, including safeguarding the independence of the Bank of Korea (IMF 2009a: 21-22). Given the short track record of its formal independence, the ubiquity of inter-personal influences and doubts about independence in reality, it might indeed be a problematic signal to subordinate the central bank to a new 'council' that would probably be dominated by a representative of the president of the republic or indeed by him personally.

To mitigate the impact of the crisis, the Korean government has set up a Bank Recapitalisation Fund to support the recapitalisation of banks by purchasing subordinated bonds of banks, hybrid bonds and preferred stock. The fund is put up by capital from the Bank of Korea and by the Korea Development Bank, a governmental policy bank, with a total of up to 20 trillion won (roughly US$14 billion) (Bank of Korea, undated). In the first quarter of 2009, eight banks drew a total of 4 trillion won. The Fund has played a positive role in helping to raise the capital adequacy ratio of banks to almost 13 percent (IMF 2009a: 21); the availability of such funds has also indirectly helped some banks to tap the international capital markets once again. There has also been some criticism, however, because the possibility of drawing capital from the Fund has been linked to offering new credit lines or roll-overs to SMEs. This has contributed to the efficiency problems of support for ailing SMEs. The government realises such problems and wants to readjust the conditions for support.

Korea already possesses an organisation to buy up toxic assets, a remainder of the 1997-8 crisis. The Korea Asset Management Corporation (KAMCO) is able to raise some 40 trillion won to buy up non-performing loans and other troubled assets. Major private banks announced in August 2009 that they were setting up their own 'bad bank', able to purchase some five trillion won of troubled assets (Oliver 2009). According to the Korea Federation of Banks, the motivation is to create a more transparent market, overcoming the monopoly position of KAMCO. There are concerns that the mechanism would be used to set higher prices for the distressed assets, thus allowing the banks, which have been currently facing a significant squeeze on their profitability, better sales prices for such assets.

4 THE PRELIMINARY IMPACT OF THE POLICY RESPONSE TO THE CRISIS

The Korean economy has made a good recovery from the shockwave of the Lehman collapse in September 2008. According to Bank of Korea figures for the third quarter of 2009, GDP increased 2.6 percent quarter-on-quarter, where the median estimate of the Bloomberg survey had been 1.9 percent. Already in the first quarter of 2009 some improvement could be noticed. While the current account moved into negative territory in late 2008, it already registered a surplus of 4.5 percent in the first quarter of 2009. Government consumption and construction investment rose by 3.75 percent and 5.25 percent (quarter-on-quarter) respectively, supported by the government stimulus measures, thus avoiding a technical recession (negative growth) in the first quarter of 2009 (IMF 2009a: 7). This positive development was repeated in the second quarter (Bank of Korea 2009c): GDP grew by 2.6 percent in comparison to the first quarter, while exports rose by almost 15 percent. Facilities investment showed a hefty 10.1 percent growth, certainly, to some extent, related to the earlier low levels. Final government consumption registered an increase of 7.1 percent in the second quarter of 2009 compared to one year earlier. This improvement from extremely low values has been hailed as a dramatic turnaround. Observers found it to be the fastest second quarter income growth in 21 years (Lee 2009).

It is difficult to judge whether government measures or the rebounding global economy have played a more decisive role in bringing about this turnaround up to the third quarter of 2009. Looking at the performance of economic activities during this quarter in comparison to the corresponding quarter of 2008 (Bank of Korea 2009d), it is noticeable that exports of goods and services have actually increased by 0.9 percent, while imports have decreased 8.7 percent. Korean export strength and international recovery have thus been a major force in the recovery. This is in line with reports that major Korean exporters like Hyundai Motors and Samsung Electronics have been reporting surging profits again. Government consumption has also increased significantly (4.9 percent in the third quarter of 2009 year-on-year), but given the relatively small share of the government sector, exports have been the stronger force, combined with inventory changes, at least once the immediate financial shockwave in late 2008 was overcome thanks to government initiative.

The recovery of the economy has been faster than originally expected. Already by the summer of 2009, for instance, the IMF had revised its growth projection for 2009 from -3 percent to -1.75 percent. This implies that Korea has to consider exit options earlier than many other OECD economies. The situation is quite complex, however. On the one hand, stock prices have already risen considerably and even real estate prices are already rising again in Seoul and its vicinity. Raising the interest rate early may help to avoid another asset bubble, but may be premature for the real economy. On the other hand, the rebound of the real economy may not only be threatened by a W-shaped recovery of the global economy; it has also become more apparent that low-income households are suffering considerably from the impact of the crisis. President Lee Myung-bak has modified his earlier image as a 'hard-hearted" liberaliser and changed in June 2009 towards a softer approach.

Consequently, and given this dilemma, the mid-term outlook for policy directions in the second half of the 2009 fiscal year, issued in June 2009, is somewhat loose on drawing policy implications from the first months of the crisis-related response measures. The gist is to review and evaluate carefully the current policies with respect to their effectiveness (Financial Services Commission 2009b). In a statement of 9 August 2009, following the regular Article IV consultations with the Republic of Korea, the IMF encouraged or even urged the Korean government to continue its efforts to support the economy (IMF 2009b). At the same time, it noticed some problems with the effectiveness of the measures, for instance, that money borrowed by SMEs under the eased conditions Korean banks are facing may not have gone into productive investment. As the Lee Myung-bak government gained public approval by showing more concern for the weak parts of the economy during the summer of 2009, it became difficult for it to find a suitable way between continuing economic support on the one hand and avoiding an asset bubble plus safeguarding allocative efficiency on the other.

There is some concern that existing longer-term structural imbalances of the Korean economy will not improve, but may rather be aggravated. As is well known, a worldwide debate is under way on structural imbalances that may not be sustainable over the long term: some economies register large trade surpluses and capital account outflows, while others have the opposite characteristics. South Korea clearly belongs to the former camp, with a considerable trade surplus, a strong export sector, a structural capital account deficit and large, growing foreign reserves that keep the currency down and could thus work as an additional mechanism to reinforce the imbalances in the balance of payments. Because of the nature of the monetary and fiscal response to the crisis, the characteristics of the production sector remain untouched. As has been identified elsewhere (see Sections 3.2 and 3.3 above), the weakness of the SME sector has been a persistent issue for the South Korean economy. A number of support schemes for distressed SMEs have permitted many of them simply to survive the crisis, although they should have been undergoing severe restructuring. According to government screening in the early summer of 2009, of 861 SMEs evaluated, 77 were found to need restructuring and 36 were found to be unviable (IMF 2009a: 23). For political reasons, it is questionable whether a competitiveness-based restructuring is feasible for the time being.

On the positive side, the usual recipe for export-reliant economies is to strengthen their domestic economy further. It is difficult to achieve this for domestic consumption, as household debt is very high by international standards. On the supply side, the Korean government announced a programme in May 2009 to strengthen the service economy (Ministry of Strategy and Finance 2009d). In particular, it plans to support education, content-providing, IT services, design, consulting, medical services, employment agencies, logistics, broadcasting and communication. Because of the crisis, this project may receive a strong boost from the state. However, there has to be some assurance that a new layer of basically inefficient companies is not created. For that reason, the opening of the service sector to domestic and foreign competition will play an important role. It remains to be seen whether new free trade agreements with the US and the European Union are allowed to play a constructive role in this respect.

5 POLITICAL-ECONOMIC BOUNDARY CONDITIONS

A look at the political-economic boundary conditions of Korea's crisis economic policy measures will help in understanding the political economy of crisis response in Korea's case and allow us to form an opinion about the role of learning from the earlier 1997-8 crisis.

As pointed out in Section 2, at the outbreak of the financial crisis in September 2008, the new government under President Lee Myung-bak was not even one year in office. The president had been elected with a comfortable 49 percent of the vote in late 2007, and the presidential party (Grand National Party) also achieved a majority in the parliamentary elections of April 2008, winning 153 of 299 seats. From this perspective, the Lee-led government was able to work with a stable majority in any kind of crisis. Nevertheless, Lee faced considerable opposition before the financial crisis set in. For instance, his cabinet including the prime minister felt compelled to hand in their letters of resignation in June 2008, after major public protests over the re-admittance of US beef imports. As a Korean president has only a single five-year term, he can, however, act somewhat more freely on the political stage than leaders in other countries who have to consider their re-election chances.

The usual mechanisms were involved to handle the crisis. Building on the tradition of a strong executive wing under the president, in January 2009 a weekly 'emergency economic meeting', personally headed by President Lee Myung-bak, became the ultimate forum through which to respond to the unfolding crisis (Na 2009). By 17 September 2009, 31 meetings had been held.

Government bodies were not prevented from acting swiftly. Indeed, it may be considered one of the strengths of the South Korean government system that the government can act speedily and decisively if backed by the Blue House, i.e. by the president—though this, of course, can easily turn into a weakness as well. It is thus all the more surprising that the government has been criticised from various quarters for having acted too slowly—a criticism voiced not only by opposition politicians, by also by a number of economists from Korea and abroad (Yoo 2009). The reason for any delay in decision-making is probably twofold. First, Korean observers were truly surprised at how vulnerable the South Korean economy was in face of the financial crisis, despite large currency reserves and a fairly sound banking system.

Second, economic policy had to practically change full course from fighting inflation to countering a deep recession.

In short, the government could act fairly freely to counter the crisis, without formal mechanisms having to change. The domestic opposition—apart from some 'noise'—acted with restraint, and consequently the general sense of imminent economic danger, deepened by the memory of the 1997-8 crisis, allowed the government to go ahead proactively.

While the president himself does not have to face re-election, in passing laws he depends naturally on the support of his party members and his party's parliamentarians. While no immediate parliamentary election was coming up apart from by-elections, politicians close to the government could be expected to become seriously concerned about public sentiment towards governmental policies, and here the government's communication policies and approval ratings become important. As is to be expected in a democracy, the government does communicate its policies to the public. During the first weeks of the crisis, announcements were somewhat confused, but given the complex nature of an unprecedented type of global economic crisis, this may not be surprising. It may be fair to add that the sophistication of conveying policy details to the public and communicating with the domestic and international public has not yet reached a similar level as in some other advanced Western economies. In some sections of a 'critical' public—almost irrespective of the policy field under investigation[5]—there is quite widespread dissatisfaction with the government and how honestly it communicates its policies. Indeed, in autumn 2008, government sources agreed that communication of the crisis responses had not been handled well; as a consequence, a public-relations firm was hired (*Economist* 2008).

In the summer of 2008, President Lee Myung-bak had reached an absolute low point in public approval. Interestingly, during the months of the economic crisis he was able to improve his ratings, with an approval level of some 30 percent (well below earlier highs, however). The economic crisis did not harm him further; possibly there was some sense of national solidarity amidst international turmoil, although views are split on this interpretation.

---

[5] Critical websites include the following: http://www.gobada.co.kr, http://nocanal.org/bloglounge.

A wave of public discontent broke in the late spring of 2009. An important rallying point was the death of former president Roh Moo-hyun by suicide, following investigations into his behaviour during his presidency (Hwang 2009). It was suggested that these investigations had been excessive (although some members of Roh's close family were indeed found to have misbehaved). Public mourning over Roh by millions of citizens turned into anger against the Lee government and its alleged 'coldness'. Public events were accompanied by critical statements of thousands of professors, writers, civic groups and others, often following the partisan demarcations so typical of the Korean political system. The loss of a by-election in late April, while not endangering the majority of the government party in parliament, showed that the ruling groups faced a dramatic decline in popularity, and that many parliamentarians would not survive the next general election, putting additional pressure on President Lee. While Lee has faced criticism from the left, his later changes in particular have also provoked critical comments from conservatives and liberals. One issue has been Lee's growing reliance on capable bureaucrats, particularly from the former Ministry of Finance ('Mofia'), a choice that seems to run counter to his liberal roots.

Around mid-2009, Lee's approval ratings increased considerably, a development often explained by political factors (such as the skilful handling of the funeral of the late President Kim Dae-jung), but also by an improvement in the economic situation in general and a 'softer' approach to support low-income citizens affected by the crisis (Ser and Kim 2009). Since the summer and autumn of 2009, the government has been trying to find a way between the various political camps. For instance, in summer 2009 it sought to extend from two to four years the period for which companies can use contracts for temporary labour. This initiative was justified by fighting unemployment (because those employed earlier with two year-contracts might soon face dismissal), but it was also motivated by an urge to make the labour markets more flexible, a policy to be expected from a pro-market government. (This legislation has been blocked by the opposition, partly because the expected negative impact of dismissals has not yet been experienced.)

6 AN EFFECT OF 1997-1998?

Did the legacy of the 1997-8 crisis influence reaction to the most recent economic crisis? Korea was hit unexpectedly hard by the unfolding of the Lehman collapse. On the one hand, investors withdrew funds from Korea to mend problems elsewhere, the stock market fell and the won depreciated strongly; on the other hand, for the real economy, the large exposure of the Korean market to the world market implied an extremely fierce decline in exports. The memory of 1997 hardly cushioned people against experiencing surprise in 2008. Each crisis is different—otherwise, it would probably never evolve into a 'crisis'. In Korea's case, the mixture of liquidity and solvency issues of 1997 was very different from the situation in 2008 (see Table 3). The expectation that any danger that might arise would come from a constellation similar to 1997 may actually have contributed to being less concerned in 2008—when so many Korean policy makers believed that Korea was not much imperilled this time around, because of its much more comfortable level of finance regulation and of foreign reserves compared to 1997.

The very first reaction of the government, particularly with respect to monetary and financial issues, was rather insecure, but it did the job of stabilising the flow of funds by the end of 2008. Fiscal measures were better prepared, involved a major stimulus (also compared to many other OECD economies), and were executed in timely fashion, despite criticism from the opposition. The government was aware of the necessity of acting speedily and decisively, and this feeling was probably amplified by the traumatic memory of 1997, when Korea had to rely on foreign support with its considerable collateral damage. The government reacted quickly to unfolding challenges (Table 4). Despite different ideological inclinations, the government also reacted fairly constructively to the evolving social unrest in 2009.

It would, however, be too easy to attribute the success in handling the first year after the September 2008 shock to the legacy of 1997-8 alone. The government profited from several factors: a strictly top-down administrative system that allows decisions to be quickly made and executed; the absence of forthcoming elections; the president's safe position and a majority in parliament; the reaction of the opposition and of the trade unions, which, while certainly not mild, may have been somewhat muted by the sense of a national crisis. Moreover, Korea enjoyed a low public debt and has interest rates well above zero, so fiscal deficit spending as well as monetary policy could be expected to work reasonably well. Finally, it can also be reasoned that the current crisis was so widespread that there was perhaps less of a sense of 'victimisation'.

Table 3 The 1997-1998 and the 2008-2009 economic crises of South Korea—a comparison

	1997-98 Asian crisis	2008-09 Global financial and economic crisis
Background/ reasons	• *International* liquidity issue (speculation against won; lack of short-term funding) • *Internal* solvency issue (over-exposure to debt without adequate returns)	• *International* liquidity issue (pull-out of foreign investors because of their liquidity shortage) • Brisk decline of major *export* markets
Foreign support	Major IMF-led rescue programme (of dubious quality)	Fairly little support necessary: Swap agreements to potentially access reserve currencies
Major policy instruments	Interest rate hike to defend the exchange rate; painful structural reforms to regain international market trust	Organising short-term liquidity; major fiscal programme including 'green' components
Domestic political situation/ boundary conditions	President Kim Dae-jung newly elected with 'left-wing' support	Relatively new conservative/liberal president already facing decline of public support; recent parliamentary elections
Economic performance	Relatively speedy recovery under severe social cost	Relatively speedy recovery under considerable social cost

Source: Author's own compilation.

Established institutional mechanisms proved quite able to handle all issues, while the new Recapitalisation Fund helped banks to recapitalise. An asset management organisation to purchase toxic assets had already been in place since the 1997-8 crisis and can be viewed as having helped face the challenges of 2008.

Table 4 The sequencing of economic problems and Korean policy responses during the 2008-2009 economic crisis

Economic disturbance	Visibility of impact	Policy timing
Finance: capital outflows and stock market decline	Strong and immediate; September 2008	Almost immediate (less than one month delay, with some irresolution about relevant measures)
Real economy: decline of exports and growth	Fast and unexpected; ca. November 2008	Rather fast; stimulus package in early November 2008
Socio-economy: layoffs, etc.	Protests: token protest of opposition parties in winter 200-09, massive public protests in late spring 2009	Social policy elements already in stimulus programme of early 2008-09; profile significantly raised in summer 2009
Economic structure	Still not easily visible, as short-term effects and longer-term implications are difficult to distinguish	No significant discussion during the year following the crisis (debate on Green New Deal, for instance, dominated by other concerns and interests)

Source: Author's own compilation.

Summing up, the legacy of the traumatic crisis of 1997-8 can be noticed on at least two levels. First, there are lasting formal institutional effects such as stronger regulation of the financial sector and the presence of a state-run organisation to purchase toxic assets. Second, at an attitudinal level, there seems to be a strong national drive to avoid a similarly harmful situation at all cost. As the policy-making process in Korea is much more personalised than in many other democracies, thanks to the strong role of the president, individual-psychological effects like the imprinting of attitudes through the experience of an earlier crisis could play a significant role. From an academic perspective, these latter aspects are particularly interesting, and they should be scrutinised by more substantial research.

REFERENCES

ADB (Asian Development Bank) (2009), *Asian Development Outlook 2009*, Manila
Bank of Korea (undated): 'Expansion of Banks' Credit Supply Capacity', undated. Online: http://eng.bok.or.kr/user/util/print_pop_eng.jsp (accessed September 2009)
Bank of Korea (2008), 'Financial Stability Report', October 2008. Online: http://eng.bok.or.kr/contents/total/eng/boardView.action (accessed September 2009)
Bank of Korea (2009a), 'International Investment Position at the End of 2008 (Preliminary)', 20 February 2009, Seoul
Bank of Korea (2009b), 'Policy Response to the Financial Turmoil'. Online: http://eng.bok.or.kr/user/util/print_pop_eng.jsp (accessed September 2009)
Bank of Korea (2009c), 'Gross National Income: the 2nd Quarter of 2009 (Preliminary)', 3 September 2009. Online: http://www.korea.net/image/news/today/20090903005L.pdf (accessed September 2009)
Bank of Korea (2009d), 'Real Gross Domestic Product: the 3rd Quarter of 2009 (Advance)', 26 October 2009. Online: http://ecos.bok.or.kr/EIndex_en.jsp (accessed October 2009)
Chang Jae-chul (2008), 'Global Financial Crisis and the Korean Economy', Samsung Economic Research Institute, 29 October 2008. Online: http://www.eucc.or.kr/board/down.php?db=data&filename=data_file_416.pdf&PHPSESSID=4b73f1cc94869008074bbe44fa298ed3 (accessed September 2009)
Channels (2009), 'Moody's May Up Korea Sovereign Rtgs If Econ Improves', 16 September 2009. Online: http://www.channelstv.com/newsdetails.php?news_id=14213 (accessed October 2009)
Cheong Wa Dae (Presidential website) (2009), 'Goals'. Online: http://english.president.go.kr/government/goals/goals.php (accessed June 2008 and September 2009)
Chung, Myung-je (2009), 'Gov't Finalizes Blueprint for 17 New Growth Engines', 14 January 2009. Online: http://www.korea.net/news/news/newsView.asp?serial_no=20090114004 (accessed September 2009)
The Economist (2008), 'Happy Travels: A Nasty Downturn, but Politics as Usual', 20 November 2008
The Economist (2009), 'Paranoid Seclusions: A Prophet without Honour in Seoul', 15 January 2009
Financial Services Commission (2009b), 'Economic Policy Directions for Second Half of 2009', 26 June 2009. Online: http://www.korea.net/news/news/newsView.asp?serial_no=20090626005 (accessed September 2009)
Germany Trade and Invest (2009), *Koreanische Regierung hilft in Not geratenen Werften und Reedereien*, Datenbank Länder und Märkte, 4 September 2009
HSBC Global Research (2009), 'A Climate for Recovery: The Colour of Stimulus Goes Green', 25 February 2009
Hwang, Jang-jin (2009), 'President Lee Gravitates to Political Center', in: *Korea Herald*, 13 August 2009. Online: http://www.koreaherald.co.kr/NEWKHSITE/data/html_dir/2009/08/13/200908130018.asp (accessed October 2009)
IMF (2009a), 'Staff Report for the 2009 Article IV Consultation', IMF Country Report no. 09/262, August 2009. Online: http://imf.org/external/pubs/ft/scr/2009/cr09262.pdf (accessed October 2009)
IMF (2009b), 'IMF Presses Korea to Continue Rebalancing Economy', 9 August 2009. Online: http://www.imf.org/external/pubs/ft/survey/so/2009/car080909a.htm (accessed September 2009)

Kim, Yoon-mi (2009), 'Korea to Cut Tax Incentives for Large Firms', in: *Korea Herald*, 26 August 2009
Klepper, Gernot et al. (2009), 'Konjunktur für den Klimaschutz? Klima- und Wachstumswirkungen weltweiter Konjunkturprogramme', *Kieler Diskussionsbeiträge*, Nr. 464, April 2009
Kusev, Petko et al. (2009), 'Exaggerated Risk: Prospect Theory and Probability Weighting in Risky Choice', in: *Journal of Experimental Psychology: Learning, Memory, and Cognition*, 35 (6), pp. 1487-1505
Lee, Hyo-sik (2009), 'Second-Quarter Income Growth Fastest in 21 Years', in: *Korea Times*, 3 September 2009. Online: http://www.koreatimes.co.kr/www/news/nation/2009/09/123_51233.html (accessed October 2009)
Lybecker, Leif Eskesen and Erik Lueth (2009), 'Republic of Korea—Selected Issues', IMF Country Report no. 09/263, August 2009. Online: http://www.imf.org/external/pubs/ft/scr/2009/cr09263.pdf (accessed September 2009)
Ministry of Strategy and Finance (2008), '2009 Economic Policy Directions', 16 December 2008. Online: http://english.mofe.go.kr/news/pressrelease_view.php?sect=news_press&sn=6114 (accessed September 2009)
Ministry of Strategy and Finance (2009a), 'Realizing 2009 Policies: Action Plans by the MOSF', 18 December 2008. Online: http://english.mofe.go.kr/news/pressrelease_view.php?sect=news_press&sn=6137 (accessed September 2009)
Ministry of Strategy and Finance (2009b), 'Briefing on the Green New Deal for Foreign Correspondents', 19 January 2009
Ministry of Strategy and Finance (2009c), 'KRW 6 Trillion to Support Low-income Families', Press Release, 13 March 2009
Ministry of Strategy and Finance (2009d), 'Gov't Announces Plans to Boost Service Industries', 8 May 2009. Online: http://www.korea.net/News/news/newsView.asp?serial_no=20090508014&part=101&SearchDay= (accessed October 2009)
Na, Jeong-ju (2009), 'Cabinet Asked to Pool Wisdom for Economic Revival', in: *Korea Times*, 8 January 2009. Online: http://www.koreatimes.co.kr/www/news/include/print.asp?newsIdx=37541 (accessed September 2009)
New York Times (2008), 'Chronology of Korean Responses to the Financial Crisis', 19 October 2008. Online: http://www.nytimes.com/2008/10/19/business/worldbusiness/19iht-wonchrono.17073102.html (accessed September 2009)
OECD (Organisation for Economic Cooperation and Development) (2008), *OECD Economic Survey Korea 2008*, Paris
OECD (2009), 'Report on the Strategic Response: Strategies for Aligning Stimulus Measures with Long-Term Growth. Meeting of the Council at Ministerial Level, 24-25 June 2009', 17 June 2009, C/MIN(2009)9/ANN2, Paris
Oliver, Christian (2009), 'S Korea Set for Private Bad Bank', in: *Financial Times* online, 20 August 2009. Online: http://www.ft.com/cms/s/0/cc78145a-8d93-11de-93df-00144feabdc0.html (accessed September 2009)
Park, Hyun-soo (2009), 'How to Ride Out the Financial Crisis', Samsung Economic Research Institute. Online: http://www.seriworld.org/01/wldContV.html?&mn=A&mncd=0301&key=20090731000001&pubkey=20090731000001&seq=20090731000001&kdy=E5JjH5a6=&sectno=3 (accessed September 2009)
Rakow, Tim and Ben Newell (2010), 'Degrees of Uncertainty: An Overview and Framework for Future Research on Experience-Based Choice', in: *Journal of Behavioral Decision Making*, 23, pp. 1-14
Ser, Myo-ja and Kim, Jung-ha (2009), 'Lee's Popularity Ratings Improve', in: *JoongAng Daily*, 14 September 2009. Online: http://joongangdaily.joins.com/article/view.asp?aid=2910033 (accessed September 2009)

Starbuck, William (2009), 'Perspective-Cognitive Reactions to Rare Events: Perceptions, Uncertainty, and Learning', in: *Organization Science*, 20 (5), pp. 925-37

UN News Service (2009), ' "Green" Stimulus Plans by Japan and Republic of Korea Hailed By UN Environment Chief', 9 January 2009. Online: http://www.un.org/apps/news/story.asp?NewsID=29505&Cr=climate&Cr1=change# (accessed September 2009)

Wassener, Bettina (2008), 'South Korea Earmarks $10.9 Billion to Aid Growth', in: *New York Times*, 3 November 2008

Yoo, Soh-jong (2009), '[First Anniversary of Lee Government (12)] Is the Lee Administration on the Right Track?', in: *Korea Herald*, 4 March 2009

'GREEN GROWTH': SOUTH KOREA'S PANACEA?

David Shim

ABSTRACT

To overcome the global economic crisis, many governments enacted comprehensive stimulus packages in the beginning of 2009. Parts of these recovery plans were devoted to 'green' economic programmes to account for the environmental sustainability of future growth policies. According to the United Nations Environmental Programme, two-thirds of these 'green' stimulus packages have been committed in the Asia-Pacific region. South Korea's 'green' share of its recovery scheme amounts to 80 percent, which represents the largest share in the world. This 'green' stimulus package is part of the country's so-called Low Carbon Green Growth strategy, which President Lee Myung-bak announced on the occasion of the 60th anniversary of the foundation of the Republic of Korea. 'Green Growth' was accordingly set to become South Korea's development paradigm for the coming decades. However, the 'Green Growth' concept appears to be double-edged, raising questions the government has not answered yet. This paper examines the objectives of 'Green Growth' and reviews the implications of this strategy on other policy areas. It identifies potential pitfalls and raises questions regarding the consistency of the concept itself.

1 INTRODUCTION

In 2008 the global economy was confronted with what some observers called an unprecedented global economic crisis not seen since the late 1920s, when the stock market crash on Wall Street led to the 'Great Depression' (e.g. World Bank 2010: 58). Many governments enacted comprehensive economic stimulus packages in the beginning of 2009 to overcome the economic downturn. The members of the Organisation for Economic Development and Cooperation (OECD) and major emerging economies such as China, Brazil and Russia pledged to spend in total US$2.193 trillion to reanimate their economies (OECD

2009a: 6). Among the OECD, the size of the fiscal package of the Republic of Korea (ROK—South Korea), which comprised tax cuts, government investments, and transfers to the private and industrial sectors, was, at 5 percent of its Gross Domestic Product (GDP), the second highest after the United States (US) (ibid.: 5).

Parts of the global recovery plans were devoted to 'green' initiatives and economic programmes intended to account for the environmental sustainability of future growth policies. According to the United Nations Environmental Programme (UNEP), two-thirds of these 'green' stimulus packages have been committed in the Asia-Pacific region. South Korea's 'green' share of its total recovery scheme amounts to 80 percent, which is the largest share in the world (HSBC 2009: 13). This 'green' stimulus package is part of the country's so-called Low Carbon Green Growth strategy (hereafter 'Green Growth'), which President Lee Myung-bak outlined in August 2008 on the occasion of the 60th anniversary of the foundation of the ROK. In his speech Lee declared the strategy of 'Green Growth' would become the national development paradigm for the next 60 years, succeeding the 'Miracle on the Han River' (Lee 2008). Through massive investments in 'green' technologies and industries, South Korea would transform its current growth model, based on the consumption of fossil fuels such as oil and coal, into a more sustainable concept that would consider the compatibility of economic growth and environmental protection.

In terms of economic theory, 'Green Growth' can be rooted in the Keynesian economic model, after which instruments of the government's and the central bank's fiscal and monetary policies should be applied to ease the impact of external shocks on the national economy. Especially during the global economic crisis many governments implemented Keynesian economic policies and intervened accordingly in their economies. The symbiosis of economic growth and development with environmental preservation appears to have emerged as a strategic priority for governments and international organisations around the world. The OECD (2009b) in its 'Declaration on Green Growth' laid out a strategy to assist its members to 'identify the policies, the incentives and the frameworks that can achieve clean resource efficient, low carbon economic growth and development', according to OECD Secretary-General Angel Gurria (Gurria 2009). The scope of 'Green Growth' addresses key economic issues such as human resource development ('green collar jobs'), investment ('green financing'), taxation ('green fiscal policy'), trade and research and development ('green technologies', 'green innovation'). The UNEP with its 'Green Economy Initiative', in which South Korea emerged as a major partner, and the World Bank with its appeal for a 'green stimulus' also set up an international campaign to 'green' national economies.

However, the question of whether 'Green Growth' provides a coherent policy concept, which might serve as a new international growth model, or is rather a mere buzzword to 'green-wash' old policy practices, remains debatable. For the putative environmental sustainability of future policy approaches should not be the only criterion for this strategy since the question regarding what counts as 'green' is a highly political issue. For instance, while for many states, including South Korea, nuclear energy is considered a 'green' or clean technology, which, with its assumed zero carbon emissions, contributes to the preservation of the environment, for many others, due to the unresolved question of the management of nuclear waste, it does not.[1]

The significance of 'Green Growth' for South Korea's future development not only appears to serve the purpose of mitigating the economic crisis, but supports also a range of other policy issues and areas. For Lee's vision of a new national growth concept should not be understood as oriented strictly towards domestic or economic policy. It has also a strategic and a foreign policy dimension with, for instance, the propagated claim to increase the country's self-sufficiency in energy, focus on 'green' development assistance and serve as a global role model. Like a panacea, 'Green Growth' resembles the administration's attempt to find a cure for several national symptoms since it shall help to:

- overcome the economic downturn by developing new growth engines and related technologies
- protect the environment and alleviate climate change
- enhance the country's energy security by reducing dependence on foreign oil resources
- improve the quality of the standard of living, and

---

[1] For example, UNEP (2010: 24-6) in its latest annual report on the development of a 'Green Growth' strategy does not list nuclear energy as a 'green' technology. Furthermore, under the Kyoto protocol nuclear energy is not included as a greenhouse gas-reducing instrument in the Clean Development Mechanism (CDM) (UNFCCC 2001: 20-24).

- elevate South Korea's international standing by serving as a role model for other countries.

The 'greening' of South Korean politics was further made visible when the government pledged to reduce the emissions of greenhouse gases (GHG) voluntarily. This announcement was noteworthy insofar as South Korea is not obliged under the United Nations Framework Convention on Climate Change to cut its GHG emissions. It was also the first developing country to formulate concrete, though not legally binding, reduction goals.

However, as it will be shown later, the 'greening' of South Korea politics appears to be double-edged, sparking questions the government has not answered yet. The following sections examine and discuss the objectives of 'Green Growth' and review its implications for other policy areas. The paper identifies pitfalls and raises questions regarding the consistency and substance of the concept.

2 Initiatives and Implications of 'Low Carbon Green Growth'

2.1 *Domestic policy*

In the beginning of 2009 the Lee administration approved an economic stimulus package to prevent the domestic economy from falling into recession and lay the ground for a new way of national development. While, for example, the US and Germany reserved 11 and 13 percent respectively of their stimulus packages for 'green' investments, about 80 percent of South Korea's recovery package was devoted to environmental themes (HSBC 2009: 13). About US$38.5 billion of this so-called 'Green New Deal' were to be invested over the next four years in selected areas such as transport, recycling and infrastructure and would create about 950,000 jobs (PCGG 2009a). The core project of the 'Green New Deal' focuses on infrastructure development with the restoration of the country's four main rivers, the Han, Naktong, Kŭm and Yŏngsan. About US$17.3 billion of this infrastructure project will be allocated, for instance, on the alleviation of water scarcity, prevention of floods and the construction of multi-purpose spaces for the local population.

Six months later the government presented a more comprehensive plan, which expanded the 'Green New Deal' with additional projects and investments. The 'Five-Year Plan for Green Growth' integrates the funding of other related strategies and policy areas such as economy and science and technology (S&T) into the government's long-term plan. For example, together with the current S&T promotion plan the gross domestic expenditure for research and development (R&D) of 'green' technologies will be increased to 5 percent of the GDP by 2012 (MEST 2008).[2] The five-year conception is reminiscent of South Korea's early development period of the 1960s and 1970s, when the then government under Park Chung-hee formulated economic policies for the promotion of specific industry sectors. It indicates the current administration's hope that 'Green Growth' will also be the main agenda of succeeding governments (PCGG 2009b; see also Government of the Republic of Korea 2009). The aim is to become one of the world's top seven 'green' economic powers by 2020. With total investments of US$86 billion in selected areas such as climate protection, energy supply and environmental technologies, up to 1.8 million jobs are estimated to be created by 2013. The volume of the mid-term plan represents the annual spending of 2 percent of GDP and is twice the amount suggested by the UNEP for 'green' investments (UNEP 2009: 23). The persistence of the government's 'green' development strategy will be ensured also through the legislative process. In January 2010 President Lee signed the 'Basic Law on Low Carbon and Green Growth', providing the legal and institutional basis for adjusting regional and national ruling with the new strategy. The new law, which is expected to go into effect in April 2010, not only establishes the legal setting for the government's 'Green Growth' initiatives, but is also meant to highlight South Korea's ambitions for international leadership in this area.

However, the administrative structure of South Korea's political system has already been adapted to the introduction of 'Green Growth'. Several panels with representatives of government, business, civil society and academia have been established. For the planning and implementation of the new policy the 'Presidential Commission on Green Growth' (PCGG) was created in February 2009. It is the

---

[2] South Korea's total investments in R&D were in 2008 already one of the highest in the world with about 3.5 percent of GDP (OECD 2009c). For a critical review of whether quantitative input leads to an increase of qualitative output of R&D activities see Conlé and Shim 2009.

highest decision-making body and nodal point for consultation on related matters. The commission is responsible for the above-mentioned five-year plan and developed also the long-term strategy for 'Green Growth' (PCGG 2009b). In addition every ministry has a 'Chief Green Officer', who, at the general level of director, coordinates communication between the respective ministry and the presidential commission. It is planned to establish this post in all public institutions (PCGG 2009a).

As the development blueprint for the coming decades, 'Green Growth' points to a comprehensive governance approach, the scope of which might go beyond institutional, ministerial or administrative boundaries. This more horizontal policy setting would have to reconcile the possibly conflicting imperatives of different policy areas such as the economy, the environment, society or foreign policy and co-ordinate the interplay of governmental agencies, industry, academia, civil society and possibly international actors. This framework would entail a strengthened role for the government in co-ordinating the different functions of its agencies and non-governmental sectors to ensure the systematic and consistent realisation of 'Green Growth'. The approach to a more integrated and coherent policy framework resembles the OECD's concept of its so-called third generation of innovation policy, which calls for a broader and more comprehensive perspective on structural change and adaptation (OECD 2005). In particular, the balance or effective integration of assumed opposed policies would be the task of this policy setting. It would enable governments to implement long-term strategies and create a distinct environment, in which innovation is 'stimulated across a number of governmental or policy areas' (ibid.: 20).[3] To increase the efficiency and co-ordination of governmental bodies President Lee adapted the governance structure shortly after his inauguration, with for instance the centralisation and merging of competencies in the Ministry of Education, Science and Technology (MEST) and the Ministry of Knowledge Economy (MKE).

---

[3] The first generation of innovation policy is seen as a linear process, in which increasing research and development expenditure would result quasi-automatically in more patents, products and technologies. The second generation focuses more on systems and infrastructure, which require the formulation of an institutional framework conducive to innovations. The second generation, which is more commonly known as the national innovation system approach, is the predominant policy setting of major economies.

2.2 Foreign policy

The government's efforts to advance its new growth model are not restricted only to the domestic realm, but also include initiatives and activities that are aimed to elevate South Korea's international standing. In this respect 'Green Growth' reveals its function for South Korea's foreign policy, since it will enable the government to achieve the long-standing goal of becoming an internationally recognised role model for other nations that would play a bridging role between developing and developed countries. To this end the government fosters 'Green Growth' on many occasions at the international level. For example, under the chairmanship of South Korea the OECD ministerial council meeting in June 2009 formulated a strategy on 'Green Growth' to help its members achieve sustainable economic growth (OECD 2009b). At the UN climate summits in New York and Copenhagen, President Lee presented his policy as the 'most effective way to address global climate change and at the same time to overcome the economic crisis' (Lee 2009a; see also Lee 2009b). As the host of the G20 summit, which is to take place in Seoul by the end of 2010, the government will not miss the chance to bring 'Green Growth' as a sustainable development concept on to the summit's agenda. Indicative are the remarks of the then prime minister, Han Seung-soo, during the 2009 East Asia World Economic Forum, in which he underlined Seoul's claim to international leadership by proposing 'Green Growth' as a blueprint for the international community (Han 2009a):

> I believe that low carbon, green growth must be a paradigm not only for Korea, but for the international community as a whole [...] the primacy of the current global economic downturn should not deter our focus from effectuating a low-carbon, green growth agenda. Rather, we must seek intensive cooperation and unprecedented commitment from all stakeholders. Korea is not only ready to its part; it is ready to lead this process.

In the efforts to push 'Green Growth' as a global development concept the official development assistance of the government appears to be play an important role. For instance, at the 2008 G8 Extended Summit in Japan, President Lee announced a development assistance initiative, which would help 'developing countries in East Asia, least developed countries (LDCs) and small island states (SIDs)' to establish environmental technologies and implement joint projects to reduce carbon emissions (PCGG 2009a). In addition to this US$200 million 'East

Asia Climate Partnership', the government pledged to increase its economic development co-operation fund over the next four years to US$1.45 billion in support of 'Green Growth' in developing countries (*Korea Herald*, 7 October 2009). According to the summit meetings of 2009 between South Korea and the Association of Southeast Asian Nations (ASEAN), the African Union (AU) and countries from Latin America, 'green' co-operation and development assistance would characterise future relations. For example, at the Korea-ASEAN summit, held in June 2009 to commemorate the 20th anniversary of mutual relations, President Lee proposed to turn the relationship into 'a new era of green partnership' (Lee 2009c; ASEAN 2009). He called on ASEAN leaders to co-operate in the development of low carbon technologies, which would provide the opportunity for South Korea and ASEAN to emerge in partnership as the 'world's green research hub' (Lee 2009c). At the second Korea-Africa Forum, held between South Korea and the AU in November 2009, the 'Korea-Africa Green Growth Initiative' was adopted as part of a broader development co-operation agreement. It stipulates the transfer of environmental technologies and the implementation of joint development projects in the area of water supply, sewerage and waste management (KAF 2009). Representatives from the government, business and environment sectors of Central and South America met with their Korean counterparts at a forum to find ways of fostering environmental co-operation (*Korea Herald*, 11 November 2009). Furthermore, on overseas trips to Australia, New Zealand and Indonesia in March 2009 President Lee had campaigned for his 'Green Growth' vision, tempting the *Korea Herald* to call his foreign policy 'green diplomacy' (*Korea Herald*, 5 March 2009).

The government is well aware that publicity, international recognition and foreign opinion are crucial for its goals of giving an example to other countries and advancing its growth model. To this end it canvasses major international media to influence positive reporting and opinion among the foreign public. In June 2009 the administration invited researchers and journalists from the US (*New York Times*), Japan (*Asahi Shimbun*), Russia (*Rossiyskaya Gazeta*), Netherlands (*De Telegraaf*), France (*Le Figaro*) and other countries to attend a workshop 'to export its vision of green growth' (Kim 2009; see also Han A-ran 2009). At another workshop held in October 2009 the culture ministry invited about 20 international journalists to introduce them to South Korean environment-friendly projects for tourism and culture.[4] The importance of the 'Green Growth' coverage by foreign media can be seen in the counting of articles reporting on the administration's strategy. The official website of the government *korea.net* shows who and what kind of information was reported on 'Green Growth' (Ro 2009a, 2009b). It points out that *Le Figaro* and *Asahi Shimbun*, who participated in the June workshop on 'Green Growth', reported positively on South Korea's strategy. It also cites other foreign newspapers from Spain (*El Mundo*), China (*Liaowang*), Singapore (*Straits Times*), Japan (*Nihon Keizai Shimbun*) and Germany (*Financial Times Deutschland*) that covered Seoul's 'green' policy.

However, domestic newspapers go a step further and align themselves directly with the government, providing a quasi-advertisement platform for the dissemination of official positions on 'Green Growth' (and other policy issues). A clear example of this government-journalism alignment is the joint project between the Presidential Council on Nation Branding and the *Korea Times* to publish a series of government-friendly articles on 'Korea's growing international status and its vision of becoming an advanced country', which features also a story on 'Green Growth' (*Korea Times*, 12 December 2009).

3 Evaluation of 'Low Carbon Green Growth'

In light of the above-described developments it appears reasonable to speak of proactive efforts by the South Korean government to promote its 'Green Growth' policy. To raise its ecological profile the Lee administration has started many national and international activities and initiatives since its inauguration in the beginning of 2008. As the first developing country to do so, it has announced voluntary GHG reduction goals and established the 'East Asia Climate Partnership' to promote regional co-operation on ecological development. The proposed measures have prompted some to speak of a South Korean 'green leadership' (Scarlatoiu 2009). In addition the under-secretary-general for economic and social affairs of the United Nations stressed South Korea's pioneering role in the global efforts for environment-friendly growth and expected Korea 'as a leader to come up with experiences, sometimes even lessons' for other countries (*Korea Herald*, 10 September 2009). Furthermore, in August 2009 UNEP published an in-

---

[4] I would like to thank Max Borowski for pointing me to this workshop.

terim report, which praised the government's 'green' policy and concluded that the country 'is demonstrating engagement and leadership at the international level by boosting global efforts towards achieving a green economy' (UNEP 2009: 30). However, a closer look at 'Green Growth' reveals its rather double-edged character and points to implications that could thwart the government's strategy. It also raises questions that are as yet unanswered.

3.1 New policy?

First of all, it should be noted that 'Green Growth' is not an entirely new concept to South Korean politics, but is based on an initiative of the former Roh Moo-hyun administration to provide a regional consultative body on sustainable development. Already in 2005 the Ministry of Environment had introduced 'Green Growth' at the 5th Ministerial Conference on Environment and Development in Asia and the Pacific organised by the United Nations Economic and Social Commission for Asia and the Pacific (UNESCAP 2005). This proposal was then adopted by the ministerial meeting and later embraced by UNESCAP as the 'Seoul Initiative Network on Green Growth' (SINGG). Since then the SINGG convenes annually to consult on the issue of the compatibility of economic growth and environment protection. Its last gathering was held in Seoul in August 2009.

3.2 Ambitious policy?

As already mentioned, as part of the 'Green Growth' strategy the Lee administration has pledged to reduce its GHG emissions voluntarily. South Korea, which is formally not obliged under the UN convention on climate change to decrease its GHG outputs, would be the first developing country to announce such goals. After a longer consultation process, in which the government together with several research institutes identified three possible reduction scenarios, the government revealed its concrete reduction targets in November 2009, declaring it would decrease emissions by 30 percent from the level projected for 2020 if GHG emissions increase at the current pace. While President Lee called this decision a 'historic moment' that would elevate Korea's international status by giving an example for other developing countries, the *Korea Times*, for instance, described it as a 'bold plan' of the administration (PCGG 2009c; *Korea Times*, 17 November 2009). The headlines of other major domestic newspapers such as the *Chosun Ilbo* (18 November 2009), *JoongAng Ilbo* (18 November 2009) and the *Korea Herald* (18 November 2009) also referred to the announcement, suggesting the country would lower emissions by 30 percent by 2020.

However, what the government, but also domestic newspapers emphasise much less is the fact that only 4 percent of emissions will be cut if compared to the reference year 2005. Indicative is the press release of the government on the announcement of its reduction goals, which does not mention the 4 percent reduction compared to 2005 levels (PCGG 2009c). In the period between 1990 and 2007, South Korea's carbon output grew at the fastest pace among OECD members, making it in 2007 the ninth largest CO_2 emitter in the world (IEA 2009). Further, the 'voluntary' reduction of emissions has a flipside. On the one hand, it could be seen as a decision to act as an early mover in international climate politics—a rationale that has always played an important role in the considerations of the government. On the other hand, these commitments are not legally binding, such as the Kyoto protocol is, and therefore are easier to neglect than legal obligations. The economy minister and business associations have already warned of putting too many strains on the domestic economy, which would curtail its international competitiveness (Yonhap, 30 October 2009).

From an international comparative perspective, South Korea's climate targets do not seem as ambitious or exemplary as the government wishes them to be. Other developing countries formulated—though likewise not binding themselves legally—higher GHG reduction goals than South Korea. Taking 2005 as the reference year, India, Indonesia, China and Brazil, for instance, declared they would decrease their emissions between 20 and 45 percent up to 2020 (*Kyodo News*, 3 December 2009; *Jakarta Post*, 3 October 2009; *Financial Times*, 26 November 2009; Reuters, 13 November 2009). Domestic environmental groups such as the Korean Federation for Environmental Movement and Green Korea have criticised the government's goals for being too modest and called for a 25 percent decrease from 2005 levels (*Hankyoreh*, 6 November 2009). Especially in the run-up to the Copenhagen climate summit, where national governments attempted unavailingly to negotiate a successor agreement to the Kyoto protocol, which is due to expire in 2012, South Korea was pressed to join the group of so called Annex I parties, who are compelled to lower GHG outputs under the current climate convention. The European Union (EU) in particular called for a redefinition of South Korea's developing status to include it in the Annex I category (*Korea Times*, 20 September 2009). The EU argues that the country, as an OECD member, should make its reduction commitments commensurate with its economic status (Lefevere 2009). Against this background the government appraised the outcome of the climate talks in Copenhagen as a partial success since, according to South Korea's ambassador on climate change, '[o]ne of the accomplishments of Korea at the meeting is that we remain a Non-Annex 1 country that has no obligatory emissions reduction target' (*Korea Herald*, 22 December 2009).

3.3 *'Green' policy?*

Another controversial issue related to Korea's reduction targets concerns how to achieve them. On the one hand the government willingly states it will promote the development of renewable energies within its 'Green Growth' framework, which would help in lowering GHG emissions. To this end the share of regenerative energy sources such as solar cells, wind, and geothermal energy in total energy production would be more than doubled by 2020 (PCGG 2009b: 13). However, given the already low ratio of 2.7 percent of renewable energy in total power generation in 2009, the intended rise to 6 percent would be still low. According to UNEP the EU and China, for instance, want to increase their quota of regenerative energy in total energy production by 20 percent by 2020 (UNEP 2009: 27). The UN's environmental programme concludes in its otherwise positive report on South Korea's 'Green Growth', that the 'current plan on renewable energy does not appear to be particularly ambitious' (ibid.).

On the other hand, the government does not regard regenerative energy as promising or helpful in achieving the goals of 'Green Growth'. According to the then economy minister, Lee Yoon-ho, renewable energy would take time to establish these goals as 'viable sources of energy'. Lee lamented the need for subsidies that alternative energy would require in order to be commercially feasible and warned of budget constraints without having corresponding benefits. Since there would be 'no energy source as good as nuclear power in terms of efficiency and ecology', he campaigned for a 'renaissance of nuclear energy' (*Korea Times*, 3 July 2009). Likewise his successor, Choi Kyung-hwan, claimed that the development of alternative energy would be ill conceived and therefore required investment in the nuclear industry. For this reason nuclear power would be chosen to fuel South Korea's 'Green Growth' (Yonhap, 29 December 2009).

According to the 'National Basic Energy Plan', which sets out the parameters of the country's energy supply until 2030, investment into nuclear energy would be massively expanded (MKE 2008). In this US$100 billion plan the share of nuclear power in total energy generation would be raised from 36 percent in 2007 to 59 percent in 2030 (ibid.: 12). While the increase will be met by the construction of ten or 11 new atomic power plants, the state-run operator Korea Hydro & Nuclear Power intends to add in total 18 new facilities to the already existing 20 units by 2030 by investing US$32-40 billion (WNA 2009). The massive expansion of nuclear energy represents a strategic decision to increase South Korea's energy security. About 97 percent of the country's total energy needs have to be imported, making it highly depended on foreign suppliers and prone to market fluctuations. For example, as the fourth largest oil consumer in the world, South Korea imports 100 percent of its crude oil from abroad with the Middle East providing 82 percent (Kang Seon-jou 2008: 2). 'Green Growth' reveals here its overlapping with another foreign policy initiative of the government. With South Korea's so-called Energy Cooperation Diplomacy, the government attempts to diversify and secure a stable supply of energy and resources (MOFAT 2009: 137-141). In the long term dependence on foreign resources would be decreased, while energy self-sufficiency would be increased. However, with the government's orientation towards nuclear energy it seems debatable whether reliance on foreign resources can be reduced since all fuel for South Korea's nuclear plants likewise has to be imported.

With the government's heavy investment in nuclear energy, which it deems to be a green or clean technology, it hopes not only to reduce carbon emissions and dependence on oil, but also to produce cheap energy and export technology, equipment and components for the emerging nuclear market.[5] The appreciation of atomic energy by the

---

[5] South Korea is a newcomer in the global nuclear industry, competing with more established countries such as France, Japan or the US. However, recent developments

government is also reflected in a recent proposal put forward at the 2009 General Conference of the International Atomic Energy Agency (IAEA) by the minister of education, science and technology to establish an international 'Day of Nuclear Energy' (*Korea Herald*, 16 September 2009).

3.4 Trouble-free policy?

According to a report of the International Energy Agency (IEA), South Korea's nuclear plants are considered safe and reliable (IEA 2006: 140). However, recent incidents suggest that the domestic nuclear industry is not necessarily immune to trouble-free operation of its facilities. In January 2009 reactors at the country's oldest nuclear power plant in Pusan had to be shut down because of technical problems. Operations at the same facility had already had to be stopped a month earlier because of a false alarm in one of its turbines. In a similar incident, another reactor in Kyŏngju was shut down for two days due to a problem with the power supply (*Korea Times*, 29 January 2009). In October 2009, a generator at the nuclear facility in Yŏnggwang was closed down by a malfunctioning in its control rods (Yonhap, 24 October 2009). Although no radioactivity was reportedly leaked during the incidents, recent episodes point also to the risky side of nuclear energy generation.[6] Furthermore, questions of nuclear waste disposal, of public acceptance but also of operating safety still remain open. Domestic environmental groups such as the Korean Federation for Environmental Movement criticise the selection process of repositories for atomic waste and the decisions to extend the runtime of nuclear facilities as lacking in transparency. After a long search of 20 years, in 2007 the government began with the construction, in Kyŏngju, of a repository for mid- and low-level nuclear waste. With the establishment of the Korea Radioactive Waste Management Corporation in early 2009, the institutional process to resolve and forge a

---

indicate the competitiveness of domestic nuclear know-how. For instance, in December 2009 a South Korean consortium won one of the largest projects of the nuclear industry, to built nuclear power plants in the United Arab Emirates. Orders worth up to US$40 billion were involved (*Korea Herald*, 27 December 2009).

[6] Not least to ease public concerns regarding the safety of atomic plants, the Ministry of Education, Science and Technology in December 2009 opened its fourth nuclear disaster centre to prevent and cope with contingencies (Yonhap, 21 December 2009).

national consensus on high-level waste and its disposal has just started. As a researcher in the state-run Korea Atomic Energy Research Institute (KAERI) puts it, '[a]lthough the government has made its commitment to nuclear power clear, the discussion over storage solutions for radioactive waste has been virtually non-existent' (*Korea Times*, 1 October 2009). According to a report by KAERI, total storage capacity of atomic waste passed the 10,000-tons mark in October 2009, with the saturation of existing stocks expected for 2016 (ibid.). The lack of sufficient storage capacity for nuclear waste could require the stoppage of operations at atomic plants, which in turn could thwart the government's 'Green Growth' plans.

One way to reduce current stocks of nuclear waste is the recycling of used nuclear materials. This approach is favoured by the administration, because reliance on nuclear imports would be lessened. As Kang and Feiveson (2001) show, from the beginning of its nuclear programme in the 1970s South Korea has been interested at times in reprocessing spent nuclear fuel. However, the enrichment and reprocessing of spent atomic fuel is politically delicate since it involves eventualities of nuclear proliferation. While materials separated from reprocessing can be recycled for nuclear energy generation, they are also usable for the building of nuclear weapons—a security issue that has been discussed for years within the Six Party Talks, a multilateral forum consisting of the US, China, Japan, Russia and the two Koreas on the denuclearisation of the Korean peninsula. In this way the orientation towards nuclear energy as part of the 'Green Growth' concept reveals the implications it has for South Korea's foreign policy. Concerns over proliferation safety, which attached themselves almost naturally to North Korean nuclear ambitions, were also raised after the revelation of 'South Korea's nuclear surprise' (Kang et al. 2005). In 2004 the South Korean government had to admit that from the 1980s until 2000 scientists of the state-run KAERI had conducted secret nuclear experiments and activities, which involved the conversion and enrichment of uranium and the separation of plutonium (ibid.: 45). Although the experiments conducted had no official authorisation from the government and the amount of nuclear materials involved was marginal, the report of the director-general of the IAEA investigating the activities found their nature and the failure by the administration to report these activities a 'matter of serious concern' (IAEA 2004: paragraph 41). The admission showed that past South Korean governments not only failed to abide by the safeguards system of the

IAEA and the Non-proliferation Treaty, but also intentionally misled the IAEA and violated international agreements (Kang et al. 2005). For Kang and his fellow authors these revelations entail 'a major re-evaluation of what governments and analysts around the world thought they knew about South Korea's nuclear history' (ibid.: 42). Furthermore, after North Korea's first nuclear test in 2006, discussions emerged in South Korea concerning the South's technical ability to produce its own nuclear weapons (Shim 2006). In the beginning of 2008, the Ministry of Foreign Affairs and Trade (MOFAT) released classified documents showing the ambition of former president Park Chung-hee to develop nuclear weapons (*Korea Times*, 15 January 2008). These developments are not meant to suggest that 'Green Growth' would conceal the intentions of the South Korean government to pursue atomic weapons, but do point to the political implications of 'Green Growth' with its reliance on atomic energy.[7] Moreover, they show that questions and concerns of nuclear proliferation, nuclear development and non-disclosures of nuclear activities are not unfamiliar to South Korean politics (see also DiMoia 2009).

The efforts of the government to expand its nuclear programme for its 'Green Growth' strategy has already encountered US opposition and could emerge as a sticking point between South Korea and the US (McGoldrick 2009). In the 1970s the two countries signed an agreement for nuclear co-operation, which expires in 2014. Under the accord the US provided South Korea with nuclear technology and know-how, while South Korea agreed to refrain from reprocessing nuclear materials. However, given the 'Green Growth' goals and the expected saturation of atomic waste stockpiles in 2016, the Lee administration finds action urgent and therefore seeks for an inclusion of reprocessing capabilities in the nuclear co-operation agreement. To this end the Korean government has formed a special task force to revise the terms of the current treaty. The economy minister Choi Kyung-hwan has already called for seeking 'nuclear sovereignty' and suggested ending the self-imposed restrictions in the field of nuclear development (*Chosun Ilbo*, 31 December 2009). To counter concerns, rooted in the above-mentioned developments, that the administration may seek revision of the treaty for purposes other than civilian, the foreign minis-

---

[7] Interestingly, in January 2009 the South Korean government sent a delegation to Pyongyang to discuss the possible purchase of unused nuclear fuel rods from North Korea (*Korea Times*, 13 January 2009). I would like to thank one of the editors for pointing me to this visit.

ter Yu Myung-hwan explained the need as readjustment to the challenges of climate change. However, the US has approved reprocessing of US-supplied nuclear fuel only in the EU, Japan and India (McGoldrick 2009: 5). Furthermore, the Obama administration has already indicated its objection to altering the agreement in this respect (*Chosun Ilbo*, 1 July 2009). A permit for reprocessing would also counter the 1992 'Joint Declaration on The Denuclearization of The Korean Peninsula' between North Korea and South Korea, which the US has considered as particularly important for the stability of the Korean peninsula. The declaration states that 'South and North Korea shall not possess nuclear reprocessing and uranium enrichment facilities' (MOU 1992). Even though North Korea has not abided by the agreement, Seoul dare not risk following suit at any price.

4 Conclusion

With its heavy dependence on exports South Korea's economy was hit hard by the global economic downturn of 2008-09. With 'Green Growth' the government hoped to find a cure for an ailing South Korea. In the words of the then prime minister, Han Seung-soo, the administration sought 'to catch three birds with one stone' (Han 2009b). It would create new growth engines, while ensuring environmental sustainability and contribute to global efforts against climate change. Since the announcement of 'Green Growth' a range of measures and initiatives have been undertaken, prompting some to speak of a Korean role model for other countries (UNEP 2009, Scarlatoiu 2009). In this vein, it was argued, the policy concept should not be understood as oriented solely domestically. It underlines South Korea's claim to play an active and more acknowledged role in issues of global concern such as climate change, economic development and energy security (see also Shim 2009).

However, the self-proclaimed greening of South Korean politics also has its pitfalls. The decision of the government to choose nuclear energy as the backbone for its 'green' strategy provokes questions such as the disposal of atomic waste, which no country in the world has answered yet. Concerns over the safe operation of nuclear plants remain, diminishing public acceptance. Moreover the US has to be convinced it should consent to nuclear reprocessing. From a comparative perspective, South Korea's GHG reduction targets or investments in renewable energy appear rather modest and contest the government's claim of giving a 'green' example for other countries. In interviews with Korean researchers of the Science and Technology Policy Institute in August 2009 it became apparent that intended programmes and projects are green coated rather than being veritable ecologically sensitive and involved plans such as were introduced already under former president Roh Moo-hyun. Other critics stressed 'Green Growth' would only focus on projects for the development of the national infrastructure such as the restoration of rivers and the construction of high-speed train lines. They complained it would damage the environmental sustainability and create temporary jobs only for low-qualified workers (Yun 2009; *Korea Times*, 4 May 2009).

Questions regarding the longevity of 'Green Growth' can also be raised, since South Korean politics have seen many long-term strategies dawning and disappearing. Since various governmental bodies formulate their own development strategies, which are suited to serve their institutional interests and background, the variety of development models lacks co-ordination, resulting in a rather weak commitment to the implementation of mid- to long-term development strategies (Moon 2009). The preceding administration under the late Roh Moo-hyun unveiled in August 2006 a comprehensive long-term development strategy, called 'Vision 2030—Korea: A Hopeful Nation in Harmony' (MOFE/MOHW/MPB 2006). This large-scale project, worth 1.100 trillion won (US$1.15 trillion), was intended to lay the ground for a paradigm shift in the nation's growth path. By 2030 per capita GDP was to reach US$49,000, making South Korea a leading country in the world. Economic growth and welfare standards would be developed in tandem to raise living standards and to cope with current and upcoming challenges such as the widening socio-economic gap, low fertility rate and a fast-ageing society. Moreover, in the realm of science and technology policy the South Korean government, under the then president Kim Dae-jung, disclosed in 2000 its long-term S&T development plan 'Vision 2025' (MOST 2000). This strategy represented a comprehensive innovation policy approach, which would manage South Korea's transition to an advanced, prosperous and knowledge-based economy (Schüller and Shim 2010).

These strategies disappeared or were reformulated several times. Moreover, the recent overhauls of South Korea's innovation system in 2004 under Roh Moo-hyun and in 2008 under Lee Myung-bak point to the short lifespan of long-term projects in South Korean politics.

Given the ephemerality of South Korean development strategies, with two years remaining in office for President Lee, it will be interesting to see if 'Green Growth' will be the central motto for the next government. Generally it appears debatable to formulate long-term strategies in an environment which is said to be characterised by structural change and constant adaptation.

REFERENCES

ASEAN (Association of Southeast Asian Nations) (2009), *Joint Statement of the ASEAN-Republic of Korea Commemorative Summit*, Cheju Island, 2 June 2009. Online: http://www.aseansec.org/JS-AK-Commemorative-Summit.pdf (accessed 6 June 2009)

Chosun Ilbo, 1 July 2009, 18 November 2009, 31 December 2009. Online: http://english.chosun.com

Conlé, Marcus and David Shim (2009), 'Globale Trends in der Innovationspolitik: Best Practices für alle?' [Global trends in innovation policy: best practices for all?], in: *GIGA Focus Global*, 1/2009, Hamburg: GIGA German Institute of Global and Area Studies

DiMoia, John P. (2009), '"Atoms for Sale": From "Atoms for Peace" (South Korea) to "Weaponized" Plutonium (North Korea), 1955-2009', in: Rüdiger Frank, James E. Hoare, Patrick Köllner and Susan Pares (eds), *Korea Yearbook: Politics, Economy and Society 2009*, Leiden: Brill, pp. 117-141

Government of the Republic of Korea (2009), *Green Growth, Green Korea*, Seoul

Gurria, Angel (2009), 'The Korean G-20 leadership: Assessing the key issues for the 2010 – New sources of sustainable and balanced growth', speech to Korea G-20 Leadership Conference, Seoul, 17 November 2009. Online: http://www.oecd.org/document/18/0,3343,en_33873108_33873555_44080146_1_1_1_1,00.html (accessed 6 January 2010)

Han, A-ran (2009), 'International journalists, academics map out Green Growth', in: *korea.net*, 17 June 2009. Online: http://www.korea.net/News/News/newsView.asp?serial_no=20090617006 (accessed 20 July 2009)

Han, Seung-soo (2009a), 'Opening Remarks for the Plenary Session on "Setting Asia's Green Growth Agenda" of the East Asia World Economic Forum', speech to East Asia World Economic Forum, Seoul, 19 June 2009. Online: http://www.pmo.go.kr/eng.do?menuSID=267&tabIDX=&step=View&bbsSID=40943&refSID=0&pageNum=2&searchCategory=&searchField=&keyword=&searchDate= (accessed 20 June 2009)

Han, Seung-soo (2009b), 'On "Green Growth"', Paris, 25 June 2009. Online: http://www.pmo.go.kr/eng.do?menuSID=267&tabIDX=&step=View&bbsSID=40823&refSID=0&pageNum=2&searchCategory=&searchField=&keyword=&searchDate= (accessed 26 June 2009)

Hankyoreh, 6 November 2009. Online: http://english.hani.co.kr

HSBC (2009), *Building a green recovery*, London, 24 May 2009. Online: http://www.hsbc.com/1/PA_1_1_S5/content/assets/sustainability/090522_green_recovery.pdf, (accessed 15 December 2009)

IAEA (International Atomic Energy Agency) (2004), *Implementation of the NPT Safeguards Agreement in the Republic of Korea*, Vienna, 11 November 2004

IEA (International Energy Agency) (2006), *Energy Policies of the IEA Countries: The Republic of Korea 2006 Review*, Paris. Online: http://www.iea.org/publications/free_new_Desc.asp?PUBS_ID=1921, (accessed 15 June 2009)

IEA (2009), *CO2 Emissions from Fuel Combustion: Highlight 2009 Edition*, Paris. Online: http://www.iea.org/publications/free_new_Desc.asp?PUBS_ID=2143, (accessed 14 January 2010)

JoongAng Daily, 18 November 2009. Online: http://joongangdaily.joins.com

KAF (Korea-Africa Forum) (2009), *Korea-Africa Green Growth Initiative 2009-2012*, Seoul, 24 November 2009. Online: kaforum.net/board/_data/pds/61/pds_61_0_1259893073.pdf, (accessed 30 November)

Kang, Jung-Min and H.A. Feiveson (2001), 'South Korea's Shifting and Controversial Interest in Spent Fuel Reprocessing', in: *The Nonproliferation Review,* 8 (1), pp. 70-78

Kang, Jung-Min, Peter Hayes, Li Bin, Tatsujiro Suzuki and Richard Tanter (2005), 'South Korea's Nuclear Surprise', in: *Bulletin of the Atomic Scientists,* 61 (1), pp. 40-49

Kang, Seon-jou (2008), 'Korea's Pursuit of Energy Security', Paper prepared for the 2008 Northeast Asia Energy Outlook Seminar, Korea Economic Institute Policy Forum, Washington DC, 6 May 2008. Online: www.keia.org/Publications/Other/KangFINAL.pdf (accessed 26 August 2009)

Kim, Hee-sung (2009), 'Korea to export its vision of green growth', in: *korea.net,* 11 June 2009. Online: http://www.korea.net/News/News/NewsView.asp?serial_no=20090611008&part=101&SearchDay=&source= (accessed 11 June 2009)

Korea Herald, 5 March 2009, 10 September 2009, 16 September 2009, 7 October 2009, 11 November 2009, 18 November 2009, 22 December 2009, 27 December 2009. Online: http://www.koreaherald.co.kr

Korea Times, 15 January 2008, 13 January 2009, 29 January 2009, 4 May 2009, 31 May 2009, 3 July 2009, 20 September 2009, 1 October 2009, 17 November 2009, 12 December 2009. Online: http://www.koreatimes.co.kr

Lee, Myung-bak (2008), 'Address by President Lee Myung-bak on the 63rd anniversary of national liberation and the 60th anniversary of the founding of the Republic of Korea', Cheong Wa Dae, Seoul, The Republic of Korea, 15 August 2008. Online: http://www.korea.net/News/issues/issueMoreList.asp?serial_no=712 (accessed 20 July 2009)

Lee, Myung-bak (2009a), 'Address by H.E. Mr. Lee Myung-bak President of the Republic of Korea at the 64th Session of the General Assembly of the United Nations', New York, 23 September 2009. Online: http://www.un.org/ga/64/generaldebate/pdf/KR_en.pdf (accessed 25 September 2009)

Lee, Myung-bak (2009b), 'President Lee Myung-bak's Keynote Speech at the UN Climate Change Conference in Copenhagen', Copenhagen, 17 December 2009. Online: http://english.president.go.kr/pre_activity/speeches/speeches_list.php (accessed 20 December 2009)

Lee, Myung-bak (2009c), 'Green Partnership for Future', *Korea Times,* 31 May 2009. Online: http://www.koreatimes.co.kr/www/news/special/2009/10/275_46015.html (accessed 15 June 2009)

Lefevere, Jürgen (2009), 'The road to Copenhagen and its expected outcome: An EU perspective', paper presented at 'Korea-EU Workshop on Climate Change Policies & Business Contribution', Seoul, 14 September 2009

McGoldrick, Fred (2009), 'New U.S.-ROK Peaceful Nuclear Cooperation Agreement: a Precedent for a New Global Nuclear Architecture', November 2009, Washington DC: Center for U.S.-Korea Policy. Online: http://www.asiafoundation.org/resources/pdfs/McGoldrickUSROKCUSKP091130.pdf (accessed 4 December 2009)

MEST (Ministry of Education, Science and Technology) (2008), *Science and Technology Basic Plan of the Lee Myung-bak Administration,* Seoul, 2 December 2008

MKE (Ministry of Knowledge Economy) (2008), *National Basic Energy Plan, Korea 2008-2030,* Seoul

MOFAT (Ministry of Foreign Affairs and Trade) (2009), *2009 Diplomatic White Paper,* Seoul

MOFE/MOHW/MOPB (Ministry of Finance and Economy, Ministry of Health and Welfare, Ministry of Planning and Budget) (2006), *Vision 2030—Korea: A Hopeful Nation in Harmony*, joint press release, Seoul, 30 August 2006

Moon, Tae-hoon (2009), 'Korea's Sustainable Development Strategy', in: *Korea Observer*, 40 (1), pp. 85-114

MOST (Ministry of Science and Technology) (2000), *Vision 2025—Korea's Long-term Plan for Science and Technology Development*, Seoul

MOU (Ministry of Unification) (1992), *Joint Declaration on The Denuclearization of The Korean Peninsula*, Seoul

OECD (Organisation for Economic Co-Operation and Development) (2005), *Governance of Innovation System, Volume 1: Synthesis Report*, Paris: OECD. Online: http://www.oecd.org/document/25/0,3343,en_2649_34269_35175257_1_1_1_1, 00.html (accessed 4 May 2009)

OECD (2009a), *Policy Responses to the Economic Crisis: Stimulus Packages, Innovation and Long-term Growth*, Paris, 11 May 2009. Online: www.oecd.org/dataoecd/59/45/42983414.pdf (accessed 2 December 2009)

OECD (2009b), *Declaration on Green Growth*, Paris, 24-25 June 2009. Online: http://www.olis.oecd.org/olis/2009doc.nsf/LinkTo/NT00004886/$FILE/JT03267 277.PDF (accessed 14 July 2009)

OECD (2009c), *Main Science and Technology Indicators 2009/1 edition*, Paris. Online: http://www.oecd.org/dataoecd/9/44/41850733.pdf (accessed 14 November 2009)

PCGG (Presidential Committee on Green Growth) (2009a), *Green Growth A New Path for Korea*, Seoul. Online: http://www.korea.net/kois/eng_il_read.asp?book_no=92, (accessed 8 June 2009)

PCGG (2009b), *Road to Our Future: Green Growth National Strategy and the Five-Year Plan (2009-2013)*, Seoul. Online: http://www.greengrowth.go.kr/download.ddo?fid=bbs&bbs_cd_n=17&bbs_seq_n=40&order_no_n=1 (accessed 13 December 2009)

PCGG (2009c), *Republic of Korea Sets its Mid-term Greenhouse Gas Reduction Goal for 2020*, press release, Seoul, 17 November 2009

Ro, James (2009a), 'Foreign media report Korea's green growth plan', in: *korea.net*, 16 July 2009. Online: http://www.korea.net/News/News/newsView.asp?serial_no=20090716001 (accessed 20 July 2009)

Ro, James (2009b), 'Green Korea grabs headlines in int'l media outlets', in: *korea.net*, 1 September 2009. Online: http://www.korea.net/news/issues/issueDetailView.asp?board_no=21089&menu_code=A (accessed 6 September 2009)

Scarlatoiu, Greg (2009), 'Korea's Green Leadership', in: *Insight*, April 2009, Washington DC: Korea Economic Institute. Online: www.keia.org/Publications/Insight/2009/09April.pdf (accessed 9 September 2009)

Schüller, Margot and David Shim (2010), 'The Innovation System and Innovation Policy in South Korea', in: Rainer Frietsch and Margot Schüller (eds), *Competing for Global Innovation Leadership: Innovation Systems and Policies in the USA, EU and Asia*, Karlsruhe: Fraunhofer Verlag, pp. 169-88

Shim, David (2009), 'A Shrimp amongst Whales? Assessing South Korea's Regional-power Status', in: *GIGA Working Papers*, 107, August 2009, Hamburg: GIGA German Institute of Global and Area Studies

Shim, David (2006), 'China und die nukleare Herausforderung Nordkoreas' [China and the North Korean nuclear challenge], in: *Journal of Current Chinese Affairs*, 6/2006, pp. 48-61

UNEP (United Nations Environment Programme) (2009), *Overview of the Republic of Korea's Green Growth National Vision*, August 2009, Seoul

UNEP (2010), *2009 Annual Report: Seizing the Green Opportunity*, February 2010, Nairobi
UNESCAP (United Nations Economic and Social Commission for Asia and the Pacific) (2005), *Report for the Ministerial Conference on Environment and Development in Asia and the Pacific*, 28-29 March 2005, Seoul
UNFCCC (United Nations Framework Convention on Climate Change) (2001), *Report of the Conference of the Parties on its seventh session—Part two: Action taken by the Conference of the Parties*, vol. II, 29 October-10 November 2001, Marrakesh
WNA (World Nuclear Association) (2009), 'Nuclear Power in Korea', London, December 2009. Online: http://www.world-nuclear.org/info/inf81.html (accessed 14 December 2009)
World Bank (2010), *World Development Report 2010: Development and Climate Change*, Washington DC
Yonhap news agency, 24 October 2009, 30 October 2009, 21 December 2009, 29 December 2009. Online: http://english.yonhapnews.co.kr
Yun, Sun-jin (2009), 'UNEP should engage in independent research', *Hankyoreh*, 27 August 2009. Online: http://english.hani.co.kr/arti/english_edition/e_opinion/373377.html (accessed 24 December 2009)

SOUTH KOREA'S ECONOMIC RELATIONS WITH INDIA: TRENDS, PATTERNS AND PROSPECTS

Durgesh K. Rai

ABSTRACT

Although the Republic of Korea and India established formal diplomatic relations in 1973, bilateral economic relations only started deepening during the years following India's economic reforms in the early 1990s, and particularly after the Asian financial crisis of 1997-8. Bilateral trade increased greatly during the 1998-2008 period, along with changes in the composition of exports and imports. Although Indian investment to Korea has grown in recent years, it is largely a one-way flow from Korea to India. The absolute size of Korean investment in India increased over the period but its share in total foreign direct investment (FDI) in India has decreased. The composition of Korean investment, moreover, is quite different from that of FDI in India in general. The growing economic ties have been mainly driven by structural changes in the economies of both countries, especially India's, and by increasing trade complementarity and other measures. They have also been accompanied and facilitated by various bilateral treaties and agreements. The recently concluded comprehensive economic partnership agreement (CEPA) is expected to give a significant boost to the economic exchanges between the two economies.

1 INTRODUCTION

India and Korea are the third and fourth largest economies in Asia[1] and share a strong and growing economic relationship. The economy of the Republic of Korea (ROK—South Korea, henceforth Korea) is highly dependent on trade,[2] and India with its fast growing economy

---

[1] http://www.tendersinfo.com/global-asia-tenders.php (accessed 2 April 2010).
[2] According to the World Trade Organisation, trade to gross domestic product ratio for Korea was more than 90 percent for the period 2006-08. Online: http://stat.wto.org/CountryProfile/WSDBCountryPFView.aspx?Language=E&Country=KR (accessed 2 February 2010).

and large population provides a huge market and investment destination for Korean companies. For India, Korea is not only an export market but an important source of investment and technology transfer. Although Korea and India have shared a close relationship for a long time, bilateral economic ties gained momentum only during the early 1990s when India started its wide-ranging economic reforms. The period since those years has witnessed a manifold rise in trade between the two countries. Merchandise trade has increased more than six times during the decade 1998 to 2008 (UNCOMTRADE database, accessed 9 January 2010). Bilateral investment relations have also improved over that period. Though Indian companies have started investing in Korea in recent years, it has largely been a one-way flow from Korea to India. These developments have resulted in a significant increase in the importance to both countries of each other's economy.

This paper is an attempt to investigate the trends, patterns and prospects of the bilateral economic ties between Korea and India. The main objective is to examine the nature and evolution of the trade and investment relations between the two countries, especially after the Asian financial crisis of 1997-8. The paper contains four sections, of which this introduction is the first. The second section analyses the nature and evolution of trade relations, the third section examines investment and technological co-operation between the two countries and is based on an analysis of trends in economic flows and co-operation between the two. The fourth section looks at the future prospects for economic ties, with a final concluding remark. The paper is analytical and qualitative in nature. Important data sources include the United Nations Commodity Trade (UNCOMTRADE) database, World Investment Reports by the United Nations Conference on Trade and Development (UNCTAD), and the Department of Industrial Policy and Promotion (DIPP) of the Ministry of Commerce and Industry, Government of India.

2 Trade relations

2.1 *Trade policy*

2.1.1 *Korean trade policy*

Since the beginning of its first five-year plan in 1962, Korea has followed an export-oriented economic policy that not only led to a high rate of economic growth for many years but also continuously enhanced its economic integration with the world economy (Harvie and Pahlavani 2006). However, the Asian financial crisis of 1997 exposed many weaknesses in the economy and the Korean government was forced to introduce many IMF-led economic reforms (Cargill 2009). In December 1997, Korea shifted from a managed to a free-floating exchange rate system and since then has pursued exchange rate stabilisation. It further liberalised its investment regime to enhance foreign investment inflows. Korea also undertook reforms in trade and related policies through the implementation of commitments undertaken at the impetus of the World Trade Organisation (WTO), International Monetary Fund (IMF) and Organisation for Economic Co-operation and Development (OECD), as well as of bilaterally agreed arrangements. The general thrust of its trade and investment policies has been greater liberalisation, including the further opening of its economy to international trade and foreign investment during 1998-2008. However, some protectionist measures still continue to exist in the economy, especially in the agricultural sector. State ownership, moreover, has persisted in the telecommunications and transport services, which have maintained insufficient competition (WTO Secretariat 2008).

The customs tariff is Korea's main trade policy instrument and is an important source of revenue (4.6 percent of total tax revenue in 2007). Tariff rates have been adjusted to accord with Korea's binding commitments to WTO. Tariff transparency has improved as almost all the tariff lines have become ad valorem. However, the tariff structure remains relatively complex, embracing a multiplicity of rates often involving small rate differences and decimal points. Also, no unilateral most favoured nation (MFN) tariff liberalisation has been undertaken in recent years. The applied MFN rate averaged 12.8 percent in 2008 (the same as in 2004), which is high by OECD country standards. Peak ad valorem rates have remained unchanged and apply to agriculture, where tariff rates range from zero to 887.4 percent, and 86.6 percent of rates were 10 percent or below in 2008. Korea applies tariff rate quotas under its multilateral agricultural market-access commitments; in-quota tariff rates range from zero to 50 percent. Although 90.8 percent of tariff rates are bound, the predictability of the tariff is eroded by the leeway to raise applied tariffs that the average gap of 4.3 percentage points (9 percentage points for agricultural items) between applied and bound MFN rates encourages. Korea has continued to use this gap to apply higher MFN duties (e.g. adjustment duties) termed 'flexible tariffs', which the authorities maintain are within WTO bindings (WTO Secretariat 2008).

However, the post-Asian financial crisis period in Korea has witnessed a major departure from the previous trade policy of opposing preferential trade agreements and has increasingly focused on regional and bilateral trading arrangements. In response to the growing trend of regionalism, Korea considers these agreements as a means to liberalise its trade and investment regime in order to rejuvenate the economy, secure export markets and promote regional integration (Sohn and Yoon 2001). The present Lee Myung-bak government, which came into power in February 2008, decided on the construction of a 'global free trade agreement (FTA) network' as its core foreign-trade policy (Cheong and Cho 2009). To strengthen its position in Asia the government has also launched a 'New Asia Policy'. Presently Korea has a number of FTAs either concluded or under negotiation. Its first FTA was with Chile, effective from April 2004. Other important countries and blocs with which Korea has FTAs are Singapore, Peru, European Free Trade Agreement (EFTA), European Union (EU), the United States (US) and the Association of Southeast Asian Nations (ASEAN), and it has recently concluded a comprehensive economic partnership agreement (CEPA) with India. It is also in the process of negotiating FTAs with other countries or blocs such as Canada, Mexico, China, the Gulf Cooperation Council (GCC) and Japan.

Table 1 Korean engagement in FTAs/regional trade agreements (RTAs)/other agreements

Status	Country/Region/Economic Block	Progress	Remarks
Concluded	Asia Pacific trade agreement	Implemented (1976)	
	Chile	Implemented (April 2004)	
	Singapore	Implemented (March 2006)	
	EFTA	Implemented (September 2006)	
	ASEAN	FTA covering goods implemented in June 2007	FTA with Thailand is under ratification
	US	FTA officially signed (June 2007)	FTA with US is under ratification
	India	Officially signed (August 2009)	
	European Union (EU)	FTA negotiations are completed and the agreement was initialled on 15 October 2009	
Under negotiation	Mexico	Under negotiation	
	Canada	Under negotiation	
	ASEAN	Gradual progress in other areas	Currently negotiating on investment issues. Services agreement signed in November 2007
	GCC	Under negotiation	
	New Zealand	Under negotiation	
	Peru	Under negotiation	
	Australia	Under negotiation	
	Canada	Under negotiation	Negotiations will possibly resume in near future
	Japan	Under negotiation	Negotiations will possibly resume in near future
Official discussions	Mercado Común del Sur (MERCOSUR)	Agreement to start official talks	Joint report in May 2006
	People's Republic of China (PRC)		May possibly start negotiations in near future
	Russia		Joint study in 2008
Long-term FTAs	PRC-Japan-Korea		Joint study under progress since 2002
	EAFTA		Joint study since 2005

Source: Cheong and Cho 2009.

2.1.2 Indian trade policy

For a long time since its independence in 1947, India has followed an inward-looking economic policy or an import-substitution-policy to promote and protect domestic industry (Mohan 2006). However, in 1991, India started a new economic policy that was more externally oriented, and introduced a number of economic reforms. Since then it has continuously liberalised its trade and investment regimes to enhance trade and investment flows. During this period India continuously reformed its export-import policy and rationalised the tariff regime (WTO Secretariat 2007). It has substantially reduced the barriers to imports, and tariffs have become important tools of trade policy. Although tariffs remain an important source of tax revenue, their share is continuously declining. The overall average applied MFN rate has declined from over 32 percent to below 16 percent between 2001-02 and 2006-07. However, when ad valorem equivalents of non-ad valorem rates are taken into account, the overall average tariff was around 17.5 percent in 2007, reflecting these relatively high tariffs. As the overall applied MFN tariff declines, the gap between the bound and applied rates continues to grow. India's bound tariff rates are high, especially for agricultural products. As a result of completing the implementation of its Uruguay Round commitments, India's overall bound rate is currently at 48.6 percent. The use of import restrictions, maintained under Articles XX and XXI of the former General Agreement on Tariffs and Trade, has declined, with around 3.5 percent of tariff lines subject to such measures. India's use of anti-dumping and countervailing measures has also declined in recent years, although it is still one of the largest users of these instruments. Attempts are being made to harmonise national standards with international norms (WTO Secretariat 2007).

Until 1998, when India signed its first FTA with Sri Lanka, India had been a strong supporter of the multilateral trading system and played a very active role in all the multilateral forums like WTO and general agreements on trade in services. However, under the pressure of continued failures in multilateral negotiations at WTO and growing trends of regionalism, especially in Asia, India has also started taking a keen interest in the growing phenomenon of economic regionalism in terms of forging foreign and regional trade agreements (FTAs/ RTAs) with various countries or economic blocks. In fact, India is currently among the countries having the greatest number of such agreements either in place or under negotiation. As of now (2010), the total cumulative number of India's FTAs/RTAs is 31. Out of this figure, 11 have been proposed and in five cases the framework agreement has either been signed or is being negotiated; six FTAs have been under negotiation without having a framework agreement, four have been signed and five are under negotiation. The majority of India's RTAs are with Asian countries. It has recently concluded a CEPA with Korea and FTA in goods with ASEAN. Along with Korea, India is one of the founding members of the Bangkok Agreement of 1975, which was one of the first preferential trading arrangements in Asia. Subsequently, India joined various other regional trading arrangements such as the India-Sri Lanka FTA, the South Asian Free Trade Area, the India-Thailand FTA, and the India-Singapore comprehensive economic co-operation agreement (CECA). Currently, India is in process of negotiating several other regional and bilateral trade agreements such as the Bay of Bengal Initiative for Multi-sectoral Technical and Economic Cooperation (BIMSTEC), the India-GCC framework agreement on economic co-operation, the India-Australia trade and economic framework agreement, the India-Israel preferential trade agreement (PTA), the India-Japan CECA/CEPA, and others. In addition, India has set up various joint study groups to review the possibilities of economic co-operation with several other countries such as China, Malaysia and Indonesia.

2.2 *India and Korea in global trade: a comparative picture*

The conscious policy efforts by both India and Korea to step up their trade and investment flows have significantly enhanced the importance of trade in their respective gross domestic product (GDP) and their weight in the world economy. The economic policies of both countries have sought to improve the competitiveness of their export industries in the world market by following an open-market policy. The share of trade in the GDP of each has increased at a fast pace in recent years for both economies, but at a faster rate for India than for Korea. As can be observed from Table 3, that share has increased for both countries from 24.0 percent and 79.5 percent in 1998 to 54.3 percent and 107.0 percent in 2008 for India and Korea respectively,

Table 2 Indian engagement in FTAs/RTAs/other agreements

Partner country/ countries	Type of agreement	Status
BIMSTEC, GCC	FTA	Under negotiation
Asia-Pacific Agreement	Trade agreement	Under implementation
China, Australia, New Zealand	FTA	Under consultation and study
Afghanistan, Chile, MERCOSUR	PTA	Signed
Columbia, Israel, Uruguay, Venezuela	PTA	Under consultation and study
Egypt, Southern African Customs Union (SACU)	PTA	Under negotiation
EU	Trade and investment agreement (TIA)	Under negotiation
Indonesia	Comprehensive economic co-operation	Under consultation and study
Japan	CEPA	Under negotiation
Mauritius	Comprehensive economic co-operation and partnership agreement	Under negotiation
Russia	Comprehensive economic co-operation agreement	Under consultation and study
Singapore	CECA	Under implementation
Sri Lanka, South Asia	FTA	Under implementation
Nepal	Trade treaty	Under implementation
Malaysia	CECA	Under consultation and study
India-Korea	CEPA	Signed
India-ASEAN	FTA	Signed in goods. Under negotiation in services and investment

Source: Department of Commerce, Ministry of Commerce and Industry, Government of India (accessed 15 January 2010).

Table 3 Importance of trade (goods and services) in GDP

	India						Korea					
Year	1998	2000	2002	2004	2006	2008	1998	2000	2002	2004	2006	2008
Trade (% of GDP)	24.0	27.4	30.0	37.9	47.4	54.3	79.5	74.3	64.8	77.6	78.0	107.0
Exports (% of GDP)	11.2	13.2	14.5	18.1	22.2	24.0	46.2	38.6	33.1	40.9	39.7	52.9
Imports (% of GDP)	12.8	14.2	15.5	19.9	25.2	30.3	33.3	35.7	31.7	36.7	38.3	54.1

Source: World Bank (2009), World Development Indicators.

making both economies more and more trade dependent over the period. Although Korea's dependence on the world economy is very high, India's dependence is growing faster. As Table 3 shows, India's trade-to-GDP ratio has more than doubled from 1998 to 2008. Another interesting aspect of the trade-to-GDP ratio of both countries is the fact that the share of imports in GDP is higher than that of exports. Moreover, in India the importance of imports in GDP is not only higher than that of Korea but is increasing at a faster rate.

Both countries have become important exporters and importers in the global economy. In 2008, India ranked 18th and 11th and Korea ranked seventh and fifth among the largest exporters and importers of merchandise goods in the world. In the same year, Korean exports to the world had a value of US$422 billion and had grown by 14 percent over the previous year; its imports were valued at US$435 billion and had grown by 22 percent, again over the previous year. On the other hand, Indian exports to the world stood at US$179 billion and had grown by 22 percent and its imports had a value of US$292 billion and had increased by 35 percent over the previous year (WTO International Trade Statistics 2009).

The importance of both countries in the global economy has also augmented in terms of their shares in world trade (in both goods and services). As can be observed from Table 4, the Indian and Korean shares have increased in total world merchandise exports, but growth has been more substantial in the case of India. Korea, however, is still a more important player in global merchandise trade than India. For instance, as the table shows, despite a significant increase in India's share in total world merchandise exports, Korea's share was more than double India's in 2008. A similar situation exists in total world merchandise imports. However, where trade in services is concerned, India has outperformed Korea. As can be observed from the table, India has not only been able to increase its share in total world services exports but has also become a bigger exporter than Korea since 2006. On the other hand, the Korean share has improved marginally from 1.79 percent in 1998 to 1.94 percent in 2008, a much lower rise when compared to the increase in India's share of global services exports.

Table 4 Trade integration (share in %)

Year	India's share in world						Korea's share in world					
	1998	2000	2002	2004	2006	2008	1998	2000	2002	2004	2006	2008
Merchandise exports	0.61	0.66	0.76	0.83	1.00	1.11	2.40	2.67	2.50	2.75	2.68	2.62
Merchandise imports	0.76	0.77	0.85	1.05	1.40	1.76	1.66	2.41	2.28	2.37	2.51	2.67
Services exports	0.80	1.06	1.19	1.70	2.66	2.72	1.79	1.96	1.70	1.81	1.71	1.94
Services imports	1.05	1.28	1.33	1.66	2.42	2.40	1.78	2.23	2.31	2.33	2.61	2.66

Source: World Bank (2009); WTO International Trade Statistics (2009).

2.3 *Bilateral trade*

Bilateral trade between the two countries has increased continuously during the post-economic reform period of the Indian economy, particularly after the year 2000. Exports and imports have grown rapidly in both goods and services. The period has also witnessed a substantial change in the trade basket (Sahoo et al. 2009a). Although the Indian merchandise export basket has changed in favour of manufactured products, its exports consist largely of low value-added manufactured goods. Data on the trade in bilateral services are not available, but looking at the growing importance of services in both economies and at the complementarities in several sectors, it can be surmised that bilateral trade in services might also have increased in the recent past.

2.3.1 Merchandise trade

The increasing liberalisation and fast growth in the Indian economy have led to a significant spurt in the trade and investment flows between the two countries. The launch of Indian economic reforms in the early 1990s was considered very timely from the Korean companies' point of view. This was the period when such companies were looking for other destinations to hedge their investment risk as an alternative to China, which up till then had been the primary destination for their investments (Pattnaik 2006). These developments led to a significant surge in the trade volume between the two sides. Between 1998 and 2008, the value of Indian exports to Korea rose from a mere US$307.78 million to US$3,768.11 million. On the other hand, Indian imports from Korea increased from US$1,395.68 million to US$8,350.47 million during the same period (UNCOMTRADE database, accessed 9 January 2010).

Presently, India ranks 11th among the largest export destinations and 16th among sources of imports for the Korean economy.[3] The surge in bilateral trade relations between the two economies can be attributed to several factors in recent years, including a substantial increase in Indian per capita income, a continued reduction in trade barriers, increasing intra-industry trade and trade complementarity between the two economies. For instance, the trade complementarity index of India with Korea has increased from below 38 percent in 1995 to about 60 percent in 2006. This indicates that India-Korea export-import structures are increasingly becoming compatible with each other, which is likely to benefit further the economic exchanges between the two economies (Sahoo et al. 2009a).

One notable feature of India-Korea trade relations is that the trade balance has always been in favour of Korea and has increased continuously during 1998-2008. As can be observed from Figure 1, during this period India's trade deficit with Korea grew by more than four times from US$1,087.90 million to US$4,582.36 million, and both exports and imports increased substantially after 2001 along with the trade deficit. The big trade deficit between the two countries can be partially attributed to the bilateral structure of exports and imports along with the faster growth in India's imports from Korea than in its

---

[3] http://www.andhranews.net/India/2008/January/17-China-Korea-30055.asp (accessed 15 January 2010).

exports to Korea. The Indian export basket to Korea is largely composed of low-value products, in comparison to the relatively high value-added products of its import basket.

Figure 1   India-Korea trade relations (US$ million)

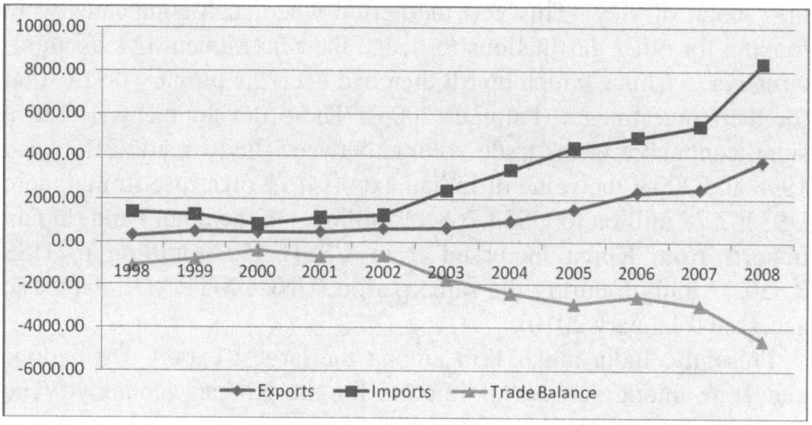

Source: UNCOMTRADE database.

Another important feature of the two countries' bilateral trade relations is that during 1998-2008 not only has the absolute amount of trade increased but the share of both countries in each other's total trade has also improved significantly, a recognition of the growing importance each country has in the other's economy. Korea's share of total Indian exports has more than doubled, having increased from 0.93 percent in 1998 to 2.07 in 2008. However, the Korean share of total Indian imports has declined from 3.68 percent to 2.82 percent during the same period. As Figure 2 demonstrates, Korea's share in Indian total imports has not shown any persistent trend and decreased till 2000 but then started rising and reached its highest level in 2004. After that it declined continuously before marginally increasing in 2008. By contrast, Korea's share in India's total exports has shown a lasting trend and improved continuously during the 1998-2008 period.

During the period 1998-2008, India became an increasingly more important trading partner for Korea. India's share in total Korean exports and imports grew continuously, rising from 1.12 and 0.35 percent in 1998 to 1.99 and 0.87 percent respectively in 2008. As

Figure 3 shows, there was a remarkable growth in India's share in total Korean exports and imports after the year 2000.

Figure 2   Korea's share (in %) in India's total merchandise exports and imports

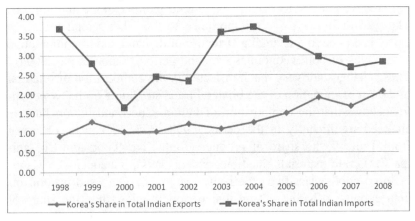

Source: UNCOMTRADE database.

Figure 3   India's share (in %) in Korea's total merchandise exports and imports

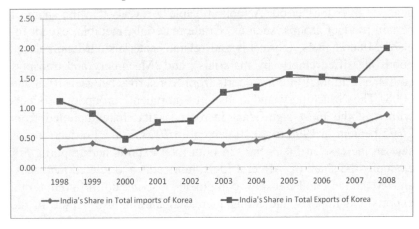

Source: UNCOMTRADE database.

It is evident from the preceding discussions that not only did the absolute size of exports and imports between the two countries increase during 1998 to 2008 at a rapid pace, but the share each country has in the other's total exports and imports has also expanded significantly. Although India's share in total Korean exports and imports is growing, it is well below Korea's place in total Indian exports and imports. The growth in each one's importance to the other's total trade has partly been due to a changing structure of demand and to comparative advantages of both economies over the period (Sahoo et al. 2009a).[4] These changes are very much reflected in the composition of bilateral trade. An examination of the bilateral trade structures of the two countries shows that the composition of Indian export and import baskets changed significantly in the period 1998-2008. As can be observed from Table 5, the share of product groups like 'Food and live animals', 'Crude materials, inedible, except fuels', 'Chemicals', 'Manufactured goods classified chiefly by materials', decreased in total Indian exports to Korea during that period. Against that, the share of product groups such as 'Mineral fuels, lubricants and related materials', 'Machinery and transport equipment' and 'Animal and vegetable oils and fats' increased substantially during the same period. The most dramatic increase was found in the 'Mineral fuels, lubricants and related materials' group, the share of which rose from a mere 0.01 percent in 1998 to 41.26 percent in 2008.

Similarly the composition of India's imports from Korea also changed over the period. A look at Table 5 reveals that the share of certain product groups, such as 'Crude materials, inedible, except fuels', 'Mineral fuels, lubricants and related materials', 'Manufactured goods classified chiefly by materials', and 'Machinery and transport equipment' in total Indian imports from Korea rose between 1998 and 2008. The 'Machinery and transport equipment' group of products witnessed the most significant increase as its share mounted from 26.75 percent in 1998 to 40.40 percent in 2008. Some product groups saw an increase in their share in both total exports and imports. For example, the share of 'Mineral fuels, lubricants and related materials' and 'Machinery and transport equipment' rose in both of India's total exports and imports, indicating increased intra-industry trade in the sector (Sahoo et al. 2009a). As is noted in Section 3.1 below, these

---

[4] This is truer in the case of India, where the rate of change has been faster compared to Korea.

sectors are among the most important attracting a maximum amount of Korean FDI in India, which further strengthens the case for developing intra-industry trade between sectors.

Table 5 Composition of India's exports to and imports from Korea between 1998 and 2008

Product group	Exports		Imports	
	1998 (Share %)	2008 (Share %)	1998 (Share %)	2008 (Share %)
Food and live animals	20.57	8.89	0.05	0.02
Beverages and tobacco	0.02	0.79	0.00	0.00
Crude materials, inedible, except fuels	10.05	5.21	2.56	3.18
Mineral fuels, lubricants and related materials	0.01	41.26	2.67	9.09
Animal and vegetable oils and fats	0.33	0.60	0.05	0.00
Chemicals	20.58	9.30	20.63	11.37
Manufactured goods classified chiefly by materials	41.61	24.60	23.83	26.77
Machinery and transport equipment	4.31	7.03	26.75	40.40
Miscellaneous manufactured articles	2.16	0.82	3.25	2.82
Commodities & transactions not classified elsewhere	0.36	1.48	20.24	6.34

Source: UNCOMTRADE database.

2.3.2 *Trade in services*

As the share of services in world GDP has grown, along with increased tradability,[5] the international trade in services has also augmented. Drawing on abundant and competitive human resources and a booming information technology (IT) industry, India has become a crucial player in the world trade in services. In the last few years the

---

[5] The increasing use of IT in the world economy has made many services, such as banking and data entry, more tradable.

export of commercial services from India has been surging ahead. The total export of commercial services from India grew from US$16.0 billion in 2000 to US$102.6 billion in 2008. India's share in the world export of services has also increased rapidly. Both the export and the import of services are rising at a fast rate. One of the principle reasons for India's spectacular performance in global services trade is that the services sector has been the fastest growing segment of India's GDP over the last two decades. Growth is attributed to both demand and supply factors. As both GDP and per capita income have progressed, the demand for many services has become elastic, and with an increasing degree of economic reforms in the country the Indian economy has shown significant dynamism (De and Raychaudhury 2008).

Korea is also an important player in the international trade in services. During the period 1998-2008, although the total value of its services exports has increased, its share in world exports has remained constant at around 2.0 percent, with some fluctuations. Contrary to merchandise trade, where Korea ranks ahead of India, in services India has been doing impressively well. In 2008, India was the 9th largest exporter and 13th largest importer of commercial services in the world, whereas Korea's position was 16th and 10th respectively in world exports and imports of services (WTO International Trade Statistics 2009). It is notable that India's performance in the export of global services is not driven by traditional service sectors such as transport, travel and tourism, but by advanced service sectors such as computer and information services. For instance, with a share of more than 17 percent in the world export of computer and information services, in 2007 India was the second exporter in the world after the EU (WTO International Trade Statistics 2009).

Data are lacking for bilateral trade in services between India and Korea, but given the expanding share of services in the GDP of both countries and the growing importance of India as a services exporter in the world, it can be conjectured that trade in services between the two countries must be increasing rapidly, at least in some sub-sectors, especially in IT/software services and travel services. According to the Electronic and Computer Software Export Council of India, software exports from India to Korea in 2001-02 were US$27.53 million compared to US$8.67 million in 2000-01.[6] Industry sources report that

---

[6] http://www.expresscomputeronline.com/20021216/newsan1.shtml (accessed 15 January 2010).

Korea is not only a market for Indian software companies but it can also be utilised as a platform to establish a stronger presence in the Asia-Pacific Economic Cooperation region.[7]

Table 6   Export of commercial services

		2000	2001	2002	2003	2004	2005	2006	2007	2008
Global exports (US$ billion)		1,481.3	1,484.4	1,596.4	1,832.4	2,220.7	2,480.3	2,816.9	3,372.4	3,777.9
Exports (US$ billion)	India	16.0	16.8	19.1	23.6	37.9	52.2	70.9	87.5	102.6
	Korea	29.7	28.1	27.3	31.8	40.5	43.7	48.4	61.7	74.1
Rate of growth (year-on-year) of exports (%)	India	-	4.8	13.8	23.6	60.5	37.6	35.9	23.4	17.3
	Korea	-	-5.5	-2.7	16.1	27.6	7.9	10.7	27.6	20.1
	Korea	2.0	1.9	1.7	1.7	1.8	1.8	1.7	1.8	2.0

Source: WTO International Trade Statistics, various issues.

3   INDIA-KOREA INVESTMENT RELATIONS

3.1   Korean investment in India

The continued economic reforms in India since the early 1990s have improved the investment environment for foreign investors. To attract foreign investment into the country the FDI regime has been continuously liberalised. The government has also provided encouragement in terms of tax incentives and tax holidays to promote FDI. To protect and promote the business interests of foreign investors, several bilateral investment treaties have also been signed with various countries. India has become a member of the multilateral investment guarantee agency (Goldar and Banga 2006). Sensing the opportunity in the Indian economy, many Korean companies made an aggressive approach to the Indian market, and within a short period of time many of them

---

[7] http://www.expresscomputeronline.com/20021216/newsan1.shtml (accessed 15 January 2010).

became household names in the country. Presently many Korean enterprises such as LG, Samsung, Hyundai and others have not only established their presence but have been able to diversify their businesses in various sectors of the economy.

Data provided by the DIPP for the years 1991 to 1999 show that with a total investment of US$571.7 million, Korea's share was 3.56 percent of total cumulative FDI in India. As can be seen from Table 7, during the 1990s Korea made a substantial contribution to the total FDI received by India. After 1999, however, although the total amount of investment from Korea increased, its share in the total FDI inflow has decreased continuously and in 2007 reached as low as 0.35 percent of total FDI inflow into the country, with a marginal increase in 2008.

Table 7 FDI inflow (actual and approved) into India by year (US$ million)

Year (January-December)	Actual inflow			Approvals		
	From Korea	From all countries	Share (%) of Korea in total FDI	From Korea	From all countries	Share (%) of Korea in total FDI
Aug.1991-Dec. 1999	571.7	16,019.7	3.56	2,605.4	53,245.7	5.18
2000	17.7	2,873	0.61	9.6	4,008.6	0.24
2001	4.5	3,728.4	0.12	14.8	4,653.3	0.32
2002	37.8	3,790.7	0.99	6	2,303.8	0.26
2003	24.5	2,525.5	0.97	13.4	1,177.5	1.4
2004	26.7	3,753.4	0.71	3.5	1,900.3	0.66
2005	66	4,360.2	1.51	15.3	1,795.4	0.85
2006	64.7	11,108.4	0.58	23.1	5,111.2	0.45
2007	67.95	19,309.89	0.35	15.7	4,772.8	0.32
2008	148.10	33,039.8	0.44	0.0	9,685.8	0.0

Source: DIPP.

There also exists a difference between FDI approvals and the actual inflow of Korean FDI into India. As Table 7 shows, the Korean share in FDI approvals during August 1991-December 1999 was quite substantial, with more than 5 percent of total FDI approvals. This was in contrast to 3.56 percent in actual FDI inflow. Korea's share (both in actual inflows and approvals) has fluctuated during the post-1999 period and declined continuously after 2005, reaching, in fact, a zero share in total FDI approvals in 2008. According to one estimate, the average realisation rate for investments from Korea was found to be around 24 percent for the period 1991 to March 2003.[8]

Turning to the sectors in which Korean companies have been investing in India, FDI has reached some selected industries. Figure 4 shows the major sectors that have constituted the large proportion of Korean FDI and the share of the same sectors in total FDI in India. As the figure shows, the important sectors that have received maximum amounts of Korean FDI include the automobile and metallurgical industries, electronics, housing and real estate, and industrial machinery. However, if one looks at the composition of FDI directed from the world into India, the share of the above mentioned sectors is less than 16 percent of total FDI received from the world. This highlights how Korean interests are different from those of other countries investing in India. Furthermore, as many of these sectors also appear in top trading sectors between India and Korea there seems to be a correlation between the composition of India-Korea bilateral trade and the composition of investment. The sectoral composition of FDI approval for Korea in India is different from the actual inflow. For example the major sectors attracting FDI approvals from Korea were the transportation industry, fuels (power and oil refinery), electrical equipment (including computer software and electronics), chemicals, and commercial, office and household equipment.

---

[8] FICCI (accessed 2 February 2010).

Figure 4   Composition of FDI inflow into India from Korea and the world

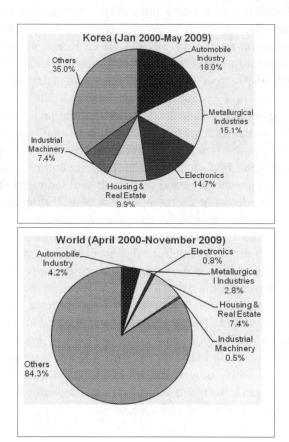

Source: DIPP.

3.2 *Indian investment in Korea*

In contrast to its trade performance, particularly in merchandise trade, Korea does not fare well in attracting foreign investment into the country. Korea scored poorly on the inward FDI performance index for 2005-06 and is ranked 130th (UNCTAD 2010). Although Korea is the 11th largest economy in the world and accounts for 1.8 percent of world GDP, it attracted only 0.8 percent of global FDI in 2005.[9] In comparison with other East Asian economies, Korean policy-makers give preference to loan-based investments over direct investment (Ahn 2008). For example, during the years 1962 to 1986, total cumulative long-term foreign capital in Korea amounted to US$49 billion. Of that amount, commercial loans and borrowings from development agencies represented 65 percent and 32 percent respectively, while FDI accounted for a mere 3.9 percent. The share of FDI inflow both in Korea's gross fixed capital formation and in its GDP has been substantially lower than that of the world and most of the East and Southeast Asian economies. For instance, in 2007, Korea's inward FDI as percentage of its gross fixed capital formation was a mere 0.9 percent, whereas the same for Malaysia and Singapore was 26.6 percent and 60.0 percent respectively. Moreover, although, after the Asian financial crisis, Korea switched to a more pro-active FDI regime, the ratio of inward FDI stock to GDP was still one of the lowest in the world, far lower, in fact, than the global average or that of developing economies.[10]

Following sluggish economic growth in the mid-1990s and the Asian financial crisis in 1997, Korea was forced to shift its policy direction from conventional loan-based borrowing to an FDI-based growth strategy (Ahn 2008). Korean policy-makers realised the importance of foreign investment in economic growth and enacted a new comprehensive foreign investment promotion act in 1998. This was to provide foreign investors with lucrative incentives, which include tax exemptions and reductions, financial support for employment and training, cash grants for research and development projects, and exemptions or reductions in leasing costs for land for factory and business operations for a specified period. Korea has also created several new institutions such as Invest KOREA and the Office of the Foreign Investment Ombudsman to facilitate foreign investment in the country. Presently, foreign companies play a pertinent role in the Korean economy and are recognised as an essential source of export growth. Korea has a liberal FDI regime which allows all kinds of FDI includ-

---

[9] http://www.keia.org/Publications/Insight/2006/december%2006.pdf (accessed 4 February 2010).

[10] For instance, according to UNCTAD (2008), the ratio of inward FDI stock to GDP for world, developed and developing economies was 27.8 percent, 27.2 percent and 29.8 percent respectively in 2007.

ing establishment, stock acquisitions, mergers, and long-term loans (WTO Secretariat 2004). FDI restrictions on most of the sectors are relaxed apart from radio and television broadcasting and rice and barley growing, which are completely closed to FDI. Some of the infrastructure sectors are also partially closed and have foreign equity limits (WTO Secretariat 2004). Although all these measures have induced foreign investment in Korea, inward FDI, as a percentage of both gross fixed capital formation and absolute amount, has decreased in the last few years. On the other hand, outward FDI as a percentage of both gross fixed capital formation and absolute amount increased during 2005-2007 (UNCTAD 2008).

The EU is the largest source of FDI to Korea followed by the US and Japan. In fact these three regions/countries constitute more than 80 percent of total FDI inflow to Korea (Ahn 2008). India's share in Korea's total FDI inflow is substantially lower. Although Indian investment in Korea is almost negligible, and India does not figure among the major investors in Korea, the growing prowess of Indian companies and their eagerness to expand their global presence means many Indian companies are establishing themselves in Korea through different means such as merger & acquisition. For instance, in February 2004, Tata Motors of Mumbai signed an agreement to acquire Daewoo Commercial Vehicles based at Kunsan in Korea at a cost of US$102 million.[11] The Indian IT industry sees a lot of opportunities in Korea and is viewed as a stable plank for those looking to establish a stronger presence in the APEC region. Some IT companies, such as Aptech, already have their centres in Korea.[12]

3.3 *Technical collaboration*

Technology transfer from the advanced to the developing world has been a major source of technology acquisition and upgrading for industries in the developing countries. In the case of India-Korea economic relations, Korea has been a major partner of India for technological collaboration. According to the DIPP, 230 technical collaboration projects were approved for Korea, which accounted for 2.85 per-

---

[11] FICCI (accessed 2 February 2010).
[12] http://www.expresscomputeronline.com/20021216/newsan1.shtml (accessed 4 February 2010).

cent of the total collaboration approved for the period August 1991 to March 2009. It is important to note that compared to its share in total FDI approval (2.90 percent) in India, Korea's share is slightly lower in technical collaboration. The highest number of technical collaboration initiatives has been in the transportation industry, followed by electrical equipment (including computer software and electronics) and chemicals (other than fertiliser).

Table 8 Share of top five sectors attracting technology transfer from Korea in India (August 1991-March 2009) (number of approvals)

Rank	Sector	No. of technical collaboration projects approved	% of technical collaboration projects approved for Korea
1	Transportation industry	57	24.78
2	Electrical equipment (including computer software & electronics)	48	20.87
3	Chemicals (other than fertiliser)	19	8.26
4	Miscellaneous mechanical & engineering	14	6.09
5	Metallurgical industries	13	5.65

Source: DIPP.

According to the Federation of India Chambers of Commerce and Industry (FICCI), there exists tremendous potential for enhancing technological transfers/collaboration between the two sides. Huge possibilities exist for Korean companies, and they can look at joint ventures as well as sub-contracting arrangements with Indian companies, especially in the small and medium enterprise (SME) sectors. Opportunities also exist for Korean SME companies to synergise with Indian SMEs in the areas of semi-conductors, plastics, auto parts, agricultural implements, textiles, multi-media, ceramic products, software, etc. Korean participation can also be invited in the special economic zones in India (Sahoo et al. 2009a).

Opportunities to set up joint collaborative projects between the two sides are specially high in the infrastructure sectors such as power, ports, telecommunications, ship building and ship repair, petrochemicals, automobile ancillary industries, electrical and electronics, office equipment, banking and financial services and software as well as iron and steel. Development of the Indian infrastructure is a high priority and requires both advanced technology and massive investment. Given the strong financial and technological capacities of Korean companies, there is great scope for them to participate in these projects. The participation of Korean companies in the Indian infrastructure sector has increased substantially in recent times. Out of 44 contracts awarded for the National Highway Development Project, nine have been won by Korean companies in collaboration with Indian companies or independently. Recently, Hyundai Heavy Industries won two mega-projects including a pipeline project worth US$600 million.[13]

4 CO-OPERATION AND FUTURE PROSPECTS FOR BILATERAL ECONOMIC RELATIONS

The increasing economic exchanges between the two countries have been accompanied and facilitated by various co-operative measures that both countries have taken to strengthen bilateral relations. Since the establishment of formal diplomatic ties in 1973, both countries have signed various agreements or treaties. To promote trade, investment and technical co-operation both countries signed an Agreement on Trade Promotion and Economic and Technical Co-operation in 1974. Under this agreement both countries provide MFN status to each other. Other important co-operation agreements include the Agreement on Co-operation in Science and Technology in 1976, a Convention on Double Taxation Avoidance in 1985, and a Bilateral Investment Promotion/ Protection Agreement in 1996, among others.

In August 2009, the two countries concluded a CEPA that covers trade in both goods and services, and investment. The agreement proposes the abolition and reduction of tariffs on 90 percent of Indian goods and 85 percent of Korean goods in terms of value by the end of

---

[13] http://www.economywatch.com/world_economy/south-korea/indo-south-korea-trade-relation.html (accessed 15 February 2010).

2019 (Sahoo et al. 2009b). This is likely to improve significantly the trade volume between the two economies. The CEPA proposes to reduce considerably the tariff rates on some of the products that constitute a major proportion of Korea's exports to India. These include products such as vehicles, rail- and tramways, and iron and steel. India is also likely to gain substantially in sectors like textiles and agriculture. Both countries have undertaken commitments to provide market access and national treatment[14] in several service sectors, such as professional services and communication and telecommunication services, a move likely to give a considerable boost to trade in services between the two countries. The CEPA also proposes to enhance services and investment flows by reducing distortions in trade and to facilitate co-operation in various sectors of mutual interest such as renewable energy, infrastructure and transport, and health care. It is expected that this agreement, along with changing demand and supply structures of both economies, will substantially improve the economic relations between Korea and India.

There also exists a synergy in the global and regional outlook of both countries. India and Korea are committed to enhance Asian economic integration and co-operation. To strengthen its engagements with East Asian countries India started its 'Look East Policy' in 1992 and Korea is regarded as an important partner in this process. The 'New Asia Initiative' of the present *Lee* Myung-bak government further underlines the importance that Korea bestows on co-operation with Asian countries including India. Both countries have also been active members of ongoing Asian economic integration and co-operation processes such as the East Asia Summit.

This article has shown how economic relations between India and Korea have improved continuously after 1998, driven mainly by the fast pace of growth in the Indian economy, structural changes in both economies and the rising trade complementarity between the two countries. As most of these factors remain strong, especially in India, bilateral economic ties between the two countries are likely to improve further.

---

[14] The WTO defines national treatment as 'the principle of giving others the same treatment as one's own nationals'.

REFERENCES

Ahn, Choong Yong (2008), 'New Direction of Korea's Foreign Direct Investment Policy in the Multi-Track FTA Era: Inducement and Aftercare Services', OECD Global Forum on International Investment, 27-28 March. Online: http://www.oecd.org/dataoecd/24/37/40400795.pdf (accessed 20 January 2010)

Cargill, Thomas F. (2009), 'The Impact of U.S. Financial and Economic Distress on South Korea', in: Korea Economic Institute and Korea Institute for International Economic Policy, *Korea's Economy*, 25, pp. 15-24. Online: http://www.keia.org/economy.php (accessed 28 January 2010)

Cheong, Inkyo and Jungran Cho (2009), 'The Impact of Free Trade Agreements (FTAs) on Business in the Republic of Korea', *ADBI Working Paper Series*, no. 156, October

De, Prabir and Ajitava Raychaudhury (2008), 'Is India's Services Trade Pro-poor? A Simultaneous Approach', *Macao Regional Hub Working Papers*, no. 16, December. Online: http://www.unescap.org/tid/artnet/markhub/WP/wp16.pdf (accessed 4 April 2010)

DIPP (Department of Industrial Policy and Promotion, Ministry of Commerce and Industry, Government of India). Online: http://dipp.nic.in/fdi_statistics/india_fdi_index.htm (accessed 15 January 2010)

FICCI (Federation of Indian Chambers of Commerce and Industry). Online: http://www.ficci.com/ (accessed 28 January 2010)

Goldar, Bishwanath and Rashmi Banga (2006), 'Impact of Trade Liberalisation on Foreign Direct Investment in Indian Industries', paper presented at CESS Silver Jubilee Seminar, 'Perspectives on Equitable Development: International Experience and What Can India Learn?', Hyderabad, 7-9 January. Online: http://www.ris.org.in/India_Globalisation_Impact_of_trade_liberalization_on_FDI_in_Industries_RBanga%20BN%20Goldar.pdf (accessed 4 April 2010)

Harvie, Charles and Mosayeb Pahlavani (2006), 'Sources of Economic Growth in South Korea: An Application of the ARDL Analysis in the Presence of Structural Breaks – 1980-2005', *University of Wollongong Economics Working Paper Series*, WP 06-17

Mohan, Rakesh (2006), 'Economic Reforms in India: Where are We and Where do We Go?', paper given at public seminar organised by Institute of South Asia Studies, Singapore, 10 November. Online: http://rbidocs.rbi.org.in/rdocs/Speeches/PDFs/74043.pdf (accessed 28 January 2010)

Pattnaik, Rohit (2006), 'India-South Korea: The State of Affairs', *IDSA Comment*, 22 September. Online: http://www.idsa.in/idsastrategiccomments/IndiaSouthKoreaTheStateofAffairs_RPattnaik220906 (accessed 2 February 2010)

Sahoo, Pravakar, Durgesh K. Rai and Rajiv Kumar (2009a), 'India-Korea Trade and Investment Relations', *ICRIER Working Paper*, no. 242

Sahoo, Pravakar, Durgesh K. Rai and Rajiv Kumar (2009b), 'Gains from India-Korea CEPA', in: *Foreign Trade Review*, 44 (3), pp. 57-78

Sohn, Chan-Hyun and Jinna Yoon (2001), 'Korea's FTA (Free Trade Agreement) Policy: Current Status and Future Prospects', Korea Institute for International Economic Policy, Discussion Paper 01-01

UNCOMTRADE (United Nations Commodity Trade) database. Online: http://wits.worldbank.org.witsweb (accessed 9 January 2010)

UNCTAD (2010), Inward FDI Performance Index: Results for 2005-2007. Online: http://www.unctad.org/templates/webflyer.asp?intitemid=2471&lang=1 (accessed 28 January 2010)

UNCTAD World Investment Report (2008). Online: http://unctad.org/en/docs/wir2008_en.pdf (accessed 2 February 2010)

WTO International Trade Statistics (various issues). Online: http://www.wto.org/english/res_e/statis_e/statis_e.htm (accessed 15 January 2010)

WTO Secretariat (2007), 'Trade Policy Review, India'. Online: http://www.wto.org/english/tratop_e/tpr_e/tpr_e.htm (accessed 28 January 2010)

WTO Secretariat (2004), 'Trade Policy Review, Republic of Korea'. Online: http://www.wto.org/english/tratop_e/tpr_e/tpr_e.htm (accessed 28 January 2010)

WTO Secretariat (2008), 'Trade Policy Review, Republic of Korea.' Online: http://www.wto.org/english/tratop_e/tpr_e/tpr_e.htm (accessed 28 January 2010)

World Bank (2009), 'World Development Indicators'. Online: http://web.worldbank.org/WBSITE/EXTERNAL/DATASTATISTICS/0,,menuPK:232599~pagePK:64133170~piPK:64133498~theSitePK:239419,00.html (accessed 15 January 2010)

ON THE TRAIL OF THE MANCHURIAN WESTERN

Mark Morris[1]

ABSTRACT

In recent years South Korean mainstream cinema has seemed to show a softening of mood towards the Korea of the colonial era. A variety of commercial films have portrayed a sepia-toned world of Koreans in snappy suits, broad-brimmed hats and slinky dresses managing to outwit the clumsy efforts of the Japanese to dominate their lives. Director Kim Ji-woon's film *The Good, the Bad and the Weird* (2008) shares some of the mood of colonial nostalgia and joins that lighter-hearted approach to the Korean past with the conventions of the action film. An all-Korean production, set in the wild west of Manchuria sometime during the colonial era, it is a clever mix of genres. Beyond that, however, *The Good, the Bad and the Weird* provides pointers back down the genealogical trail to earlier Korean/Manchurian westerns. A number of films made during the Park Chung-hee years were set in or near Manchuria of the colonial and wartime period. Made by skilled directors such as Im Kwon-taek and Lee Man-hee, they provided a sense of adventure and escape from the claustrophobic political and cultural atmosphere of those years, while associating the action film with serious questions of national and personal identity not always associated with genre entertainment.

1 PROLOGUE

'Manchuria offered the Japanese opportunities akin to what Americans had found in the great expanses West of the Mississippi.'
    Yoshihisa Matsusaka, *The Making of Japanese Manchuria, 1904-1932* (Matsusaka 2003: 397).

---

[1] I wish to acknowledge the great help and advice concerning illustrations that I have received from Rosanna Morris.

'... all of Manchuria is a very unsettled place. I can't help feeling that it's tremendously dangerous' // 'That's because a lot of different people are converging there.'

    Dialogue in Natsumei Sōseki's *The Gate* (1910).

'The visual motif of *The Good, the Bad and the Weird* is the image of men racing through the vast plains; we don't know why but they're racing relentlessly.'

    Kim Ji-woon in interview, 2008 (Kim Hyung-seok 2008: 135-6).

You run off into the future, and look at the past—do you run into the past and see the future? Running off into the future is not identical to running into the past; running into the future is running into the past.

    Yi Sang, 'Reflections on Lines 5' (1931).[2]

2 INTRODUCTION

Figure 1
KOFA exhibition 2008

In August 2008 the Korean Film Archive (KOFA) presented an unusual retrospective of Korean genre films. Publicity material (Figure 1) urged people to buy their tickets and 'Head for the continent' through this special exhibition of Manchurian westerns (KOFA 2008). The fourteen films ranged from the debut film of Im Kwon-t'aek, *Farewell Tumen River* (*Tumankanga chal ittgŏra*) of 1962, to the 1971 *Break the Chain* (*Soesasŭrŭl kkŭnhŏra*), one of the last films of Lee Man-hee (Yi Man-hŭi). The latter was one of the most significant directors of the 1960s and 1970s. While his films have yet to gain recognition outside the country, they are much appreciated by knowledgeable cinephiles and students within it. The former, Im Kwon-t'aek, is the best-known survivor of the film industry from the leaner, poorer, more censored days

---

   [2] Sōseki text from Rubin (2001: 372); lines from the Yi Sang poem 'Sŏnaekwanhan kaksŏ 5' (Reflections on Lines 5), translated from Yi (2004: 50).

before the arrival of the New Korean Cinema that has developed as a major cultural and financial force since the late 1990s. Not only did the retrospective offer a chance to see Im's very first film, two more of his earlier and rarely screened films were part of the same programme.

In terms of historical era, these Manchurian westerns were located in the 1930s and 1940s, when Korea was a Japanese colony and officially a part of the Japanese empire. Some of the action may be set in Korea, from Seoul to the borderlands near the northeastern provinces of China. Geographically and geo-politically, most of the action takes place over the border, in the area which in the West was often referred to as Manchuria and which Korean people, as Japanese people with the term *Manshū*, referred to as *Manju* (滿州).

3 THE GOOD, THE BAD AND THE WEIRD

Whatever the attraction these old Korean/Manchurian genre films might have for cinema buffs or film historians, the tactical and timely motivation for screening them in August 2008 was provided by a blockbuster action film that had appeared on hundreds of screens only the month before: *The Good, the Bad and the Weird* (see Figure 2).

In recent years, South Korean mainstream cinema has seemed to show a noticeable softening of mood towards the Korea of the colonial era. Films such as the spy-adventure pastiche *Once Upon a Time in Korea* (2008), the horror film *Epitaph* (2007), *Radio Dayz* (2008) or the 2009 hit *The Private Eye* portray a sepia-toned world of young Korean men in snappy suits and broad-brimmed hats matched by young women in slinky dresses, all managing to outwit, at least for a while, the clumsy efforts of the Japanese to dominate their lives. This is in marked contrast to films from only a few years before such as *2009 Lost Memories* (2002) or *Hanbando* (2006): the former portrayed a dystopic future in which Korea had been absorbed wholly within a victorious Japanese empire; the latter was a similarly dystopic, stridently nationalistic attempt to cast Japan as a villain blocking Korean reunification (Morris 2007, 2009).

One other film which might be added to this provisional list is the biggest of all films in 2008, *The Good, the Bad and the Weird* (*Chohŭn nom nappŭnnom isanghan nom*), directed by Kim Ji-woon (Kim

Chi-un). *The Good, the Bad and the Weird* was the number two hit at the South Korean box office in 2008, was chosen to represent the country at that summer's Cannes Film Festival, then went on to open the London Korean Film Festival. It evokes, albeit in helter-skelter fashion, a more cinephilic, colonial nostalgia rather than any sense of bitterness concerning the colonial past, and joins that lighter-hearted approach to the conventions of the action film, particularly the post-apocalyptic variety. In various interviews, Kim Ji-woon acknowledged his debt to films such as *Blade Runner* and *Mad Max* (Kim Ji-woon 2009; Kim ji-woon nd).

Figure 2
The Good, the Bad and the Weird

Story: Three characters become involved in a treasure hunt, following the uncertain information contained in an ancient map. The map is supposed to take the winner of this colourful, violent, full-speed competition to the location of the treasure hoard of the deposed Qing dynasty. The 'weird' character is played by Song Kang-ho (Figure 2, centre), one of Korea's most gifted comic actors; the 'bad' role goes to Lee Byung-heon (Yi Pyŏng-hŏn) (Figure 2, right), a major star of both film and television drama; the 'good' is played by the inexpressive but athletic Jung Woo-sung (Chŏng U-sŏng) (Figure 2, left). They careen through various encounters with one another, Chinese bandits and Japanese mounted soldiers. The bad character is the leader of a Korean-Chinese bandit gang, whom the black-clad Lee imbues with reptilian threat; he has been commissioned to find the map and treasure by a Korean collaborator with the Japanese colonial army. The treasure is also sought by some of the Korean Independence Army, who play a role in sending Jung's good bounty hunter on its traces. The weird character stumbles into possession of the map first, and only realises what he had after it has been stolen from him. The protracted ending of the film places the three characters, battered but still able to point their guns, in a final showdown at the site where the treasure was supposed to be but where they find nothing—or so they think.

An all-Korean production, set in the open spaces of Manchuria (and in reality, filmed at locations in western China) sometime during the colonial era, mixing together Korean outlaws, Japanese soldiers, Chinese and Russian bandits, *The Good, the Bad and the Weird* is a clever pastiche in genre terms; spectacular cinematography and the kinetic display of stunts, fights and chases predominate over narrative coherence. The film may have, as its title proclaims, connections closer to the cinema of Sergio Leone (*The Good, the Bad and the Ugly*) than to the Hollywood western. However, as the *Cine 21* reviewer Kim Hyaeri emphasised upon the film's release, *The Good, the Bad and the Weird* is also 'a genre film which carries on the bloodline of the Manchurian Westerns' of Korea's own cinematic past (Kim Hyae-ri 2008).

Kim Ji-woon was planning the sort of film spectacle he hoped to make, combining the more exciting, action aspects of favourite films—from spaghetti westerns or Sam Peckinpah's violent variations on the genre, to films mentioned above, *Mad Max* or *Blade Runner*—when he turned to sources closer to home. 'I found out that at KOFA [Korean Film Archive] there were in fact action films made in Korea in the early 1970s called 'Manchurian Westerns'. Watching those films, I realised that I must have seen them in my childhood; it convinced me that a Korean Western was possible, and that I could make it if the film were set in 1930s Manchuria' (Kim Ji-woon 2009).

4 REPRESENTATIVE FILMS FROM THE MANCHURIAN WESTERNS

4.1 *Lessons from popular culture*

Below, I will describe and comment on some representative works from the repertoire of Manchurian westerns, emphasising some of the things we can learn about Korean society, politics and history through the medium of popular culture. I think these old films are worth looking at in some detail for several reasons.

While *The Good, the Bad and the Weird* may in fact be a hodgepodge of many films and genre possibilities, it is a mistake to reduce it, as quite a few foreign critics and reviewers have done, to simply 'a remake of Sergio Leone's spaghetti western masterpiece *The Good, The Bad and The Ugly*, but given an Asian flavour' (Alexander Pashby: see Kim Ji-woon nd).[3] Nor is it entirely accurate to assert, as Korean film journalist Kim Hyung-seok has, that Kim Ji-woon's film is a 'Korean-style 'Manchurian Western' ... which is a copy of the spaghetti western which came from the classical western' (Kim Hyung-seok 2008: 40). Even the New Korean Cinema has a history, and some of that history is tied up with earlier decades of Korea's own film tradition.

A second reason to consider the earlier genre films is the dramatic if oblique angle they offer on the ideological climate and structure of feelings of South Korean life in the 1960s and 1970s, during which the first Manchurian westerns were produced. A big-budget film, backed by world-class technology and enlivened with locations in western China: it would have been an undreamed-of possibility within the narrower horizons of Park Chung-hee's country. What film-makers could accomplish back then, in their socially and geographically constricted spaces, was limited. While the films may have been set mainly in colonial-era Manchuria, they convey much about the longing for action, colour and freedom of movement of the society that produced and consumed them. In contrast, we can move from these old films to the blockbusters of today and take some measure of the changes that may suggest.

One last reason to consider the old Korean/Manchurian westerns is that it does not require the kind of effort it once took to see them. You can watch at least some of them seated at your computer. The Korea Film Archive (KOFA) has thrown open the doors. Their website, in both Korean and English, now allows video-on-demand (VOD) access

---

[3] One simple way to get a sample of UK and American critical opinion is via the website *Rotten Tomatoes*: http://uk.rottentomatoes.com/. British critics such as Philip French (*The Observer*) and Edward Parker (*The Sunday Times*) were generally positive if bemused. *The Guardian*'s head reviewer Peter Bradshaw agreed: 'Here is a real one-off: a full-blooded Korean take on the spaghetti western, complete with 10-gallon hats, repeater rifles and reach-for-the-sky shootouts.'

to hundreds of old 'classic' films and provides a service that allows cultural historians or just plain film fans to access the audio-visual past of South Korean popular culture. No other country has made available anything like this cinematic archive.[4] The kind of advanced technology that has allowed Korea to produce the blockbusters of the New Korean Cinema allows us to look back down the trail and take the measure of some of its humbler origins.

4.2 *Korean heroes, Chinese bandits, Japanese soldiers, patriotic armies and some very patient women, and horses, too*

4.2.1 *Farewell Tumen River*, director Im Kwon-t'aek, 1962, black and white (see Figure 3)

Figure 3
Farewell Tumen River

Story: An idealistic group of Korean students from Keijō Imperial University (Keijō being the Japanese name for colonial-era Seoul) decide to take action against their Japanese colonial masters. Their small band of Independence fighters (*tongniptan*) carries out sabotage on military installations. When the Japanese react, our hero Yeong-u (Yŏng-u) and his closest friend say farewell to family and girlfriends and head across the Tumen river into Manchuria in order to join up with the Independence guerrillas already there. On their way, they are helped by Korean villagers. But they need to move on, as the Japanese

---

[4] In referring to Korean films below, I will indicate those available for online VOD viewing by the reference '(KOFA VOD)'. (The English database provides less information, but still allows you to locate VOD films: http://www.kmdb.or.kr/eng/index.asp.) Unless otherwise stated, information on the films is based on my own viewing, or Korean-language material such as plot summaries, notes and commentaries found on the KOFA database pages(s) for the individual films, at http://www.kmdb.or.kr/. Where appropriate, and to simplify references, Korean interpretive material will be cited as '(film title, kmdb)'.

close in, beating and killing some of the farmers who aided them. Later, in Manchuria, when Yeong-u is wounded, he and his comrades are given shelter by a kindly Korean father and daughter, two isolated representatives for the Korean diaspora scattered through Northeast China. Our Yeong-u's girlfriend Kyeong-ae (Kyŏng-ae) makes a desperate bid to join him, after her evil collaborator uncle has betrayed Yeong-u's identity to the Japanese; they in turn torture the boy's mother for clues to his whereabouts; she dies as a result. The uncle, and eventually the Japanese *kenpeitai* military police and soldiers go on the track of Yeong-u and comrades all the way to Manchuria. Kyeong-ae is eventually forced to shoot her uncle to save her own life. All the characters and forces finally converge in a battle on the banks of the Tumen. After their dramatic clash, Yeong-u dies in the wounded Kyeong-ae's arms. She, his best friend and the friend's son are the only ones left alive of all the Independence fighters, their family members and Japanese soldiers.

Comment: This was Im Kwon-t'aek's first film as a fully-fledged director. Its success, some 90,000 admissions in Seoul alone, helped spur other directors and producers and Im himself to try their hands at something similar. Thus are genres born. Over the years, Im has tended to talk the film down. Back in the late 1990s he grudgingly agreed to have it screened for his friend, the doyen of Japanese film critics, Satō Tadao. Satō recalls the director declaring the film 'a waste of time' and being tempted to tell the man in charge of the screening to pretend that they could not actually locate the print of the film. Im found looking back down his own cinematic trail painful: he left the screening almost immediately (Satō 2000: 37-8).

Im had worked as assistant director to Cheong Ch'ang-hwa (Chŏng Ch'ang-hwa). Cheong was the single most significant director of action films in Korea during the 1950s and early 1960s. He later took these skills on to Hong Kong where he made an international reputation and better money. The martial arts 'classic' *Five Fingers of Death* (also called *The King Boxer*), which Cheong made for the Shaw Brothers in 1972, became a worldwide hit after Warmer Brothers released it across the United States. A year later Bruce Lee arrived on the scene with *Enter the Dragon*, and the martial arts/kungfu genre took off. Later, many Korean stuntmen and martial arts experts would dash, tumble, punch and above all kick (the t'aekwondo contribution to action films everywhere) their way thorough as least as many Hong

Kong productions as Korean ones. For better or worse, the 'kungfu' film always carried significant Korean cinematic DNA.

Im had been assistant director on Cheong's now lost *Horizon* (*Chip'yŏnsŏn*) only the year before his debut. The plot involved a young Korean patriot who leaves his country behind to join a partisan band fighting the Japanese in the Manchurian heartland around Harbin. With *Farewell Tumen River*, Im's contribution towards the proto-genre seems to have been to take the trappings of the patriotic action film confidently outdoors: rather than in the streets of Seoul or Harbin or in small farming villages set in a tame landscape, the action takes place on rough country roads and rugged hilly scenery, in a borderland with all that that suggests of freedom and possibilities of movement, where there is room for men to dash about on horseback with their insurrectionary heads held high. Above all, and most viscerally, it gives Korean men a chance to strike back against their oppressors.

Im also added a reasonable dose of romance and allows for gradations of both heroism and villainy rather than staging a one-dimensional showdown between thoroughly good Koreans and completely bad Japanese. That said, the Japanese officers, soldiers, *kenpeitai* and regular police plus yakuza gangs, who will punch, rape, shoot and stab the good people of Korea in most Manchurian westerns no doubt have their prototypes in works by Cheong and this debut success by Im.

The final battle scene includes an attack by Independence fighters zooming down a snowy slope, rifles blazing at the Japanese troops. The battle by the riverbank leaves bodies scattered all over the snow and ice. The Japanese soldiers seem almost as vulnerable and doomed as their opponents. Coming as they did only a decade after the end of the Korean War, these scenes of mutual carnage inflicted by Koreans and their enemies impressed audiences at the time. They are powerfully constructed and effectively filmed. It is of course unlikely that anyone could aim a rifle with any accuracy while travelling downhill on skies. The way the soundtrack music shifts to 'Auld Lang Syne' as requiem for the fallen strikes the wrong note for audiences now. We look back and see a twenty-five-year-old director still learning his craft.

4.2.2   *The Soviet-Manchurian Border* (*Somangukkyŏng*), director Kang Beom-gu (Kang Pŏm-gu), 1964, black and white (KOFA VOD)

Story: Towards the last stages of World War II, the Korean Independence Army in North Manchuria has been suffering defeats. The commander is forced to send his son and one other soldier into Harbin to attempt to rescue an important comrade from the clutches of the Japanese and to locate a box full of gold which they need to keep their struggle going.

When the plot to spring their comrade is discovered, they are rescued by a mysterious figure, half-gangster, half-patriot: Kwon Chunju (Kwŏn Ch'un-ju), played by Jang Dong-he (Chang Tong-hŭi). He turns out to be a former Independence fighter, brother-in-law of the commander's son, and had disappeared with a stash of patriotic funds several years before. He rescues only to hold captive his former comrades: it appears Kwon intends to keep this second load of gold for himself as well. In order to escape the Japanese security net around Harbin, he manages to enlist the aid of a band of bald-headed bandits; he will split the patriotic funds with them. The bandits ride into Harbin on horseback, firing submachine guns and rifles and swinging huge swords. Kwon hits the road, headed for the Soviet border, with the loot and his captives. He is in a more than average hurry, since not only has he infuriated the Japanese commander at Harbin, but he has cheated the bandits out of their share of the gold as well. There is a final battle, just after we have learnt that it was the bandit chieftain who actually stole the first pot of gold; Kwon had been tricked, and ended up taking to a life of crime, unable to face his comrades. Kwon shoots the evil chieftain, but his men eventually forgive him. With zeal they join Kwon and his mates to hold off an assault by Japanese troops who have tracked them to their hideout. They are almost overrun by the Japanese, but the Independence Army comes riding to the rescue. Too late, however, for Kwon; he dies surrounded by wife, little daughter and the patriotic soldiers, recognised as a true Korean.

Comment: Rip-roaring action, co-incidental encounters, plot twists, mounted bandits, reliably bad but believable Japanese opponents, the sultry café singer Kwon leaves behind, and the pretty, ever-patient wife who still cares—there is a kind of frenetic genius in the variety of elements crowded into two hours' worth of celluloid. The Manchurian western came up with a number ways of depicting not only the Korean settlers but also adventurers, gangsters and patriotic fighters in conflict with the Japanese rulers. As to who else belongs in the Manchurian landscape or in its towns and cities, the obvious answer would be the Chinese, the numerically dominant inhabitants, then as now. But the action film preferred its Chinese to come in bandit packages, or, as in this film, suggested that the Manchu or Mongolians might make a better, more primitive and scary alternative. The bald bandits of The Soviet-Manchurian Border are a strange hybrid: posited as archetypically autochthonous Manchurians (or maybe Mongolians?), but with hints of a wild band of North American braves on the loose.

4.2.3 *The Burning Continent* (*Pulpunnŭn taeryuk*), director Lee Yong-ho (Yi Yong-ho), 1965, black and white (KOFA VOD)

Story: Dong-min (Tong-min) (played by Jang Dong-he) is an undercover agent of the Independence Army. He follows a Korean spying for the Japanese from Harbin to Seoul, kills him and steals an important list of secret agents. A Japanese officer orders Ji-seok (Chi-sŏk), a Korean serving with the *kenpeitai*, to find the murderer and get back the list. Ji-seok goes in civilian clothes to Manchuria to infiltrate the Independence Army. He is befriended by Dong-min, but the latter's girlfriend suspects the new recruit is actually her long lost half-brother, abandoned years ago when her father left baby son and wife behind to work as a doctor for the patriotic forces in Manchuria. Dong-min tries to win Ji-seok over to the cause, and Ji-seok does waver but orders are orders. The two men fight it out on a cliff-top. Dong-min beats Ji-seok but sets him free, after informing him that the Japanese have killed his father. Ji-seok, reborn a patriot, volunteers along with Dong-min for a dangerous mission to blow up a bridge. Japanese soldiers almost foil the mission, but the Independence Army arrives in time. Ji-seok dies, grieved by his sister and niece. The music swells as Dong-min carries his lifeless body away from the battlefield.

Comment: A blend of spy thriller with just about enough outdoor locations and mounted soldiers to merit the Manchurian western label. While Jang Dong-he plays the patriotic soldier in the later parts of the film, earlier as undercover agent he adopts a civilian disguise that became a kind of Jang Dong-he trademark. Trilby or similar hat, sunglasses, bow tie, tweedy hunting jacket, checked trousers: the perfect sporty English gent out for a spot of espionage. This outlandish outfit, and the genre clichés of the 1960s action film it evokes, have been lovingly parodied by Ryoo Seung-wan (Ryu Sŭng-wan). His film *Dachimawa Lee* (tach'imawa li) appeared the same year, 2008, as Kim Ji-woon's *The Good, the Bad and the Weird*. It is much more faithful to the old genres, mainly the gallantry/chivalry variation of action film, with chunks of 'Manchurian' action thrown into the mix. No doubt this cinephilic faithfulness to now outmoded genre conventions, even presented in tongue-in-cheek fashion, is one reason, along with a relative lack of stars or a big advertising budget, the film failed at the box office.

4.2.4   *The Homeless Wanderer* (*Musukja*), director Shin-Sang-ok, 1968, colour and wide-screen (KOFA VOD) (see Figure 4)

Figure 4
The Homeless Wanderer

Story: A lone rider approaches an isolated farm house, seeking water from the well. He is fired upon by a resolute frontier woman who chases him off, but not before the stranger has befriended her little boy. Almost at once, the man is set upon by bandits, who take him back to their camp. The leader is an old colleague from his own outlaw days. The man, Jang (Chang), has been wandering Manchuria after a period of exile. When the bandits plan a raid on the family on the isolated farm, his conscience forces him to go to their aid. The man of the family is killed by the desperados; he entrusts wife and child into Jang's keeping. They wander to the woman's home village but are not welcomed there. They then put up at an inn, but the woman is almost raped by a drunken general, who is little more than a bandit himself. Jang finally finds the two a safe home with a family of kindly Korean farmers. When the boy falls ill from treatment he had received at the hands of the villains at the inn, Jang decides to go back to the bandits in order to earn money for medicine for the boy. He is wounded in the act of assassinating the general, and wanders once again, a price on his head. After a year he returns to the Korean farmstead, but the woman and boy are gone. She has married a warm-hearted widower and lives in the nearby town. He spies on her and her new family, then rides off into the Manchurian sunset.

Comment: Shin Sang-ok was the most significant film-maker of the 1960s. His studio, Shin Films, was the biggest and most successful production house, his wife and collaborator Ch'oi Eun-hee (Choe Ŭn-hŭi) (see Figure 5) his most reliable and bankable star. With *The Homeless Wanderer* Shin brought to the Manchurian western colour and wide-screen cinematography. He also decided to make a much more Western-looking Manchurian film than had been attempted before. There are plenty of horses, a variety of rugged landscapes, campfires, wolves that howl at night, guitar and harmonica music on the soundtrack. The homage to *Shane* (1953), one of the best-loved Hollywood westerns, is strongest in the opening scenes. The sight of Ch'oi Eun-hee stepping out of the small farmhouse, Winchester shouldered and ready to shoot, is memorable. Ch'oi is far removed from her usual *hanbok* or fashionable frocks, though still smart in frontier greens and browns. Shin Sang-ok did not have to jump squarely on the genre bandwagon, nor did he need to add too much by way of patriotism to his film. The importance of the Korean family is clear, yet the nationality of the villains is left rather vague. The story of a Korean widow and mother set adrift in a hostile world had many resonances for 1960s' film-goers. Here, melodrama has a landscape suited for cinemascope ambitions. The wanderer, played by another star of the era, Shin Yeong-kyun (Shin Yŏng-kyun), rides off into a sunset that Shin's long-lens photography makes almost beautiful enough to offset our hero's heartbreak.

Figure 5
Ch'oi Eun-hee

That the film is in a sense derivative of Hollywood westerns is obvious. But showing well-known actors doing a convincing job of acting out of their usual skins in a well-crafted, well-shot narrative film demonstrates that Korean film-makers, too, could do what Italian directors had been doing for a few years already: adopt the genre framework, costumes and props, and a natural landscape fit both for heroes and for wide-screen camera-work. They had the ability to throw on to the screen powerful, beautiful colour images holding briefly at bay the ever-encroaching competition of the small TV screen (albeit Korean television only encroaches on cinema through the 1970s) and were able to make action films sufficiently close to the Hollywood product to be recognisably the same yet different, global and local.

The fact that film-makers on the periphery of the older producers were vigorously reshaping the western in this era is partly due to the time-lag involved in developing film technology, infra-structure and capital. It is also connected to the slump in production at the Hollywood centre. By the early 1960s, American audiences and certainly American film critics sensed that the western genre was played out. Where Hollywood has turned out 54 western features in 1958, by 1962-3 the number had dropped to 11. In Italy, 'between summer 1963 and April 1964 ... twenty-five Western features were produced at Cinecittà', the great Roman film factory (Frayling 2006: 50). The Korean film industry produced in total less than two dozen Manchurian westerns. The subgenre never established anything like the hold that the melodrama, the historical film or, later on, Hong Kong-inspired action film had over audiences.

4.2.5 *Eagle of Wild Field* (*Hwangyŏŭi toksuri*), director Im Kwon-t'aek, 1969, colour and wide-screen (see Figure 6)

Story: A happy group of Korean farmers are gathered at their Manchurian homestead to celebrate the arrival of an itinerant photographer. But suddenly they are set upon by a dishevelled band of Japanese soldiers, lead by the mad-eyed Captain Yoshida. He rapes a young woman and looks on while his men take their turns, as he calmly composes a poem. They kill the entire family, taking one young boy with them. Jang (Chang) (played by Jang Dong-he), the husband of the woman, who is also the father of the stolen child, arrives to find a scene of carnage. He recovers a photographic plate that records the savagery, and sets out to revenge his people. Twenty years go by, during which he tracks down and kills three of the men. He finally locates the army unit in which Yoshida still serves. During these same years, Yoshida has raised the stolen boy as his own son, turning him into a merciless killer; he has told him that his Japanese mother was killed by bandits of the Korean Independence Army, who castrated Yoshida for good measure. Our hero, Jang, still seeking revenge, kidnaps the young man, Hundo (perhaps the Japanese name 'Hondo'?), not knowing this is his lost son. His father's brutality to a Chinese woman he has fallen in love with and other clues had begun to sow doubts in Hundo's mind about his origins and his loyalty to Japan. In a protracted final showdown, Yoshida connives to have Hundo shoot Jang, but that does not prevent both our hero and his son learning the truth of the lad's identity. Desperate when the man won't give up and die, Yoshida orders Hundo to shoot him again, but this time he turns the gun on Yoshida. Shot in turn by the last Japanese soldier still breathing after all the gunfire, Hundo dies in the arms of his real father Jang.

Figure 6
Eagle of Wild Field

Comment: Among the many Japanese villains carving their bloody path through Korean films of the 1960s and 1970s, the character of Yoshida is one of the most foul. Played by an action star almost as famous as Jang Dong-he, Pak Nou-shik (Pak No-sik) (see Figure 7), Yoshida's psychotic brutality, a penchant for watching his men rape helpless women, his alleged impotence and general all-consuming evil obliterate any sense of common humanity between the Koreans and Japanese who shared the space of Manchuria for many years. There may be something halfway serious going on as regards the theme of false paternity, some sort of phallic inheritance gone astray through

Figure 7
Pak Nou-shik as Yoshida

violence and greed. The final scene, with the patriotic *pietà* of Korean prodigal son reintegrated into the embrace of the nation, seems a somewhat bloodier version of the ending of *The Soviet-Manchurian Border*.

In his affectionate spoof of the old action films, *Dachimawa Lee*, Lee Seung-wan included a few parodic Japanese villains in uniform. In *The Good, the Bad and the Weird*, there is no major role for any single Japanese character. But plenty of Japanese suffer the old genre's pre-ordained fate. For the most elaborate of the many chase scenes in this film, one involving the three main characters, lots of bandits and what seems like half the Japanese cavalry of the World War II, Kim Ji-woon had a 30-kilometre road built for a specially equipped camera car to race along (Kim Ji-woon 2009). As it speeds along, the 'good' Jung Woo-sung rides in and out of clusters of mounted soldiers, eventually shooting down every single one—with some help from other characters—without suffering a scratch himself.

Im Kwon-t'aek has been frank about the kind of films he ended up making as the 1960s wore on, within a context of pressure for rapid production and the search for ways to cope with an increasingly strict regime of control and censorship imposed by the Park Chung-hee government:

> I shot five or six films a year. I could not think of myself as a man who could do positive things for society, a man with dreams and the means of realizing them. For me, there was no tomorrow. Just eat, drink, and shoot. Since I was making only B-grade movies, if I did an adequate job and the film did well in the regional box office, the distributors requested another one. Whatever the production company required, I would do it (Im 2002: 251).

Or, as Im put it more succinctly when reflecting on the great films he was able to make in later years: 'Lousy films had to come first' (Kim Kyung Hyun 2002: 19). We could add one other Im Kwon-t'aek film to the lousy list: *One-Eyed Park* (*Aekkunun Pak*). Part gangster film, part adventure-western, it was one of eight films the director ground out in 1970.

4.2.6 *Break the Chain*, director Lee Man-hee, 1971, colour and wide-screen (KOFA VOD) (see Figure 8)

Figure 8
Break the Chain

Story: A jeep surrounded by mounted bandits comes racing through a brown, barren landscape. Gangster and soldier of fortune T'ae-ho (played by Jang Dong-he) is chained to a wooden frame on the jeep. Another man waits in ambush: Kim Ch'eol-su (Kim Ch'ŏl-su), an undercover agent of the Independence Army, pretending to be a contract killer. Ch'eol-su guns down the bandits, but does not free T'ae-ho, whom he suspects of having some important information. T'ae-ho outwits him, knocks him unconscious and drives off in the jeep, still chained to a beam of wood. He and Ch'eol-su soon cross paths with collaborator-spy Heo Dal-geon (Hŏ Tal-gŏn). The three engage in a variety of betrayals and chases, on the trail of a valuable statue of Buddha. The statue contains a list of Independence Army personnel. Ch'eol-su seeks to find it in order to protect the Independence Army, the other two are out for personal gain. The local Japanese commander also wants the statue, so he and his men join in the hunt. Jeeps, cars, trucks and horses race about; late in the film, we find ourselves in a snowy landscape through which Japanese soldiers swoosh after our heroes and their allies in the patriotic army.

The climax is a shoot-out with the Japanese. The two potential villains finally side with Ch'eol-su and his armed comrades; the latter are led, it happens, by a pretty young woman the trio had competed for earlier in the film. When T'ae-ho and Dal-geon manage to capture the hapless commander, the Japanese are forced to back off. They retreat in ignominy after their commander botches his efforts at a face-saving *hara-kiri*. Yet T'ae-ho and Dal-geon decide not to stay with their new friends. As they ride off for more exploits and adventures (see Figure 9), Ch'eol-su makes up his mind to let the patriotic cause take care of itself, mounts up and dashes off to join them.

Figure 9
Ready to ride off

Comment: It is probably no coincidence that the poster for *Break the Chain* (Jang Dong-he in the middle) bears a more than passing resemblance to the poster for *The Good, the Bad and the Weird*. Kim Ji-woon singled this film out as the one Manchurian western that had most intrigued him when planning his own variation on the old genre:

> I enjoyed not only Leone's films but Italian Westerns from that period even in general ... The plot and the combination of the characters were influenced by the early 1970s action film Break the Chain, which I would characterise as a sort of Western. All the films I mentioned above were films I watched in my childhood. It's [my film's] not a homage to a specific film or certain film-maker (Kim Ji-woon 2009).

There is no doubt that, setting aside the value or quality of particular films, in the 1960s and early 1970s the South Korean film industry 'was one of the most profitable and active industries in Asia, producing at its peak from 1968 to 1971 over 200 films a year' (Kim Kyung Hyun 2002: 25). This level of production could of course generate problems: simplistic scenarios, little time for planning or rehearsing, and hurried editing. All of these production short-cuts leave their traces in the films I have been discussing. One other problem was the box office. Whereas novice director Im Kwon-t'aek's *Farewell Tumen River* was considered successful at 90,000 admissions, even the celebrity status of Shin Sang-ok and Ch'oi Eun-hee managed to produce only some 45,000 tickets for *The Homeless Wanderer*. The Korean Film archive registers less than 12,000 sold for *Break the Chain*.

These disappointing figures may accurately reflect the film's commercial failure. Certainly the critics, who usually valued Lee Man-hee greatly, did not much care for the film. KOFA summed up their reactions: 'It is not surprising that the film is considered something of a Lee Man-hee cult film. But the usual colouration of a Lee Man-hee film seems here blurred. This is because it is not like his artistic works of the latter half of the 1960s, where he went back to genres merely to make use of their forms. This is a genuine genre film' (KOFA 2006: 26).

4.3 Towards a genealogy of action heroes

4.3.1 Heroes and anti-heroes

Figure 10
Gallant Man

Jang Dong-he is the best known of all action heroes from this age of film-making. He was at home in the thriller or spy genre, as well the stay-at-home, urban variant of patriotic action film called most often by the Korean term *muh-yeopmul* (*muhyŏmmul*) (武俠物), or film of gallantry or chivalry. The 1969 feature *Gallant Man* (*P'altosanai*) (KOFA VOD) (Figure 10), generally taken as the successful starting point of this new sub-genre, starred Jang in a role he had been polishing in the more exotic settings of films such as *The Soviet-Manchurian Border* (see Section 4.2.2 above). When in the 1960s and early 1970s films about the Korean War became popular, though often through government sponsorship, Jang was kitted up and ready to fight.

Physically, Jang Dong-he was the most unlikely-looking of heroes (Figure 11). Film researcher Yi Ho-geol (Yi Ho-gŏl), in his notes on *Eagle of Wild Field*, has focused on the disparity, in contemporary eyes, between our expectations of a film hero and the reality of this far from handsome, dumpy, ordinary man:

He was taken as representative of Korean masculinity. It is interesting to ask, why on earth was he granted such a status? With his incongruous features, randomly wrinkled skin, peculiar eyes, excessively thick lips and heavy jaw. ... Perhaps in his image there is a blend of the gangster who seems like just an ordinary villain and that of the idealistic Independence fighter, as well as a sense of limitless human warmth and fierce cruelty. ... Koreans had a remarkably strong preference for anti-heroes in the historical images of Korean masculine genres. The colonial experience will have made a focus on anti-heroes unavoidable (*Eagle of Wild Field*, kmdb).

Figure 11
Jang Dong-he

Lee Byung-heon's character in *The Good, the Bad and the Weird* (see Section 3 above) exudes pent-up violence (see Figure 12). We are never in much doubt that he is the 'bad' one, certainly no hero, though his physique and bravado make him the most alpha of this almost entirely male cast. Jung Woo-sung's 'good' role seems tame in comparison. In contrast, Lee's villain holds the eye and seems closer to the real, focal character of the loosely-focused story. Had Kim Ji-woon decided to play things straight, rather than in post-modern pastiche mode, Lee's character had many of the ingredients of a convincing anti-hero.

Figure 12
Lee Byung-heon

Lee Byung-heon's well-chiselled body has become, like those of other young male leading actors, a major asset to his career. Men's semi-naked bodies, with dramatically defined arms and shoulders, pecs, lats and those all-important six-packs,[5] are be-

---

[5] *Ed*. Pectoral muscles, lateral muscles of the back, and rib and stomach muscles.

coming standard accessories in the once timid medium of television drama[6] as well the more adventurous cinema. Lee's more recent role in the spy-thriller drama *IRIS*, the big KBS drama series of 2009, seems to have been designed as much with his body as his acting skills in mind. Jang Dong-he would not fare well in this sexualised, body-obsessed climate. The actor who looks the most like Jang Dong-he, at least in physique if not in face, is the stocky Song Kang-ho—the 'weird', not any kind of hero.

4.3.2 *Nationalist resistance, South and North*

Nearly all Manchurian westerns leave a role for the Korean Independence Army. In *The Burning Continent*, important scenes are set at 'The Headquarters of the 17th Army of Liberation'; the uniformed men are organised into roughly company strength, and look much more like regular soldiers than the fur- and leather-clad scruffy heroes of Im's *Farewell Tumen River*. In the space of the first few years of the subgenre, the resistance guerrillas have taken on the allure of a proto-national army.

Far and away the greatest number of Koreans who took up arms against the Japanese in Northeast China during the peak years of resistance of the 1930s did so as members of the Chinese Communist Party (Lee Chong-sik 1983). In North Korea, it was precisely this struggle, suitably reshaped around Korean nationalism and the Kim Il Sung family legends, that became one central theme of film production for many years. It would not be too much of a stretch to suggest that an epic film such as the 1969 *Sea of Blood* (*P'ipada*) had some things in common with the Manchurian western. *Sea of Blood* depicts a small group of Korean villagers settled in Manchuria as they are attacked by Japanese troops when their men are suspected of organising a resistance movement. The father of one family seems to have been killed, and his wife is left to flee with her children. While an older son goes off to join the struggle, the youngest son is killed, bayoneted by a Japanese soldier. The main force of the plot invites audiences to follow this devastated woman on her journey to revolutionary consciousness and action. Scenes of isolated villages amid Manchuria's rolling hills and broad plains, secret meetings, sudden and savage attacks by

---

[6] For a good introduction to Lee Byung-heon's career and how it has been shaped by changes taking place in both film and television, see Russell (2008: 98-132).

the villains on the good people of Korea—there are obvious historical reasons that North and South should represent Korean experience of Manchuria through similar stories. Rather than offer an imaginary resolution to the contradictions and failures on the road to national independence in the form of last-ditch heroics by non-communist armies of independence—the kind of scene which rounds off a number of films in the Manchuria action genre—in the DPRK, a film such as *Sea of Blood* has a didactic political task to perform in emphasising 'the crucial impetus brought about by the leader to stir up the masses and instruct about the need to be engaged in a revolutionary struggle' (Lee Hyangjin 2000: 111).

The Manchurian guerrilla war could not be portrayed on a South Korean screen in any very realistic fashion back in the 1960s or 1970s, and has yet to receive serious treatment by South Korean film-makers. Yi Soon-jin (Yi Sun-jin), in his notes on *Female Bandits* (*Yŏmajŏk*), has noted how tricky in general the subject of nationalism could be for South Korean genre film-makers in this era. Films like the Manchuria westerns were criticised for their 'uncertain nationality' ('kukchŏk pulmyŏng'). Setting aside the gut-level ethnic-nationalism the term may have implied, it was not of course all that inaccurate. 'The space of 1930s Manchuria where Chinese, Koreans and Japanese all competed with one another cannot be resolved into any one "nationality"':

> Accordingly, it is significant that the films deal mainly with the armed struggle of the Independence Army. This is because, if representing the history of the Independence Movement shows us how the nation state of today came into being, the heroes we watch swaggering through the Manchuria of the Manchurian action films actually wage their lonely battles in order to overcome the condition of 'uncertain nationality' (*Female Bandits* kmbd).

So while the red guerrillas are absent, South Korean nationalism is always already present: most strikingly in the various battles of Independence armies of various shapes and sizes, iconically in the form of ever-present national flags, and perhaps most persistently in the form of the Korean family from which most dramas begin and in the embrace of which many conclude.

5 THE APPEAL OF GENRE FILMS

Seoul-derived statistics and Seoul-based critics may not be the best sources of information when it comes to judging the sort of popular culture represented by genre films. As Im Kwon-t'aek noted in the interview cited above, he was making his 'B-grade' films with the regional market in mind. At the beginning of the 1960s there were some 312 cinemas in the country, 56 of them in Seoul; by the end of the decade, the figures had doubled to 690 nationwide and 112 for Seoul (KOFA 2004: 193). Film-makers could try to get their films into first-run Seoul cinemas, but just as well aim for distribution through second-run theatres in the capital and major cities and the crucial regional cinema networks. (In 1968, to select one year in the middle of the Manchurian western era, there were 14 first-run, quality theatres in Seoul, 24 second-run theatres, and some 48 small third-run cinemas (KOFA 2004: 195).)

We know quite a bit about the people who made the Manchurian westerns and the actors who appeared in them, less about the people who bought the tickets. I think we can make a hypothetical sketch of this audience if we consider the way genre films came to be enjoyed in later years. An Jinsoo has written about the popularity of Hong Kong films during the 1980s. This popularity began on the margins, in the 'mini-theatres' ('sogŭkchang'): 'small, third-rate movie houses ... They are located on the outskirts of major cities and provincial towns' (An 2001: 112, n. 34). 'Unlike major urban theatres, where young females comprise the majority of the audience, the mini-theater audience is composed mainly of teen-aged males. Such an audience composition significantly affects the programming' (An 2001: 104-5).

Two general considerations arise if we posit, and there is anecdotal evidence that we can, the audience for these Manchurian action films to be largely made of young men and male teenagers. We know their popularity arose from factors other than those associated with mainstream films: 'Instead of an impassive, restrained realism, filmmakers present a caricatural version of the action that aims to carry away the spectator. A fight or chase is given a distinct, vivid emotional profile' (Bordwell 2000: 231-2). David Bordwell has even referred to the highly developed action skills of Hong Kong cinema as a form of 'kinesthetic artistry' (ibid.: 199). We can assume that in their era, the Manchurian westerns were experienced in just such a manner, viscerally, whether the action is hand-to-hand, foot-to-head or gun-versus-gun. Now, however, the fight scenes looks almost laughably old-fashioned, almost as old-fashioned as the rare love scenes in these films. The New Korean Cinema has made state-of-the-art kinaesthetic action one of the staples of its crime, action and historical genres. *The Good, the Bad and the Weird* belongs entirely to its own age in this respect.

If a young male audience was appealed to emotionally and physically by such B-grade genre fare, there was another level at which the films spoke to their fans that may be more significant in social and political terms. The ideological climate of the Manchurian genre can seem very contradictory: on the one hand, the films can project a kind of nostalgia for a colonial era that may have been worse, in the sense of conflict, violence and suppression of national identity, than the present, but did have a clear sense of good versus bad, Japanese versus Koreans. This seemed to mean all Koreans, though the only flags on display belonged to the Republic of Korea. The sheer fact of daring to be Korean could be an act of bravery.

On the other hand, if the national project which a film such as *The Soviet-Manchurian Border* prefigures was now beginning to be accomplished in the new society of Park Chung-hee's forced modernisation and police control—if this was actually *it*—then a young filmgoer might have needed all the escapism an action genre might have to offer. This was an era when actual travel outside South Korea was difficult. Few young people could afford it, and government policy was against issuing visas for men suitable for military service. The atmosphere was resolutely anti-communist and claustrophobic; the country sat like an island with one major enemy to its north, while north and west of that one, loomed China. Action genres offered escapism of the visceral type but also the imaginative and emotional variety as well, away from the realities of 1960s nationalism into the open spaces of a fictive Manchuria.

For this reason, critic and film-maker Kim Soyoung has emphasised the unpredictable, off-beat freedom implied by the ending of *Break the Chain*. Rather than joining up with the Independence fighters, the three protagonists ride off towards the horizon. One says cryptically, 'I have lived enough in the darkness. But now I follow the trail of the Sun' (Kim Soyoung 2007: 74). It may be going too far to see this conclusion not only as a lack of complicity with a conventional, happy patriotic ending, but as also an explicit rejection of the entire national project. Yet there is something refreshingly odd about the last scenes of *Break the Chain*. As the big showdown between the Japanese soldiers and the patriotic fighters kicks off, the two reprobates, T'ae-ho and Dal-geon, are busy with their own punch-up, biffing away at one another at the bullets whiz past. In is almost as an afterthought, just for a lark, that they break off and defeat the Japanese soldiers, showing the young Independence fighters how real men sort things out.

6 RUNNING INTO THE FUTURE: SOME CONCLUSIONS

The lines of poetry I cited from a poem of Yi Sang (1910-37) at the beginning of this article are cryptic. Yet from this poem and from other poems and stories by him such as 'Wings' ('Nalgae', 1936), most readers can readily detect a sense of entrapment, blockage, past and present circling around one another: states of existential tension and frustration that seem entirely appropriate to the keenest poetic sensibility of the colonial era. There may be something similar about the way many Manchurian westerns repeated their simple tales of nationalism vindicated and patriarchy justified, even when the hero's death meant the Korean family would have to be reconstructed, alongside the nation, in an uncertain future. For audiences sitting in the future of the 1960s and 1970s, the films could provide symbolic mediation, offer an entertaining way of running back into that cinematic past all the better to accept the nationalist imperative, or even a symbolic way of running away from Korea's well-policed modernisation inside the space of one's own imagination. In this sense, we may find these films old-fashioned and crudely filmed, but it would, I think, be a mistake to discount them as mere entertainment. In so many words, it is often the case with popular culture that there is something at stake, socially and politically, in mere entertainment.

If we make our own brief dash back to the 2008-present of *The Good, the Bad and the Weird*, I hope that the above discussion of the old genre films has made at least one point: Kim Ji-woon's blockbuster may assemble a bricolage of many films, but it does also connect with elements of Korea's own cinematic past. Still, the extraordinary social and political changes in South Korea, the growth of film and television into large complex industries, revolutions in visual-digital technologies, and growing sophistication in training for film directors and crews—all these mean that this up-dated version of a Manchurian western has been made and watched by people with very different experiences and expectations from the generation of their parents and grandparents. Kim Ji-woon may borrow, as do some of his contemporaries, from old genres, but he is very firmly situated in the generation of New Korean Cinema:

> Youth-oriented, genre-savvy, visually sophisticated and not ashamed of its commercial origins, the New Korean Cinema ... [is] perceived as something entirely different from the works that preceded it (Paquet 2009: 63).

I noted above that *The Good, the Bad and the Weird* had sold some seven million tickets. In 1971, the year that *Break the Chain* sold its meagre 12,000 tickets, admissions for all of Seoul added up to not much more than 12 million (KOFA 2004: 218). Not just Lee Man-hee's career but the whole industry was in a major slump from which it never really re-emerged until the late 1990s. Such has been the escalation of box-office numbers, however, since the late 1990s that seven million is no longer the mark of a hit. The new target is 10 million and counting, and that is because of the rising expenses involved in making big-budget, spectacular films. For all the successes of the new film industry, 2008 was felt to be a cinematic recession. There were 60 million admissions for the year, yet only seven films broke even out of an already reduced 40 features, down from over 100 annually in previous years (KOFIC 2008: 7). In financial terms, the seven-million tickets did not make Kim Ki-woon's film a success; it failed to break even. So the 2008 film unluckily has that also in common with the 1971 *Break the Chain*.

The fact the Kim Ji-woon took a full film crew, main actors and stuntmen all the way to western China for extensive location shooting is one sign of the ambitions and scale of investment of a major South Korean production nowadays—or at least before the cinematic recession of 2008, which preceded the one we are in now, in 2010. The Manchurian westerns had all been shot inside South Korea. Finding suitable locations was easier then: 'action films which sought to adapt ... popular Western genres [were] on a low budget, and thus often told their stories while setting the fields of the Apgujeong region—now a forest of apartments in modern-day Seoul—as Manchuria or using some deserted night street in Seoul to represent Hong Kong' (Kim Young-jin 2008: 16).

The Good, the Bad and the Weird shares little of the overt nationalism or the kinds of concerns with family and patriarchy displayed, often in a heavy-handed way, in the old genre films. The Independence Army does make a come-back in brief sections of the film, particularly in the full Korean release. Kim nevertheless less edited out one extensive patriotic back-story about the Independence Army in the slight shorter international version of the film, perhaps in recognition of how unlikely it would be for foreign audiences to understand such an element of genre nostalgia.

It seems clear that however sophisticated the technology behind its staging and cinematography, and despite a lengthy shoot in China, *The Good, The Bad and the Weird* may not have come a long way in the depiction of non-Koreans from the attitudes on display in some of the old films. As Kim Kyu Hyun (2008) pointed out, disagreeing with certain claims made about the film's success in finally escaping the burden of stereotypical nationalism:

> Song Kang-ho [the 'weird' character] does mumble something about how the *yangban* aristocrats and Japanese colonizers are hardly different from one another as rulers. But it really has nothing worthwhile or interesting to add about Manchuria as a multicultural, potentially subversive (fictive) space. In the end, [the film] reduces the Japanese opponents (along with Chinese bandits) to straw figures to be mowed down.

Kim Ji-woon has explained that, while recognising Manchuria as 'a melting pot of all races and various cultures...Manchuria was attractive cinematically as this lawless world. All this helped my imagination' (Kim Ji-woon 2009). Such a 'postmodern space', as he conceived it, allowed him to bring together costumes or sets derived from 1930s Northeast China with action films such as *Star Wars* or *Blade Runner* or allusions to older Korean films.

Play with genre conventions or clichés, knowing references to other films, focus on physical speed, the mastery of bodily movement, balletic violence, gymnastic camera-work—in form and content Kim's film inhabits its post-modern space with such panache that criticisms such as Kim Kyu Hyun's may sound hopelessly 'modern', concerned as they are with less playful, historically far from transcended aspects of representing one's others. Kim Hyae-ri (2008) makes a subtler point, but one that goes directly to one weakness of the self-consciously post-modern play with genre and action common in much contemporary film-making. I will conclude with her verdict:

> What [Kim's film] lacks is not a sense of speed but any clear sense of direction. The real intentions of the 'good' remain unclear to the end; the motives of the three characters collide, while the contrived ending is fairly uncertain. The way things happen the psychological catharsis which a conclusion would give seems weak. Psychology and narrative are by no means things distinct from the explosive power of action. Only when the motives of the characters grab the audience and the importance of the situation holds them is the pleasure of action fulfilled.

References

An, Jinsoo (20010, 'The Killer: The Cult Film And Transcultural (Mis)Reading', in: Esther C.M. Yau (ed.), *At Full Speed: Hong Kong Cinema in a Borderless World*, Minneapolis and London: University of Minnesota Press, pp. 95-113

Bordwell, David (2000), *Planet Hong Kong: Popular Cinema and the Art of Entertaining*, Cambridge MA: Harvard University Press

Frayling, Christopher (2006), *Spaghetti Westerns: Cowboys and Europeans from Karl May to Sergio Leone*, London: I. B. Tauris

Im, Kwon-t'aek (2002), 'An Interview with Im Kwon-taek', in: David E. James and Kim Kyung Hyun (eds), *Im Kwon-taek: The Making of a Korean National Cinema*, Detroit: Wayne State University Press, pp. 247-65

Kim, Hyae-ri (2008), 'Manchuwesŭt'on hyŏlmaegŭl innŭ changrŭl: *Chohŭn nom nappŭn nom isanghan nom*' ['The Good, the Bad and the Weird': a genre film which carries on the bloodline of the Manchurian westerns], in: *Cine 21*, 16 July 2008. Online: http://www.cine21.com/Article/article_view.php?mm=002001001&article_id=52098

Kim, Hyung-seok (2008), KIM Jee-woon, series Korean Film Directors, Seoul: Korean Film Council

Kim, Ji-woon (nd), '*The Good, The Bad and The Weird*: Interview', with Andrew Pashby. Online: http://www.lovefilm.com/features/detail.html?section_name=interview&editorial_id=9557

Kim, Ji-woon (2009), 'Web Exclusive: East Meets West', interview by James Bell. Online: http://www.bfi.org.uk/sightandsound/feature/49513

Kim, Kyu Hyun (2008), '*The Good, The Bad and The Weird*', review. Online: http://www.koreanfilm.org/kfilm08.html

Kim, Kyung Hyun (2002), 'Korean Cinema and Im Kwon-taek: An Overview', in: David E. James and Kim Kyung Hyun (eds), *Im Kwon-taek: The Making of a Korean National Cinema*, Detroit: Wayne State University Press, pp. 19-46

Kim, Soyoung (2007), 'Geo-Political Fantasy and Imagined Communities: Continental (Manchurian) Action Films during the Cold War', in: *2007 Trans: Asia Screen Culture Conference*, Seoul: Korean National University of Art, pp. 62-83

Kim, Young-jin (2008), *RYOO Seong-won*, series Korean Film Directors, Seoul: Korean Film Council

KOFA (2004), *Hanguk yŏnghwasa kongbu* [Korean film: studies], Seoul: KOFA

KOFA (2006), 'Imanhŭi kamdokchŏnjakchŏn, yŏnghwach'ŏnjae imanhŭi'[Exhibition of the complete films of Lee Man-hee: Film prodigy Lee Man-hee], Seoul: KOFA

KOFA (2008), Publicity brochure 'Taeryukhang t'ik'esŭl kkŭnhora! Manjuwesŭt'on t'ŭkbyŏlchŏn' [Buy up tickets for a journey to the continent! Special exhibition of Manchurian westerns], Seoul: KOFA

KOFIC (2008), *Korean Cinema 2008*, Seoul: Korean Film Council

Lee, Chong-sik (1983), *Revolutionary Struggle in Manchuria: Chinese Communism and Soviet Interest, 1922-1945*, Berkley CA and London: University of California Press

Lee, Hyangjin (2000), *Contemporary Korean Cinema: Identity, Culture, Politics*, Manchester and New York: University of Manchester Press

Matsusaka, Yoshihisa Tak (2003), *The Making of Japanese Manchuria, 1904-1932*, Cambridge MA: Harvard University Press

Morris, Mark (2007), 'The Political Economy of Patriotism: the Case of *Hanbando*', in: Rüdiger Frank, James E. Hoare, Patrick Köllner and Susan Pares (eds), *Korea Yearbook 2007: Politics, Economy and Society*, Leiden and Boston: Brill, pp. 215-34

Morris, Mark (2009), 'Melodrama, Exorcism, Mimicry: Japan and the Colonial Past in the New Korean Cinema', in: Jonathon D. Mackintosh, Chris Berry and Nicola Liscutin (eds), *Cultural Studies and Cultural Industries in Northeast Asia: What a Difference a Region Makes*, Hong Kong: University of Hong Kong, pp. 195-211, 270-74

Paquet, Darcy (2009), *New Korean Cinema: Breaking Waves*, London and New York: Wallflower Press

Rubin, Jay (2001), 'Sōseki', in: Jay Rubin (ed.), *Modern Japanese Writers*, New York and London: Charles Scribner's Sons, pp. 349-84

Russell, Mark James (2008), *Pop goes Korea: Behind the Revolution in the Movies, Music, and Internet Culture*, Berkeley CA: Stone Bridge Press

Satō, Tadao (2000), *Kankoku eiga no seishin: Im Kwon-t'aek kantoku to sono jidai* [The spirit of Korean cinema: Director Im Kwon-t'aek and his era], Tokyo: Iwanami Shoten

Yi, Sang (2004), *Isangchŏnjip 2 si sup'il sŏgan* [Collected works of Yi Sang, 2], Seoul: Garam Kihweik

All online sources accessed during April 2010.

WEBSITES

Daum (film): http://movie.daum.net/
Korean Film Archive (KOFA) 한국영상자료원
    Korean database: http://www.kmdb.or.kr/
    English database: http://www.kmdb.or.kr/eng/index.asp
Koreanfilm.org: http://www.koreanfilm.org/
Rotten Tomatoes: http://uk.rottentomatoes.com/

A META-ANALYSIS OF NORTH KOREANS MIGRATING TO CHINA AND SOUTH KOREA

Daniel Schwekendiek

ABSTRACT

While North Korea was celebrating the 65th birthday of its leader Kim Jong Il in 2007, the 10,000th North Korean was arriving in Seoul. Some ten thousand further North Koreans are illegally residing in China. This article provides a meta-analysis of comprehensive surveys carried out among North Koreans in China and South Korea. It seems that women are disproportionably under-represented in surveys conducted in China compared to those carried out in South Korea, a divergence that calls for further investigations. Yet, thanks to governmental raw data used in this article, the following paper satisfactorily depicts the migration pattern to South Korea up until 2007. These migrants lived for long periods of time in transit countries after having left North Korea at the peak of the famine. Overall, 76 percent to 84 percent came from the northeastern provinces bordering China, indicating that travel distance and information networks are major determinants for defection to both China and South Korea. Because most migrants residing in China would prefer to live in South Korea, the country should prepare for a further massive influx of North Koreans who will sooner or later be heading towards it.

1 INTRODUCTION

Ironically, while the Democratic People's Republic of Korea (DPRK—North Korea) was celebrating the 65th birthday of its leader Kim Jong Il in 2007, the 10,000th North Korean was arriving in Seoul (*JoongAng Ilbo* 2007). According to the Ministry of Unification of the Republic of Korea (ROK—South Korea), 11,641 North Koreans entered South Korea from 1990 to 2007, whereas only 607 came during the Cold War (see Table 1, below). Indeed, the rate of North Korean migrants to the South has recently surged to about 3,000 per year

(*Chosun Ilbo* 2008), with North Koreans emerging as a dynamic diaspora group in South Korea.

Table 1 Inflow of North Koreans to South Korea

Period	Persons	Persons
Before 1970	485	
1970-1979	59	
1980-1989	63	
Subtotal Cold War era	607	607
1990-1993	34	34
1994-1998	305	306
1999-2001	1,043	1,043
2002	1,139	1,138
2003	1,281	1,281
2004	1,894	1,894
2005		1,383
2006		2,018
2007		2,544
Subtotal post-Cold War era	5,696	11,641
Total all periods	6,303	12,248

Source: Lankov (2006) (second column); Bidet (2009) (third column).

Not only have North Koreans massively migrated to South Korea, the majority has migrated illegally to China. Exact numbers are almost impossible to obtain. In the early 2000s, border guards once noted that 35 to 50 persons cross the frontier on an average day (Nanchu and Hang 2003: 115), while in 1997, other guards put the number at 2,000 (Becker 1996: 330). Frequently used figures for the North Korean population in China circulating in the media were 100,000 to 300,000 as of 2002 (Smith 2002), or 100,000 to 400,000 in the late 1990s (Shim 1999). More conservative estimations—often focusing on long-term residents—put this number at about 100,000 in the early 2000s (Lankov 2004), or 70,000 to 80,000 migrants including permanent residents and marriage migrants in 2005 (Smith 2005: 34). In the mid-2000s, a working figure accepted by the US State Department was 30,000 to 50,000, whereas the figure given credit by China was as low as 10,000 at that time (Margesson et al. 2007: 4). A North Korean official who had defected put the total number of migrants in 2002 at about 100,000 (Lankov 2004: 859).

In addition to the two immigration countries South Korea and China, a smaller proportion of North Koreans is hiding in other countries in the region such as Cambodia, Laos, Vietnam, Thailand and Burma (Margesson et al. 2007: 14). Estimates are again hard to make, but their number can be expected to be rather low because these countries try to maintain good diplomatic relations with both Koreas. Hence, they are not willing to co-operate much with North Korean illegal migrants, let alone that the local population does not speak Korean (unlike in China, where some two million ethnic Koreans with Chinese citizenship are living).

This article provides a meta-analysis of comprehensive surveys conducted among North Korean migrants by assessing their socio-economic profile and basic sample characteristics. Given the aforementioned migration pattern to South Korea and China, the article focuses on respondents interviewed in these two immigration countries only. After examining the course of North Korean migration to China and the ROK from the Cold War onwards, the paper first investigates major studies conducted in China. It then investigates studies published by South Korean researchers who interviewed North Koreans in Hanawon (a facility set up by the government for incoming defectors). A comparative meta-analysis is then attempted between the two groups of studies.

More importantly, this article analyses South Korean raw data that I was able to access in my previous work (Pak et al. 2010). The dataset stems from the South Korean government, which systematically interviewed all North Korean migrants on their arrival. Thus, as distinct from other studies drawing merely from non-random interviews conducted in Hanawon, I have made use here of information comprising the entire adult North Korean migration population arriving in South Korea.

2 THE POLITICAL ECONOMY OF NORTH KOREAN MIGRATION

2.1 *Terminology*

First and foremost, the terminology for North Koreans leaving their country must be examined. Terms such as refugees, fugitives, escapees, economic migrants, or asylum seekers are applied (Smith 2002). Certainly, these terms have a political undertone if not a humanitarian implication. South Korea encourages the use of terms such as defectors or, more recently, *saet'ŏmin* (new settlers), which is a more neutral term but has neither a humanitarian connotation. Article 3 of the South Korean constitution stipulates that '[t]he territory of the Republic of Korea consists of the Korean peninsula and its adjacent islands'. Thus, by law, North Koreans are considered South Korean citizens, which largely explains Seoul's political stance and its choice of terminology. A humanitarian, political and legal discussion on this dilemma would be far beyond the scope of this paper. In this article, I have therefore opted to follow Smith (2002) by simply applying the neutral term 'migrants' when referring to North Koreans leaving the DPRK—though I certainly do not intend to belittle the plight of North Koreans in China and South Korea.

From a legal point of view, North Koreans have hitherto not been considered as political refugees and hence are ineligible for official international assistance. China does not see them as refugees, arguing that many of them return to North Korea after getting food. More importantly, however, an official acknowledgment of such people as refugees will open the door to a massive influx of North Koreans, which is certainly not in China's interest. The international community, in turn, cannot help these migrants as long as they have not received refugee status from China. Thus, humanitarian workers (and missionaries) are operating illegally in China on business or tourist visas by working undercover and at night (Shim 1999). Although China has to return all North Korean migrants to the DPRK under the bilateral repatriation agreement of 1986, it more or less tolerates these migrants and relief workers as long as they do not cause trouble (Margesson et al. 2007: 11). Since about 2002, however, faced by intrusions of North Koreans into embassies and consulates within China that were backed by foreigners and reported in the Western media, China has started to crack down on these activities and has also enforced stricter controls at the border and inside the country. In 2006,

China even set up fences to protect its border to North Korea (Beck et al. 2007: 254.). South Korea likewise has no interest in granting North Koreans refugee status—for the same reasons as China—and also because these people are technically South Koreans (see above). Though it warmly welcomed any North Koreans arriving in the South during the Cold War—celebrating them as ideological defectors or as a unique source of information on the secluded North Korean society—the recent influx of thousands of North Korean migrants per year poses an increasing economic burden for South Korean taxpayers. It seems that the South Korean authorities have started to discourage if not even prevent North Korean migration, as it nowadays only appears to arrange exit trips for high-ranking defectors (Lankov 2004). In summation, those parties most affected by the massive exodus of North Koreans, notably South Korea, North Korea and China, all have a strong interest in denying North Korean migrants official refugee status for fear of further chain migration and the economic costs, a position that largely complicates the situation for relief workers and researchers. Most importantly, it has large negative consequences for North Korean migrants per se, especially for women and labour migrants, as they are often economically and physically exploited, cannot legally marry Chinese partners, and live in constant danger of getting caught and sent back to the DPRK where they face punishment.

2.2 *Historical migration*

In the past, emigration of North Koreans has been very difficult. In the Cold War era, not only did the government restrict permission for both domestic and international travel, it also insured that North Koreans leaving the country would not defect by holding their families hostage, or requiring them to travel in pairs to monitor each other.[1] Most importantly, the government sealed off its territory: the border to South Korea is almost impermeable because of barbed wire, mine fields and armed guards. Leaving the northern half of the peninsula via the coasts is 'riskier than crossing the Pacific Ocean by boat', as pointed out by a North Korean migrant (Nanchu and Hang 2003: 145).

---

[1] Such restrictions appear still to apply. Foreign diplomats who have lived within the past decade in North Korea have observed that officials sent out of the country for training must travel in pairs and that North Korean families posted abroad often leave one child in Pyongyang (personal communication with the author, 25 March 2010).

For ideological and logistical reasons, the 1,300 km northern border to (socialist) China was not much fortified or monitored by either China or North Korea. However, back in those days, guards along the Sino-Korean border would shout and then start firing if they saw an unauthorised person (Kang and Rigoulot 2001: 197). Nevertheless, even during the Cold War, about 5-10 North Koreans per year managed to arrive in South Korea. Most of them were higher-ranking officials, diplomats, pilots and fishermen, or border guards (Lankov 2006). There are also ethnic Chinese in North Korea and ethnic Koreans in China who were visiting their relatives (Lankov 2004), allowing not only some human exchange but probably also a few defections.

In the post-Cold War era, the Sino-Korean border became permeable. Three factors have contributed to the massive influx of North Koreans to China (who then transferred on to South Korea). First, a major push factor was the outbreak of the great famine in the mid-1990s, when starving North Koreans went looking for food in China or engaged in informal cross-border trade as their only means of survival. Facing either starvation or getting caught (even killed) by security agents on their way to China, thousands of North Koreans evidently started to vote with their feet. Second, a major pull factor was that there are many ethnic Koreans living in China's Jilin province adjacent to the northeast sector of the Sino-Korean border. Some North Koreans had relatives there. During the Cultural Revolution in China from the mid-1960s to the mid-1970s, many desperate Chinese crossed the border to North Korea where they would get help (Smith 2005: 33). The Sino-Korean border region has thus had a long history of mutual assistance. In addition, after China and South Korea established diplomatic relations in 1992, a number of businessmen and tourists from South Korea came to Jilin province, making it a somewhat flourishing region in the mid-1990s. For all these reasons, North Koreans would in general find good opportunities and help there— a strong pull factor. Third, North Korean security control and enforcement mechanisms broke down partially during the crisis years. Permission for domestic travel, previously compulsory, was unnecessary in the wake of a national famine when people foraged for food or were bartering goods across districts. Moreover, the food crisis increased corruption among officials and also among North Korean border guards, who could not even be fed by the government at that time; while China historically set up only a few border guards (Shim 1999). Facing a national crisis, the DPRK largely tolerated these illegal border crossings. They served various purposes, for instance as a means to keep social unrest down by letting dissidents flee the country, to decrease the number of mouths to feed, and to engage in informal cross-border trade (which in turn generated a new border-peddler class that in fact fuelled North Korea's marketization in 2002). As a major side-effect of this, the trafficking of North Korean women emerged, a topic that will be discussed in the next section.

2.3 Migration in the post-Cold War era

With slightly open doors in the mid-1990s, a large number of desperate North Koreans left for China, some temporarily, some permanently.[2] A significant group entering China during the crisis years were North Koreans who intended to take up residence there. This group comprised labour migrants, where men would mostly fulfil '3D' jobs (dirty, dangerous and difficult) as miners, farmers or construction workers, and women—if they were lucky—watched over shops, or became employed as waitresses, dishwashers or maids (Nanchu and Hang 2003; Lankov 2004). For those who came via brokers, such employment might in addition have resulted in indebted servitude, but other labour migrants also commonly received only room and board. More importantly, a significant subgroup of North Korean long-term residents in China were probably marriage migrants: in the mid-2000s, some 50,000 North Korean females were believed to live with Chinese men (mostly on rural farms), compared to only 20,000 to 30,000 other permanent residents (Smith 2005: 34.). There are two reasons for the high demand for females in Chinese rural areas: first, as a combination of China's one-child policy (since 1979) and the strong prevalence of Confucian preference for sons, there is an overall shortage of females. Second, many Chinese women, especially if of Korean ancestry, have left the poor life in the countryside and in Jilin province to move to the boomtowns or to South Korea (Becker 1996: 330). The Sino-Korean bride trade was in most cases arranged by brokers, and

---

[2] Initially, North Koreans probably only came temporarily to look for food for themselves or their family members by bartering, begging, stealing, or receiving food from charity organisations (Shim 1999). Moreover, from the mid to end 1990s, North Korean children—most of them famine orphans and often called *kkotjebi*—were roaming the streets, with many of them crossing the Sino-Korean border multiple times to get help.

this practice has often been criticised as women trafficking. Reports for prices of North Korean women in China differ and also vary by age and time, ranging from US$120-1,200 in the late 1990s (Lankov 2004) to US$800-2,000 around the year 2000 (Rigoulot 2003: 43), or on average US$244 dollars in the mid-2000s (Chang et al. 2006: 23). This money goes entirely to the brokers, who had already contacted the women or their families in North Korea and who keep up excellent relations with the border guards.

For the sake of completeness, it should also be noted that there is some evidence of forced prostitution and kidnapping of North Korean women (Feffer 2003: 67), especially of females working as hostesses in nightclubs for South Korean tourists and businessmen in Jilin province (Becker 1996: 330). There is also some speculation about a new form of female trafficking that includes North Korean women sent to Japan's nightlife-industry with forged documents (Smith 2005: 35). Overall, it is difficult to get a clear picture of such forced migration patterns. According to a survey conducted among North Koreans in China in 1999, some 85 percent of the 1,383 respondents said they had heard of women being sold to local Chinese, and about 79 percent believed that women were getting sexually abused, i.e. 'raped' (Chang 1999). Though one should be careful in interpreting such figures, what this to some extent indicates is that exploitation of North Korean women abroad seems to be the rule rather than an exception. And yet, as pointed out by Kim (2009), one should not systematically stigmatise these North Korean women. As she argues, their image has been in fact transformed through processes of romanticisation, victimisation and vilification in the public eye, for commercial interests.

The migration pattern to South Korea differs from the one to China in many degrees. It should be noted that for cultural, linguistic, legal and family reasons, North Korean migrants generally try to move to South Korea. According to the survey conducted by Chang in China in 1999 (see above), 93 percent of the respondents indicated that their country of preference to live in was South Korea (Chang 1999). A survey in China conducted in the mid-2000s found that about 64 percent—still a clear majority—preferred to live in South Korea (Chang et al. 2006: 22). However, because the inter-Korean border is sealed off, North Koreans have to take the long route via China to get to South Korea. This has two implications. First, they need more financial resources than those planning to live in China, as they have to transfer to a ship or plane in China to reach the southern half of the peninsula. They generally have to pay brokers who arrange the trip to South Korea. These human traders either hide the migrants in Chinese boats or arrange flight tickets and fake passports, raising the costs for migration further (Lankov 2006). The average brokerage costs for a North Korean to go to South Korea were about US$3,000 dollars in 2002-04 (Lankov 2006). A survey among North Korean migrants in China conducted in the mid-2000s found that three-fourths used help to leave the country, and of those, the majority used paid assistance, indicating that bribery of officials or brokers was used (Chang et al. 2006: 20). On average, North Koreans paid only US$50-100 dollars for an arranged trip from North Korea to China in the early 2000s (Nanchu and Hang 2003: 118). Hence, an arranged migration from home to South Korea is at least 30 times more expensive than from home to China. Obviously, this is making money and connections to brokers the important variables at work in reaching South Korea.

The second implication is that all migrants arriving in South Korea are intending to resettle there for good, as remigration is almost impossible let alone too expensive. Because migration to South Korea is more expensive and a permanent decision, North Koreans arriving in South Korea will probably have stronger incentives than those migrating to China. In general, these migrants might fall into three categories: first, ordinary North Koreans who have South Korean relatives or sponsors; second, ordinary North Koreans who were sponsored by charitable organisations or missionaries, invaded embassies or consulates, or managed to safe up enough money; third and last, North Korean elites who have enough resources to migrate or who are sponsored by South Korea for their political value. Astonishingly, not much research has been done on the underlying causes of North Koreans coming to South Korea. Some 50 percent of North Koreans arriving in South Korea seem to have relatives there (Lankov 2004), suggesting that the first group is the largest. This is possibly a consequence of the Korean War (1950-53) that resulted in thousands of split families, with over 900,000 North Koreans fleeing to the South between 1945 and 1953 (Lankov 2006). As a consequence, many North Koreans seem to have family ties to the South. On top of this, it seems that North Korean females do not primarily enter South Korea as marriage migrants or forced migrants of the nightlife industry. The author of this article is not aware of any study or report of such arranged migration to South Korea. Thus, the migration pattern to South Korea largely differs from the one to China, where presumably a large proportion of long-term residents consists of North Korean women sold to Chinese farmers.

3 MIGRATION SURVEYS IN CHINA

Four comprehensive surveys have been conducted among North Korean migrants in China. Three of them were carried out during the food crisis of the 1990s in order to assess living conditions at the peak of the famine (Korean Buddhist Sharing Movement 1998; Chang 1999; Robinson et al. 2001). Two of these were carried out by religious organisations, the Christian Commission to Help North Korean Refugees and the Korean Buddhist Sharing Movement (KBSM) (Chang 1999; Korean Buddhist Sharing Movement 1998). The other two assessments were implemented by private researchers (Robinson et al. 2001; Chang et al. 2009) though sometimes with the help of relief networks. All of these studies have received much attention, because of the sensitive nature of the totalitarian North Korean system, and the overall statistical blackout of the DPRK. Most importantly, these studies were based on large sample sizes as they draw on hundreds to thousands of systematic interviews among North Koreans in China. There have also been smaller studies that can, rather, be described as field surveys; they have been discarded from the analysis here in light of their low sample sizes (at the most, a few dozens of migrants were surveyed).

First, the Korean Buddhist Sharing Movement, now renamed 'Good Friends', carried out surveys from 1997 to 1998 interviewing 1,694 North Korean migrants. Results were reported in six phases, and I here focus on the last one that also summarises the findings (Korean Buddhist Sharing Movement 1998). The aim of the study was 'to accurately describe and document the suffering, damages and loss of life endured by North Koreans on account of the food shortage'. The focus of this study was thus on mortality and related demographic indicators, but a number of socio-economic and general questions were also asked in the course of the survey. Implementation was extremely difficult because of the already mentioned legal issues in China (see Section 2.1): 'Meeting places had to be changed frequently and interviews were sometimes delayed for days.' Investigators experienced external pressure during the survey, and respondents were also afraid that the researchers could have been North Korean security agents. Thus, 'what we [the researchers] did instead was to allow them [the North Korean migrants] soothe their hunger with food and their bodies with rest, then converse with them in a natural manner' to conduct the interviews. Most North Koreans were therefore migrants initially looking for food and being recruited at sites set up by the KBSM. These sites were located very close to the Sino-Korean border 'around the banks of the river Yalu and Tuman' (that form the natural frontier with China). The survey found an alarmingly high mortality rate with about 29 percent of North Korean household members dying in the years 1995-98, with a higher mortality rate for pre-school children of 49 percent and for older people of about 76 percent.

Second, the Christian Commission to Help North Korean Refugees interviewed 1,383 North Korean migrants in 1999 (Chang 1999). The survey collected the following data: 'Demographic information, current state of living conditions, severity of famine in North Korea, and amount of food aid received, the ordeals faced after being arrested and repatriated, and the plights of women and children.' By comparison with the KBSM survey it focused more on living conditions in China than inside North Korea. Similarly, however, implementation was done under extreme circumstances because of the illegal status of both researchers and respondents. And yet, this time, a major difference was that respondents were recruited in villages, mountains or at homes of church members or missionaries. Thus, long-term residents were probably interviewed. For instance, 33 percent of the respondents indicated that they were hiding in houses. Also, unlike the previous survey, which was carried out very close to the border and streets, people living deeper inland were interviewed. Among the major findings of this survey were that almost all respondents were exposed to starvation in North Korea, with 75 percent having had at least one family member die because of the food crisis. It thus corroborated findings of the KBSM study that likewise documented the devastating effects of the great famine on the well-being of the people.

Third, researchers from Johns Hopkins University carried out a survey among 381 North Koreans in 1999 on behalf of the US non-governmental organisation Mercy Corps (Robinson et al. 2001). The purpose of the project—similar to the previous study by the KBSM—was to assess the demographic profile of North Koreans and to investigate mortality rates in North Korean households. This time, however, various sites were selected: 200 local aid networks scattered in Jilin province were contacted and several dozens co-operated for the survey.

Thus, these surveys were also carried out deeper into the interior when compared with the pioneering KBSM study. The survey found crude mortality rates rising from 6 per 1,000 in 1993, to 22 per 1,000 in 1995, to 52 per 1,000 in 1997, but declining in 1998 to 27 per 1,000 (probably because of a better harvest and international aid). As with the previous two surveys, malnutrition and food deficits were pointed out as the major causes of death by the respondents.

Fourth and most recently, Chang et al. (2009) published a survey that draws on 1,346 North Koreans interviewed at different locations in the interior of China from 2004 to 2005. The focus of this survey was to assess the exposure of stress among North Koreans, alongside basic socio-economic data. This time, evidently few short-term migrants were interviewed: only 5 percent were hiding in the mountains (Chang et al. 2006: 21) compared to 26 percent that were interviewed by the Christian Commission to Help North Korean Refugees (Chang 1999), thus indicating that it was, rather, permanent residents who were surveyed by Chang et al. (2006). Moreover, because this survey was carried out after North Korea's marketisation in 2002, there might be a structural difference in the migration patterns that cannot really be investigated through lack of underlying data. Thus, a comparison with the previous three surveys should be made with caution. Major findings of this survey were that better educated North Koreans had a more negative perception of North Korea's economic development, and that the North Korean regime is overall seen negatively by the respondents (Chang et al. 2009). In addition, a large number of respondents were unaware of (or sceptical towards) humanitarian aid programmes.

4 Migration surveys in South Korea

Several surveys have been carried out among North Korean migrants living in South Korea. However, all of them focus merely on a subpopulation of the migration population living there.[3] The fact is that

---

[3] Studies in Hanawon provide limited evidence because only a small proportion of the migrants are living in the facility at the time of the survey. In addition, some might have left the country or have died, while others simply decline to participate in the research project to protect themselves or because it does not pay off, etc. Though many surveys were carried out (Bidet 2009), there are two interesting studies that were published in notable journals and received international attention. Both were

the South Korean government has systematically and extensively interviewed all North Koreans on their arrival.

This is probably done for three reasons. First, the government screens these people to make sure they are really North Koreans. A number of ethnic Koreans living in China are seeking to enter South Korea by pretending to be North Koreans because of better living standards in South Korea than at home. Second, South Korea's national security apparatus is afraid that North Korea sends agents disguised as migrants to infiltrate the South or to recruit collaborators. Third, North Korean migrants are a unique source of information for South Korean intelligence services on the otherwise statistical terra incognita of North Korea. For political and national security reasons, not much information has been released from these comprehensive interviews. However, for a previous project on bio-social welfare in North Korea (Pak et al. 2010), some socio-economic background data could be obtained and have been used in the present project. Data comprise gender, year of arrival in South Korea, year of departure from North Korea, educational status, job status, and province of residence in North Korea. Data used pertain to all North Korean adults who were 20 years or older on their arrival in South Korea from 1999 to April 2007, yielding 7,426 valid entries for this study. Sample size and socio-economic statistics used in the present project slightly differ from those reported in Pak et al. (2010) with 6,512 entries, because biological data were missing for a few individuals for that study. Surveys were conducted by government researchers, and according to one of the co-authors of the study (Pak et al. 2010), the dataset that was retrieved was not modified by South Korean authorities. Anyhow, as only standardised and politically less important information was made available for the original study, it is not very likely that the dataset was manipulated by the South Korean authorities.

Before I compare these data to the surveys in China (which I will do in Section 5), let me take a closer look at some of the variables. Information on the year of emigration from North Korea was made

---

primarily conducted by researchers from Seoul National University and draw on considerable sample sizes. The first study was in the area of public health and investigated the biological well-being of 411 North Korean women (Ku et al. 2006). The other was in the field of economics and studied the degree of informal market activity among 700 North Koreans interviewed from 2004 to 2005 (Kim and Song 2008). Basic socio-economic and demographic information was gathered too—allowing some cross-comparison with the surveys in China—but is not reported here because I make use of data from the whole North Korean migration population.

available. Unfortunately, no geographic information on the transit countries was provided. The average time spent in transit countries was found to be 3.4 years.[4] Thus, the average North Korean has resided for a considerable time-span in other transit countries, probably China, before arriving in South Korea. This suggests that a significant number of labour migrants went to South Korea—rather than North Koreans who have South Korean relatives (who directly sent money to North Korea), as previously assumed. Table 2 shows the number of migrants by exit year from North Korea. First, not surprisingly, only a small proportion (eight individuals) left North Korea during the Cold War era. However, it is somewhat puzzling why these persons did not attempt to emigrate to South Korea earlier—some of them even lived for over a decade in transit countries. Perhaps, these individuals were embassy personnel or overseas students. Second, immigration into South Korea became pronounced over time (Table 1; see above, Section 1), whereas emigration from North Korea peaked in 1998 and then steeply declined (Table 2). Another minor peak occurred in 2003—after the introduction of reforms in 2002—which might have encouraged some individuals to leave the country as they might have felt disadvantaged by the reforms. More importantly, the high point of 1998 coincides with the timing of the great famine in North Korea (Schwekendiek 2008b) which was assumed to have peaked in 1998 after two years of natural disasters. This suggests that the majority of North Koreans entering South Korea were migrants transferring from China (or other transit countries) after having left the country at the peak of the famine. It seems that few 'new' migrants came to South Korea but rather economic migrants of the 1990s. Only 27 percent of the migrants came direct from North Korea to South Korea.[5] These migrants can be expected to have relatives or sponsors in South Korea

---

[4] Defined as the average difference between year of departure and year of arrival of the individual.

[5] Transfer time is approximately one month and might be even lower because even transportation by ship requires less than a month. There are also direct flights from Jilin province to Seoul, so North Koreans can get to South Korea in a short period of time if they find a sponsor to pay the brokers. According to a South Korean non-governmental organisation, North Koreans can reach Seoul with forged passports within just five days if they have the money (Beck et al. 2007: 274).

Table 2 Exit year from North Korea of migrants in South Korea

Year	Number	Percent
1967	1	0.01
1968	1	0.01
1977	2	0.03
1981	1	0.01
1988	1	0.01
1989	2	0.03
1990	1	0.01
1991	1	0.01
1992	2	0.03
1993	7	0.10
1994	8	0.12
1995	12	0.17
1996	92	1.34
1997	767	11.16
1998	1,292	18.81
1999	588	8.56
2000	357	5.20
2001	497	7.23
2002	582	8.47
2003	892	12.98
2004	820	11.94
2005	477	6.94
2006	459	6.68
2007 (April)	8	0.12
Total	6,870	100.00

Source: Data received from the South Korean government. For further reading, see Pak et al. (2010).

who paid the brokers and arranged the trip directly from the North to the South. The majority however, about 73 percent, seem to have spent several months and often several years outside of North Korea before arriving in South Korea. In other terms, South Korea is primarily receiving the rest of the long-term famine migrants of the 1990s— implying that the rate will decline some day once the other famine migrants residing in China (or elsewhere) have arrived. However, assuming a working number of 30,000 to 100,000 permanent migrants in China (see Section 1)—with a vast majority preferring to go to South Korea (see Section 2.3)—only a small proportion (some 13,000) has arrived in South Korea. The ROK, therefore, has probably three options: to prepare for the continuing influx of famine migrants of the 1990s who are currently waiting to come to South Korea; to crack down on the brokers and logistic transportation routes; or to shut the doors to the southern half of the peninsula by means of legislation. The latter two alternatives would certainly be at the cost of the most vulnerable, the North Korean migrants, posing a humanitarian dilemma for the South Korean government.

5 COMPARATIVE META-ANALYSIS OF MIGRANTS SURVEYED IN CHINA AND SOUTH KOREA

A comparative analysis of North Korean migrants surveyed in China and South Korea, as discussed in Sections 3 and 4, is made in Table 3. Although I have tried to find the largest common denominator among categories (varying throughout the surveys because of different classifications, see notes below Table 3) and report findings wherever possible, information could unfortunately not always be retrieved (see empty entries).

Moreover, corresponding statistics on North Korea's population were added. Facing a dearth of information on North Korea (Schwekendiek 2009), data on North Korea shown in Table 3 were unfortunately more often unavailable than available. Some population data were provided by the North Korean government in preparation for the first census in 1993, and were reported by Kim et al. (1998) and by Eberstadt and Banister (1992). The data pertain to the late 1980s (around 1987/88) and are based on North Korea's mandatory household registration system. Preliminary findings from the second and most recent North Korean census of 2008 were reported by the United Nations (UN) in a public document that was accessible in fall 2008 (see notes below Table 3). Lastly, data from a random household survey covering ten out of twelve North Korean provinces in 2002 helped to provide missing information on educational status.

Table 3 Meta-analysis of North Koreans in China and South Korea with reference to the North Korean population

Background information				Origin in %	Sex in %		Job Status in %					Education in %		
Source	Year	Age	N (original)	N. and S. Hamgyŏng	Male	Female	Manual*	Office	Military	Student	Jobless	Primary	Secondary	College**
North Korean migrants in China:														
KBSM (1998)	97-98	10+	1,694	80	52	48	59	14	0	1	15			
Chang (1999)	99	10+	1,383	77	75	25	45		3	26		29	42	28
Robinson et al. (2001)	99	18+	381	84	53	47								
Chang et al. (2006)	04-05	?***	1,313	76	48	52	87		1			44	52	2
North Korean migrants in South Korea:														
See text	99-07	20+	7,426	79	31	69	61	5	2	3	2	3	72	25
North Korean population:														
Kim et. al. (1998)	late 80s	all	21,411,800				46	9	6	2				
Eberstadt and Banister (1992)	late 80s	all	19,346,000	24	46	54								
Schwekendiek (2008a)	02	mothers	6,000											24
Preliminary UN census results	08	all	23,348,845	23	47	53								

Notes: * Manual workers = labourers and farmers, ** College incl. technical and specialised schools, *** minimum age not reported but 80% of the respondents were 25-50 years old.
Preliminary UN census results were published online: http://unstats.un.org/unsd/demographic/sources/census/2010_phc/North_Korea/2008_North_Korea_Census.pdf (accessed 17 October 2009).

Who are these migrants? First and foremost, it is striking that an overwhelming majority of them come from South and North Hamgyŏng provinces, which are located close to Jilin province (Table 3). This finding is true for migrants surveyed in both China and South Korea. About 76 percent to 84 percent of the migrants lived in the two Hamgyŏng provinces, which are actually home to only 23-24 percent of the population. There are two possible explanations for this extreme provincial bias. The first is that the four eastern provinces (including the two Hamgyŏng provinces) were cut off from public supplies during the food crisis of the 1990s as they were deemed to be of less strategic value for the military (Natsios 2001). Furthermore, these were major industrial areas in the Cold War, but were debilitated by the energy crisis and economic shocks following the collapse of the Eastern Bloc. Thus, push factors were stronger for people living in these provinces. Against this, previous research has also found that another cut-off province, Kangwŏn, actually fared quite well in the 1990s (Schwekendiek 2009a). Furthermore, multivariate analysis has cast doubt on the so-called 'triage hypothesis' because these cut-off provinces did not suffer worse when controls for a number of socio-economic effects were applied—neither during the peak of the famine (Schwekendiek 2008b) nor in the post-famine period (Schwekendiek 2008a). They were actually found to be 'average' provinces during the food crisis of the 1990s in terms of malnutrition. Living standards in the two P'yŏngan provinces, where the local mining industry collapsed, were strikingly worse (Schwekendiek 2010), but very few migrants came from there. All these findings suggest that a disproportional deterioration in regional living standards in the two Hamgyŏng provinces has not been a strong factor for migration.

Second and most importantly, geographical proximity to the Sino-Korean border seems to be a crucial factor. Both Hamgyŏng provinces are not only located close to the border, but contain stretches of lowlands (in the coastal regions), reducing travel time substantially. Interestingly, there are few migrants from Ryanggang, which is also adjacent to Jilin province and was likewise cut off from public supplies. However, this is a quite mountainous region, from which it takes several days to get even to central locations (Schwekendiek 2010). Such obstacles have probably prevented residents of this province from crossing the border into North Hamgyŏng. Considering the famine and energy crisis of the 1990s, where public transportation broke down and people in any case were barely able to afford a bus ticket, it seems that most of the migrants went on foot. According to the survey by researchers from Johns Hopkins University (see Section 3 above), the average journeying distance to the North Korean border (generally to the northeast sector) was 143 km (Robinson et al. 2001). The US Department of Defense (1997: 59) found that individuals might cover as many as 45 km in a day (a 'forced march' of 10-12 hours). It would thus take about three days to walk to the Sino-Korean border. However, considering that many migrants were already exposed to the effects of famine, they would probably need more days or might even starve on their way. It is far from clear that residents from other provinces could not make this distance on foot. The closest distance from the provincial border of South Hamgyŏng to the northeastern Sino-Korean border is already over 150 km, which explains also why more migrants from North Hamgyŏng than from South Hamgyŏng left. In sum, geographical proximity to the Sino-Korean border seems to be the dominant explanation for the large share of migrants from the northeastern province. However, it remains puzzling why few North Koreans attempted to leave the country from other provinces in the post-famine period when transportation was restored and the economy revived. A likely explanation is that the tens of thousands of short-term migrants to China—in turn also from the Hamgyŏng provinces for reasons of proximity—brought back information on life in China and how to cross the border or get in touch with human traders. Beck et al. (2007: 255) note that in addition, illegal videos and radio broadcasts from abroad are major sources of information. Of the migrants surveyed by Chang et al. (2006: 20) in China, 89 percent said that they had knowledge about China by word of mouth—suggesting that hearsay evidence is the most crucial source of information on the outside. After the great famine, the government controlled intra-migration movements again, which might explain why returning migrants could not spread so much information to the other provinces.

A further point to emerge from the analysis is that gender ratios varied widely across the surveys. According to North Korean census data, sex ratios are, as would be expected, roughly balanced in the DPRK. Sex ratios among migrants in China are also balanced, except for those studied by the Christian Commission to Help North Korean Refugees (Chang 1999), which reported almost 77 percent males. This is a surprising result, but could be explained by the finding that the respondents were often sampled in the homes of church members and were living in houses. Hence, a large share of labour migrants, typically North Korean male construction workers or farm hands, were surveyed. However, there is no clear majority of female migrants in any of the surveys conducted in China. Considering that the vast majority of migrants are assumed to be female marriage migrants (see Section 2.3), none of the surveys reflects this. Either assumptions on the degree of female trafficking are incorrect, or these individuals were largely not interviewed during the surveys. Assuming that some of these North Korean women were sold to rural farms, it is far from clear that few of them could participate in these surveys, which were primarily carried out at sites of relief networks. However, the share of female North Korean migrants arriving in South Korea was found to be 69 percent. Considering that on average these migrants have spent a couple of years in transit countries (see Table 2 above), the suggestion is there that some of these migrants somehow found a way to leave the unequal relationships with their husbands in China. This clear gender pattern also contradicts the previous assumption that primarily North Koreans with relatives in South Korea are arriving in the South: assuming an equal gender preference of South Korean relatives, the gender ratio of North Korean migrants in the South should be close to one—though almost 70 percent of the immigrants are actually females.

Job status information was also retrieved from both the population and migrant samples. It seems that disproportionably more manual labourers left their home. Some 46 percent were classified as labourers according to North Korean data, but in most surveys, the proportion is higher, up to 87 percent. As an explanation of this, one can argue that these people were worse off during the famine as many North Korean industrial centres collapsed—hence they might have had stronger incentives to emigrate. One should also keep in mind that most of the migrants were from the Hamgyŏng provinces, which were a major shipbuilding region in the Cold War. Thus, the ratios probably reflect the regional economic structure. Yet it is clear that these individuals are, rather, blue-collar and less-skilled workers. Hence, better employment possibilities for them are limited in both China and especially in South Korea.

Lastly, a focus on education (as a matter of data availability, it was generally possible to report college education): on the basis of a 2002 survey conducted in households inside the DPRK, some 24 percent of those analysed seem to have enjoyed a higher education in North Korea. Astonishingly, this rate corresponds almost perfectly to the rates reported by those conducting surveys in China and in South Korea, suggesting that North Koreans going abroad are quite representative of the population in terms of higher educational attainments. As an exception to this, Chang et al. (2006) find that only 2 percent of the respondents have had a college education. I mentioned above (see Section 3) that one should be careful in comparing this survey to the other ones because of structural breaks; it was conducted five to six years later. Even so, the extremely low rate of respondents with college education in this survey remains somewhat puzzling—calling for further investigations. In any event, the overall picture one gets is that migrants arriving in South Korea seem to be slightly better educated than those residing in China. Yet, their formal educational attainment is probably of little use in South Korea, as their degrees are generally not recognised, and their general knowledge, acquired in socialist North Korea, is limited.

6 Conclusion

This article has provided a review of major statistical surveys conducted among North Korean migrants in China and South Korea. It has discussed two assessments made by religious organisations and two studies by private researchers that surveyed a large number of North Koreans systematically in China's Jilin province where ethnic Koreans are living and North Koreans have been looking for shelter ever since the onset of the food crisis of the 1990s. Most of the studies were carried out in the interior of the province, where long-term residents live. However, a considerable number of female marriage migrants from North Korea were probably not interviewed during these surveys. Therefore, a more representative study among North Korean long-term migrants in China is still needed. Bearing in mind the heavy restrictions on research arising from the illegal status of both interviewees and interviewers, and considering China's recent shift to crack down on migration and humanitarian networks—not to mention North Korean agents operating in the region—such a task becomes admittedly quite daunting.

The migration pattern to South Korea looks completely different from the one observed by surveys in China. Basing itself on raw data, this article has attempted to track down the immigration pattern of North Koreans arriving in South Korea and being interviewed on their arrival by the government. An intriguing finding is that the current migration diaspora in South Korea seems to consist of women who have spent several years in transit countries—probably in China. Most of them left North Korea in 1998 when famine was ravaging the country. This being the case, although already 13,000 North Koreans have entered South Korea, many more North Korean women—possibly up to three or four times more—can sooner or later be expected to leave China and head to the South. In addition to these migrants, a smaller proportion of chain migrants including those with South Korean relatives paying the brokers are likely to seek shelter in the South. About 27 percent of migrants came directly from North Korea to South Korea, suggesting that they had a family sponsor from South Korea, whereas the majority consisted of mid- to long-term residents in transit countries.

Furthermore, this article has provided comparative and clear evidence that the majority of migrants come from the two Hamgyŏng provinces that are close to the Sino-Korean border. This is perhaps the only common denominator of all surveys, conducted in both China and South Korea. What this suggests is that travel distance—perhaps more than previously assumed economic push factors—seems to be a crucial factor for migration. Other influential factors seem to be information and logistic networks in that region—maybe because of returning migrants spreading word-of-mouth information, or by brokers actively recruiting North Korean women for Chinese farmers or advertising their border-crossing activities.

References

Beck, Peter, Gail Kim and Donald Macintyre (2007), 'Perilous Journeys: The Plight of North Koreans in China', in: Rüdiger Frank, James E. Hoare, Patrick Köllner, Susan Pares (eds), *Korea Yearbook: Politics, Economy and Society*, vol. 1, Leiden: Brill, pp. 253-81

Becker, Jasper (1996), *Hungry Ghosts: Mao's Secret Famine*, New York: Henry Holt and Company

Bidet, Eric (2009), 'Social Capital and Work Integration of Migrants: The Case of North Korean Defectors in South Korea', in: *Asian Perspective*, 33 (2), pp. 151-79

Chang, Christine (1999), 'A field survey report on the North Korean refugees in China', Seoul: Commission to Help North Korean Refugees in China (unpublished)

Chang, Yoonok, Stephan Haggard and Marcus Noland (2006), 'North Korean Refugees in China: Evidence from a Survey', in: Stephen Haggard and Marcus Noland (eds), *The North Korean Refugee Crisis: Human Rights and International Responses*, Washington DC: US Committee for Human Rights in North Korea, pp. 14-33

Chang, Yoonok, Stephan Haggard and Marcus Noland (2009), 'Exit Polls: Refugee Assessments of North Korea's Transition', in: *Journal of Comparative Economics*, 37 (1), pp. 144-50

Chosun Ilbo (2008), 'More Than 3,000 N. Koreans to Defect South This Year', 2 September 2008

Eberstadt, Nicholas and Judith Banister (1992), *The Population of North Korea*, Berkeley CA: Institute of East Asian Studies

Feffer, John (2003), *Nordkorea und die USA*, Kreuzlingen: Hugendubel

JoongAng Ilbo (2007), '10,000th defector arrives on Kim Jong-il's birthday', 17 February 2007

Kang, Chol-Hwan and Pierre Rigoulot (2001), *The Aquariums of Pyongyang*, New York: Basic Books

Kim, Byung-Yeon and Dongho Song (2008), 'The Participation of North Korean Households in the Informal Economy: Size, Determinants, and Effect', in: *Seoul Journal of Economics*, 21, pp. 361-85

Kim, Mikyoung (2009), 'The Social Construction of North Korean Women's Identity in South Korea: Romanticisation, Victimisation and Vilification' in: Rüdiger Frank, James E. Hoare, Patrick Köllner, Susan Pares (eds), *Korea Yearbook: Politics, Economy and Society*, vol. 3, pp. 257-75

Kim, Woon Keun, Hyunok Lee and Daniel A. Sumner (1998), 'Assessing the Food Situation in North Korea', in: *Development and Cultural Change*, 46, pp. 519-35

Korean Buddhist Sharing Movement (1998), 'The Food Crisis in North Korea. 6th Phase of Research (30 Sep 1997-15 Sep 1998)'. Online: http://www.goodfriends.or.kr/eng/report/1694e.htm (accessed 2 February 2010)

Ku, Seung-Yup, Jong Won Kang, Heon Kim, Yong Dae Kim, Byung Chul Jee, Chang Suk Suh, Young Min Choi, Jung Gu Kim, Shin Yong Moon and Seok Hyun Kim (2006), 'Age at menarche and its influencing factors in North Korean female refugees', in: *Human Reproduction*, 21, pp. 833-36

Lankov, Andrei (2004), 'North Korean Refugees in Northeast China', in: *Asian Survey*, 44 (6), pp. 856-73

Lankov, Andrei (2006), 'Bitter Taste of Paradise: North Korean Refugees in South Korea', in: *Journal of East Asian Studies*, 6 (1), pp. 105-37

Margesson, Rhoda, Emma Chanlett-Avery and Andorra Bruno (2007), 'North Korean Refugees in China and Human Rights Issues: International Response and U.S. Policy Options', CRS Report for Congress, 26 September 2007. Online: www.fas.org/sgp/crs/row/RL34189.pdf (accessed 2 February 2010)

Nanchu, with Xing Hang (2003), *In North Korea: An American Travels Through an Imprisoned Nation*, Jefferson NC: McFarland & Company

Natsios, Andrew (2001), *The Great North Korean Famine*, Washington DC: United States Institute of Peace Press

Pak, Sunyoung, Daniel Schwekendiek and Heekyoung Kim (2010), 'Height and Living Standards in North Korea, 1930s-1980s', in: *Economic History Review* (forthcoming)

Rigoulot, Pierre (2003), *Nordkorea*, Koeln: Kiepenheuer & Witsch

Robinson, W. Courtland, Myung Ken Lee, Kenneth Hill and Gilbert Burnham (2001), 'Famine, Mortality, and Migration: A Study of North Korean Migrants in China', in: Holly E. Reed and Charles B. Keely (eds), *Forced Migration and Mortality*, Washington DC: National Academy Press, pp. 69-85

Schwekendiek, Daniel (2008a), 'Determinants of Well-being in North Korea: Evidence from the Post-famine Period', in: *Economics and Human Biology*, 6 (3), pp. 446-54

Schwekendiek, Daniel (2008b), 'The North Korean Standard of Living During the Famine', in: *Social Science and Medicine*, 66 (3), pp. 596-608

Schwekendiek, Daniel (2009), 'Statistical Explorations in Terra Incognita. How Reliable are North Korean Survey Data?' in: Rüdiger Frank, James E. Hoare, Patrick Köllner, Susan Pares (eds), *Korea Yearbook: Politics, Economy and Society*, vol. 3, pp. 277-300

Schwekendiek, Daniel (2010), 'Regional Variations in Living Standards during the North Korean Food Crisis of the 1990s', in: *Asia-Pacific Journal of Public Health* (forthcoming)

Shim, Jae Hoon (1999), 'North Korea: A Crack in the Wall', in: *Far Eastern Economic Review*, 29 April 1999

Smith, Hazel (2002), 'North Koreans in China: Defining the Problems and Offering Some Solutions', KASM, 1 December 2002. Online: kasm.org/PDFs/NorthKoreansinChina_HS.pdf (accessed 2 February 2010)

Smith, Hazel (2005), 'North Korean Migrants Pose Long-term Challenge for China', in: *Jane's Intelligence Review*, June, pp. 32-35

US Department of Defense (1997), *North Korea Country Handbook*, Quantico VA: Marine Corps Intelligence Activity

TEXTUAL AND VISUAL REPRESENTATIONS OF THE KOREAN WAR IN NORTH AND SOUTH KOREAN CHILDREN'S LITERATURE

Dafna Zur[1]

ABSTRACT

Since the division of the Korean peninsula, North and South Korea have told the story of war and division in fictional and historical narratives for children. This article compares North and South Korean textual and visual representations of the Korean War in children's magazines and books in order to show how narratives about the conflict have been transformed or maintained. In its examination of South Korean children's literature, it seeks to show how the narrative trend has changed from depicting the Korean Other as the demonised enemy to emphasising ethnic unity. It also demonstrates that the 'myth of innocence' of the child in South Korea plays a central role in challenging anti-communist rhetoric. In comparison, the paper demonstrates how North Korean children's literature adheres to an interpretation of the Korean War as a war of liberation, and considers the violent illustrations through the perspective of fascist aesthetics and political cartoons.

1 THE KOREAN WAR IN NORTH AND SOUTH KOREAN CHILDREN'S BOOKS

The Korean War (1950-3) was one of the most traumatic events in the contemporary history of the Korean peninsula. After liberation in 1945, mounting tensions between Koreans of pro- and anti-communist convictions culminated in the division of the peninsula in 1948. The war, which started with the North Korean invasion of the South on

---

[1] I am indebted to Wŏn Chong-ch'an, who has most generously shared his rare primary resources with me for this project. Special thanks are also due to Dom Lee, who kindly gave his permission for the reproduction of his artwork (Figures 4, 5, 6, 7, 8). Attempts to secure permission to reproduce the artwork for Figure 1 (by Kim Yŏng-ju) and Figures 2 and 3 (artist unknown) have so far been unsuccessful. All translations from the Korean are my work.

25 June 1950 and ended in a cease-fire three years later, inflicted enormous devastation and separated the two Koreas roughly at the 38th parallel.[2] Since then, North and South Korea have told their national birth story—the story of division and war—in accordance with the political ideology that defines each. And each tells its history in, among other places, historical narratives for children.

This article examines the way in which the Korean War has been remembered in North and South Korean children's fiction. Historical fiction is a subject of ongoing scrutiny, as cultural theorists and historiographers have reassessed the constructedness of subjectivity and have complicated the possibility of representing a knowable, historically accurate truth. Fiction for children in North and South Korea demands our particular attention, since, in the immediate post-war period, both sides muted the public recounting of personal experiences of the Korean War that might diverge from the hegemonic rhetoric. Even in South Korea today, a complicated silence still hovers over those who were victimised by the South Korean government for ideological crimes.

At the same time, an examination of children's literature in postwar South Korea reveals that the hegemonic narratives have been challenged since the 1980s. Moreover, the authority that the myth of innocence still maintains in South Korean children's fiction firmly places the child protagonists in a position to pose tough questions about the nature of the conflict, while remaining, to the great relief of the reader/viewer, safe from trauma. A preliminary survey of children's fiction from 1954 until the present reveals the way in which these challenges have been mounted in contemporary South Korean fiction through 'truth-telling' uses of realism; at the same time, this fiction presents a narrow interpretation of the war, and points to the implications that such interpretations might have for the possibility of achieving a complex understanding of the conflict.

In North Korea, too, the Korean War continues to be a central topic in children's literature that subscribes, without exception, to North Korea's interpretation of the war as the struggle for liberation of the

---

[2] There are, generally speaking, two interpretations of the Korean War. The one which I note above is espoused by Bruce Cumings, who sees the Korean conflict as a civil war that was exacerbated by international superpowers; the other, promoted by William Stueck, explains the war as a Cold War conflict that involved the Soviet Union, the United States, the People's Republic of China, and the United Nations as some of the key players (cf. Cumings 1981 and Stueck 2002).

Korean peninsula from the imperialist United States (US) (see also Ryang 2009: 8). Since the 1950s, North Korean children's literature has made particular use of violent images that heighten the emotional response of their child readers and continue, to the present day, to glorify self-sacrifice and dehumanise the enemy. The article will analyse the semiotic function of violence in the text and visual imagery in North Korean children's literature.

2 IDEOLOGY IN POST-WAR SOUTH KOREAN CHILDREN'S LITERATURE

The role that ideologies play in the way that children learn to understand the world and their place in it is a subject of ongoing interest.[3] Robyn McCallum writes that an individual's consciousness and sense of identity are formed 'with the discourses constituting the society and culture s/he inhabits' and that 'the formation of subjectivity is thus always shaped by social ideologies' (McCallum 1999: 3). Children's literature lends itself particularly well to this kind of analysis because of the role that it plays in communicating and disseminating a culture's ideologies to its young. Indeed, one of the distinguishing features of children's literature is that it is written by adults who usually—though not always—write for an imagined child audience. As Deborah Thacker notes, 'the layer of adult mediation that surrounds the delivery of fiction to children places the child reader in a role of "subjection" to the controlling discourses of adulthood and society' (Thacker 2000: 11). It is necessary to identify the hegemonic discourses in post-war Korea that contributed to the shaping of national identity and to the construction of memory of the Korean War, because anti-communist ideology in Korea controlled all post-war cultural production in the South, including children's literature.

Jacqueline Rose notes that 'children's fiction emerges out of a conception of both the child and the world as knowable in a direct and unmediated way' (Rose 1984: 9). In Korea, this 'knowable child' was epitomised by the portrayal of children as innocent and angelic (*tongsimjuŭi* and *ch'ŏnsajuŭi*). Ideology has played a strong role in Korean children's literature in particular because of the persistent belief that children are innocent and are therefore malleable and in need of edifi-

---

[3] See, for example, the groundbreaking works of John Stephens (1992) and Maria Nikolajeva (2003).

cation. But the consequences of this rhetoric have been pointed out by Henry Jenkins, who writes that

> the myth of childhood innocence [...] 'empties' the child of its own political agency, so that it may more perfectly fulfill the symbolic demands we make upon it. The innocent child wants nothing, desires nothing, and demands nothing—except, perhaps, its own innocence (Jenkins 1998: 1-2).

The myth of innocence has implications not only with regard to the conspicuous presence of didacticism in children's literature; it also has deep implications for the management of trauma, as argued by Kathryn Capshaw Smith:

> Since adults often are deeply invested in a desire for childhood innocence, constructions of children's responses to trauma [...] generally adhere to two poles: Because they are imagined as innocent, they are figured almost iconographically as the ultimate victims of trauma [...] Alternatively, because children are imagined as innocent, they are also figured as the survivors of trauma, those who can offer adults spiritual advice on how to triumph over the pain through simple, honest, essential values like love, trust, and perseverance (Smith 2005: 116).

The myth of innocence in South Korean fiction, though widely criticised for its creation of sentimental and unrealistic literature, endowed fictional child characters with the authority to confront adults with difficult questions that were largely forbidden until the democratisation of the 1980s and concomitant relaxation on freedom of expression. At the same time, the myth of innocence serves to calm adult anxieties about the trauma inflicted upon children, and ultimately steers the readers away from confronting the origins of the war in all their complexity.

The myth of innocence has been widely contested by critics of children's literature, the earliest criticism being aimed primarily at Pang Chŏng-hwan (1899-1931). Pang, although credited with being the most important activist for promoting children's literature and culture, has been partially dismissed because of his portrayal of children as uncomplicated caricatures with angelic dispositions, and for his lack of engagement with children's realities under the Japanese colonial rule. However, the antipathy towards the discourse of innocence must be viewed within the context of the rise in importance of realism in Korean literature from the mid-1920s. By 1929, as Sunyoung Park emphasises, realism 'emerged as the only worthy label for a conscientious literature in Korea' (Park 2006: 182),[4] and many children's writers, such as Yi Chu-hong (1906-87) and Hyŏn Tŏk (1909-?) in the 1930s and 1940s, wrote about social class and the marginalisation of children in ways that were deemed faithful to reality and were therefore engaged in the larger project of nation-building and social improvement. The realist trend continues to influence writers in its demand that literature for children tackle social issues in order to contribute to a fuller understanding of the challenges that children face in their lives.

Socially and politically engaged writing became of critical importance to nation-building in historiography, particularly with regard to the Korean War. Shin Gi-wook and Michael Robinson write that

> [b]oth Korean states have a powerful interest in history [...] Each polices the writing of history and shapes public opinion around a general common understanding of why its system should be recognized as the true expression of Korean collective identity (Shin and Robinson 1999: 4).

South Korean writers have worked their version of legitimate history into literature for children, and their version has been reinforced both externally, through censorship exercised through the authority of state security laws, and internally, through the education system, which promoted self-censorship and the internalisation of anti-communist rhetoric. Such rhetoric grew to dominate children's literature and is central to the understanding of how storytelling was controlled in post-war Korea.

2.1 *Emergence of an anti-communist rhetoric*

The configuration of a communist North and capitalist South was not indigenous; it had to be vigorously cultivated by the governments of both North and South Korea. During the colonial period, many Koreans identified with left-leaning politics, and in the three-year period between liberation (1945) and the Korean War, right- and left-leaning writers competed over social and cultural hegemony. The ideological

---

[4] Park notes that the two main groups of writers that lay claims on the direction of the literary world in Korea 'shared a general paradigm of realism in their literary practice: they all had a conviction of knowability about the world—as well as its representability through language—and they were all committed to drawing a critical portrayal of contemporary society' (Park 2006: 172-3).

struggles in the literary field spilled over into children's literature. In her study of the anti-communist discourse in post-war children's literature, Sŏn An-na notes that the left-leaning children's writers were very active in the publishing world after liberation, and revived literary magazines for children that had been censored during the Japanese occupation (Sŏn 2007: 102-4). These magazines discussed the liquidation of Japanese colonial authorities and their Korean collaborators, the rebuilding of the nation, and the inherent evils of the class system. Left-leaning writers were particularly hostile towards the myth of child innocence, and espoused more socially engaged content in fiction. Their opposite counterparts, by comparison, were less active, less organised, and refrained from serious ideological debates in children's fiction (Sŏn 2007: 102). They, however, were the ones to take control of the publishing industry. The US pushed for the elimination of South Korean leftist movements, and the South was swept by an anti-communist rage. The National Security Law passed in 1948, branding any sentiment sympathetic to communism as an anti-state crime, curtailed the freedom of speech. Those left-leaning writers who did not flee north either were forced to undergo ideological conversion or were banned from writing at all. When war broke out in 1950, the South Korean government under President Syngman Rhee placed the entire responsibility for the violence on North Korea. The devastation of the war fuelled hatred for the enemy and encouraged an enthusiastic reception for anti-communist ideology in the South. Anti-communist discourse thus became the foundational rhetoric in the construction of the South Korean nation.

Up until the Korean War, anti-communist rhetoric existed in the political sphere, and was absent from children's literature (Sŏn 2009: 97); with the war, anti-communist content was infused into classrooms, and anti-communism became the standard rhetoric conveyed to children. Writers composing anti-communist literature for children were either South Korean soldier-writers, or writers who had fled North Korea to resettle in the South. Sŏn argues that South Korean soldier-writers generally attempted to capture moments in the lives of children or the inhumane face of the war, while the ex-North Korean writers wrote anti-communist fiction either based on traumatic experiences, or in order to establish their loyalty and secure their positions in South Korea (ibid.: 99). Ultimately, however, their work was concerned with conveying anti-North Korean messages, and not with providing insight into the lives of children caught in the war. Though the

Korean War was experienced in different ways according to gender, age, region and class, the hegemonic rhetoric overrode people's individual experiences, and forced them to deny or bury their personal memories of the war until a relative relaxation of censorship began in the late 1980s.[5]

The way in which the anti-communist discourse effectively silenced alternative narratives in the immediate post-war period is significant for the understanding of trauma. Paul Antze and Michael Lambek write:

> As memory emerges into consciousness, as it is externalized and increasingly objectified, it always depends on cultural vehicles for its expression [...] the right to establish authoritative versions never rests with the individual telling the story alone. It shifts from communal institutions and collective memory to the domain of experts and beyond —to market forces and the power of the state (Antze and Lambek 1996: xvii).

As Antze and Lambek suggest here, social and political ideologies affect people's personal stories and distort the act of remembering. Sŏ Tong-su (2006) maintains that the anti-communist rhetoric in the post-war period—rhetoric that was essential for writers who wished to stay out of jail and stay active—shaped readers' experiences through a process of internalisation of images that replaced real or lived experiences.[6]

2.2 *Anti-communist rhetoric in texts*

Anti-communist children's literature generally followed several formulaic schemes. First, it depicted North Koreans as unequivocally evil and the South Koreans as wholly good. For example, in Pak Kye-ju's story '38 sŏnsang ŭi so' (The cow of the 38th parallel) (1953), North Korean soldiers claim a South Korean cow that wandered across the border, and ignore the pleas of the cow's young master to return the

---

[5] See, for example, the work of the Truth and Reconciliation Commission, Republic of Korea (TRCK), which was formed in December 2005 and serves as an investigative body seeking resolution and compensation on behalf of these victims.

[6] Part of the rhetorical strategy, according to Sŏ, was the use of metaphors such as monsters, devils, disease, poisonous snakes, crazy hounds, bloodthirsty beasts, and murderers capable of killing their parents and relatives (Sŏ 2006: 409-12).

animal; but when a North Korean cow comes south, the same boy returns the cow to the North:

> 'It's no good to return evil with evil. You must remember how much you cried when you lost your cow. I can't forget how much it hurt, either. Go, return it.' Grandpa placed the cow's bridle back in Man-su's hand. Without a word, Man-su took the cow and walked toward the 38th parallel (Pak 1953: 23).

Second, because the anti-communist discourse reinforced the hegemonic powers of the people who circulated it, Sŏn (2009:115) notes that fiction often privileged the perspective of the wealthy landowners. Ch'oe T'ae-ŭng's story 'Oksaek chogae kkŏpjil' (The jade seashell) (1954), for example, tells the story of the turning of tables when one farmer's family gains control over their landowner's property after liberation. The children—once-poor Ch'unsili and the now impoverished landowner's daughter Yŏngbogi—stay friends despite their class differences, since, as the narrator explains, Ch'unsili and his family never held a grudge against their kindly landowners:

> Thankfully, Ch'unsili's family was sweet, unambitious and warm; they were loyal and reasonable, and would never lash out in fury against their landowners no matter how drastically their situation had changed or what kind of feelings they harboured in their hearts (Ch'oe 1954: 11).

Third, works typically valorised both citizens' and soldiers' personal sacrifices for the sake of the nation. For example, in Chang Su-ch'ŏl's 'Ŏndŏkkil esŏ maejŭn ujŏng' (Friendship forged on a hill path), published in August 1958 in *Saebŏt,* a child who has been teased suddenly becomes an object of envy because her brother is a soldier:

> What's more, not a single boy or girl in the village had a brother who was a soldier.
> 'I don't know why, but I'm so jealous of her now.' Hŭisuk finally spoke.
> 'No kidding! Suddenly she seems like such a great girl.'
> 'If only we'd known sooner! We could have played with her from the very start.'
> 'I know, and she was trying to play with us for so long! I feel bad.'
> With that, the children began to feel a renewed sense of friendship toward the girl (Chang 1958: 56-7).

This ideological momentum was necessitated by the war effort, both for mobilising citizens' participation and for justifying great losses; yet even years after the war, and even with the commercialisation and popularisation of children's literature, anti-communist rhetoric continued to be reproduced and inscribed an uncompromising anti-North Korean position for its young readers (Sŏn 2009: 115-8).

2.3 Anti-communist rhetoric in illustrations

As Perry Nodelman notes, pictures in books intended for children exist primarily 'so that they can assist in the telling of stories' (Nodelman 1988: vii). Visual images, such as illustrations in children's books, also play a part in shaping personal narratives. Yet children's book illustrations in Korea have suffered neglect. The obstacles in the post-war period—a lack of financial resources, censorship, and poor technology—stood in the way of significance development of art in children's books (Yi Ho-baek 2007: 12).

Nonetheless, despite the losses that the South suffered in the Korean War and the death and disappearance of many talented illustrators, children's magazines continued to be published with illustrations. *Sonyŏn segye*, which appeared from 1953 to 1956, was one of the magazines that provided a stage for many illustrators. Interestingly, however, none of the illustrations of the 23 anti-communist stories in *Sonyŏn segye* represent gruesome violence or exaggerate the enemy through caricatures. Figure 1, for example, is the title illustration from '38 sŏnsang ŭi so' (and is the work of Kim Yŏng-ju):

Figure 1 (Pak 1953: 20)

The boy's naked body draws the viewer's gaze from left to right, and the North Korean soldier has his back turned innocuously to the viewer. This illustration, like the others in *Sonyŏn segye*, focuses on the pathos and tragedy of the victims rather than portraying graphic violence.

One possible explanation for this can be found with the editor of *Sonyŏn segye*, Yi Wŏn-su (1911-81). Yi was a prominent writer for children and published many books and short stories. Throughout his long career, Yi maintained an anti-didactic and anti-sentimental stance in his writing; more remarkably, he was vocally opposed to division and to South Korea's involvement in the Vietnam War. His vision is captured most succinctly by his children's novel *Supsok nara*, published in 1954. This novel is a utopian vision of a world created by children in which society's open market and competition are the roots of evil. Wŏn Chong-ch'an suggests that Yi's remarkably subversive voice was permissible because of Yi's reputation and because censorship was more relaxed with children's literature (Wŏn 2001: 141). It appears that Yi's convictions and his resistance to the trend of sentimentalism and dogmatism is one explanation for the lack of blunt anti-communist illustrations in *Sonyŏn segye*.

3 POST-1980S SOUTH KOREAN CHILDREN'S LITERATURE

The early 1980s were still dominated by anti-communist rhetoric; the mid-80s, however, witnessed a significant change with the work of Kwŏn Chŏng-saeng (1937-2007). Kwŏn's bestseller from 1984, *Mongsil ŏnni* (Sister Mongsil), is today considered one of South Korea's canonical young adult novels. The novel follows the trials of a girl as she experiences the full range of traumatic events dealt to her by the late colonial period and the Korean War. It takes an unwavering and unforgiving look at life in Korea during the Korean War, and contains some of the most outspoken challenges both to post-colonial, patriarchical Korea and to the anti-communist discourse, as demonstrated in the following excerpt between ten-year-old Mongsil and a female North Korean soldier:

> 'Who's more terrible? The North Korean soldiers or the South Korean soldiers? And who is the kinder of the two?'
> There was no response.
> 'Why are the North Korean soldiers killing the South Korean soldiers, and the South Korean soldiers killing the North Koreans?'
> 'Mongsil,' answered the soldier from her bed, 'Really, they are all terrible and all kind.'
> 'What sort of answer is that?' (Kwŏn [1984] 2001: 107)

Her innocence is particularly effective in seeing through the absurdity of civil war; in her eyes, the ends do not justify the means by which

North and South Korea claim the legitimacy of their ideological claims.

The text from Kwŏn's 1985 novel, *Ch'ogajibi ittŏn maŭl* (The village of thatched houses), is accompanied by prints that cast a spotlight on the painful experiences of the war. Figure 2 captures the moment a young boy is run over by a US army truck while he tries to catch some of the chocolate and gum that the soldiers toss to the Korean children; and Figure 3 portrays a South Korean soldier stealing a chicken he has shot, just as a North Korean soldier had done not long before.

Figure 2 (Kwŏn 1985: 154)   Figure 3 (Kwŏn 1985: 163)

It is perhaps Kwŏn's picture book, *Komiwa op'undori ajŏssi* (Komi and Mr Op'undori) (2007; unnumbered pages), with illustrations by Dom Lee, that best captures this author's interpretation of the origins of the Korean War. Although this book challenges the anti-communist discourse in a manner not unlike Kwŏn's other works, its particular combination of text and illustrations presents a rather superficial understanding of the origins of the war. It manipulates the folktale genre to reinforce its claim to historical truth, but I argue that the force of its argument is weakened by the simultaneous portrayal of the child as both the ultimate victim and the survivor of trauma.

Komiwa op'undori ajŏssi is narrated by two characters: nine-year-old Komi and a man called Op'undori.[7] The two awaken atop Ch'iak mountain in Kangwŏn province of South Korea, and as they start conversing, the reader learns that both man and boy have been dead for thirty years. The boy died fleeing North Korea with his parents during an air raid on civilians, and the man, from P'yŏngan province in North Korea, died on the battlefield fighting the South Koreans. Both man and boy have open, bleeding wounds. The boy then questions the man about the war in an attempt to understand the conflict better, but Op'undori's answers are open-ended and inconclusive. When they hear the growling of a tiger, Komi recalls the folktale 'Haewa tal' (Sun and moon), a story about a brother and sister who escape from a tiger which has disguised itself as their grandmother and with the help of the heavens turn into the sun and the moon. At once, the folktale is re-enacted in front of Komi and Op'undori, but with a twist: this time there are two tigers who, after devouring their grandmother alive, come after the children. The brother and sister begin to argue, and are torn from each other's grasp and separated forever. Once this folk tale performance ends, the boy and man go back to sleep, vanish, and in their place blooms an azalea flower.

The text and artwork are fascinating for several reasons. First, the dialogue is provided here by North Korean voices, and poses an open challenge to the official account of the war, all the more striking considering that it was originally written and published in the late 1980s, when accounts contrary to the anti-communist ideology would have still been silenced:

> 'Who were you fighting?' asked Komi.
> 'The Kuk-Kun [South Korean soldiers].'
> 'What kind of people were the Kuk-Kun?'
> 'People protecting their country.'
> 'What country were they protecting?'
> 'They were people just like me, protecting the same country, only with a different name.'
> 'What do you mean, "the same"?'
> 'The same—we are all grandchildren of Tan'gun.'
> Komi was silent.

---

[7] Their names are significant in their insignificance: Komi is a nondescript 'cute' boy's name (meaning 'like a teddy bear'), while Op'undori contains negative connotations of something lacking or impaired, *op'un* being a very small amount of money or a tiny percentage ('small change'). The man's name indicates that he is one nameless victim among the countless fallen in the war.

'Only I lived in the North, and they lived in the South—that was the only difference.'
[...]
'Did South Korean soldiers die too?'
'Yes, many. We North Korean soldiers killed them. Their corpses were left in the North, and they can never return to their homeland.'
'Why did you do it? Why did you kill each other?'
Instead of replying, Op'undori shook his head.

The victims' open wounds and the recollection of their deaths are described in graphic terms, and are amplified by the book's artwork. For example, the death scenes are spread out in full-page layouts. The North Korean soldier is lying on his back in what may be blood or simply his shadow (see Figure 4), and the dead boy is depicted with his face in the snow (see Figure 5). The artwork does not valorise the soldiers, nor does it make a clear distinction between the North and South Korean soldiers. The layout of the dead bodies leads the viewer's eyes in two different directions: the adult body in Figure 4 draws the eye first to the expression on the dead man's face and then left toward the legs, in the same downward direction as the bullets. In Figure 5, the viewer's eye travels from the boy's legs down along the mountain slope, taking in additional bodies along the way; on the bottom right, a cloth creates a disturbing shadow over the dead boy's head. The fact that he is lying face down, appears to be sleeping, and is accompanied by other dead bodies is a way of detracting slightly from the gruesomeness of the child's death.

Figure 4 (Kwŏn 2007)   Figure 5 (Kwŏn 2007)

The intertextual choice of folktale re-enactment is also highly significant. Maria Tatar notes that 'the reverence brought by some readers to folktales mystifies these stories, making them appear to be a source of transcendent spiritual truth and authority' (Tatar 1992: xii). Of course, folktales are cultural products that reflect the ideologies which society has a vested interest in supporting. As such they are, as Jack Zipes suggests, 'historical prescriptions, internalized, potent, explosive, and we acknowledge the power they hold over our lives by mystifying them' (Zipes 1991: 11). The placing of the folktale in this picture book plays up its cultural authority, and this authority is enhanced by realistic artwork that supports the assumption that the version unfolding in the pages of the picture book is not just traditional lore: it is a real and terribly painful part of the past. The tiger in Figure 6 is absolutely terrifying: the eye travels from the tiger on the upper left to the grandmother on the bottom right. The tiger is tilted toward the viewer, creating the illusion that the tiger is on the descent; the grandmother is caught off guard, in terror, her hand outstretched away from the tiger.

Figure 6 (Kwŏn 2007)

The rendering of the folktale has real consequences: the siblings are lured apart (Figure 7), their resistance accentuated by centrifugal lines (joined hands, feet and—almost—braids, contrasted with their turned faces and the pull of their arms in opposite directions). The viewer is left with an image of destruction (Figure 8), symbolised by the broken doors and scattered shoes; the tigers' rumps and tails suggest that they are already moving on. The appearance of both tails is significant in that it implicates both beasts and holds them both responsible.

Figure 7 (Kwŏn 2007)   Figure 8 (Kwŏn 2007)

The artist and the author of this book have chosen a deliberately realistic approach to lend the text narrative authority and to narrow the distance between the reader/viewer. But as Nodelman explains, 'the pictures most of us would be willing to label as realistic are no less dependent upon cultural assumptions' (Nodelman 1988: 16); the realistic quality of the artwork is itself a product of a deliberate agenda. The choice of colours for the artwork in Kwŏn's picture book—earthy browns, reds and oranges for the war pictures and greys, blacks and whites for the folktale—reflects a desire to create an illusion that this is not a representation but a *documentation* of the events as they occurred. In his discussion of the role of colour in visual representation, Nodelman notes that 'we commonly associate black and white with uncompromising truth, utter absence of subjective colouring: documentary' (ibid.: 67). The artist's choice of colour for both war pictures and the folktale are a deliberate attempt to manipulate the viewer into accepting this version as the truth. Kwŏn's and Dom Lee's interpretation—that North and South Korea were siblings lured apart by false 'tigers' (the USSR and the US) with devastating consequences—is not necessarily exceptional, but from a contemporary perspective, this interpretation of the Korean War ignores the abundant research on the origins of the war, which, as Cumings notes, 'had a long gestation and occurred primarily because of issues internal to Korea' (Cumings 2004: 11).

In conclusion, then, post-war anti-communist discourse exercised extreme control over children's literature in the immediate post-war period, a control that was enforced by education and state law. However, starting in the early 1980s, Kwŏn Chŏng-saeng was able to tell the story of the Korean War in a way that challenged the hegemonic discourse by giving the North Koreans a voice. At the same time, by presenting the Korean War as a foreign conflict on Korean soil that preyed upon its unsuspecting people, and by using the innocent and undying child victim as a mouthpiece, his work raises two problematic issues. First, the book utilises folktale and realism in order to claim an authentic truth, and thus inscribes an interpretive position that fails to present a more complex understanding of the conflict such as might reflect the rich historiography on the Korean War. Second, the picture book also reflects Smith's observation that the innocent child remains outside of trauma and thus allays adult (and the child reader's) anxieties (Smith 2005: 116). In Kwŏn's text the child is at once the ultimate victim of trauma (his wound is still bleeding, his death is graphically illustrated, and his recollections of the air-raid that killed his family are heartbreaking), and its survivor (he comes alive to tell the story, watch the performance of the folktale, and then turn into the blooming azalea, a flower of cultural significance in both South and North Korea). The boy's innocence makes him capable of seeing and speaking the 'truth'. And this way, the adult and child readers are spared the horror of witnessing the young child's gruesome final moments. Smith aptly asks: 'Even when texts ostensibly expose the child reader to historical trauma, do narratives also suppress pain in order to protect a child audience? Or does such suppression serve political purposes?' (Smith 2005: 118). Kwŏn and Dom Lee suppress the child's pain by granting him eternal life, thus glossing over the complexities of the conflict such as the ideological and class struggles and the legacy of Japanese colonialism. It is important to note, at the same time, that this picture book was published as the first in a series titled *P'yŏnghwa paljaguk* (Footsteps of peace) under the auspices of the Roh Moo-hyun government, perhaps as an attempt to rethink the relationship between South and North Korea. A second volume in the series has yet to be released.

4 THE KOREAN WAR IN NORTH KOREA

The origins of the Korean War from the North Korean perspective, and the events leading up to 25 June 1950, have been dealt with in great detail in previous scholarship. Charles Armstrong argues that North Korea began preparing for an armed conflict in late 1946 and that US military intelligence noted a 'marked acceleration in military training and conscription in North Korea' in 1950 (Armstrong 2002: 231-4). Incidents of military aggression occurred frequently across the 38th parallel after the US forces' withdrawal in 1949, and Armstrong notes that 'it is conceivable that either side could have started a war; but in the event, by June 1950 the North was better prepared for war, had the backing of its patron state, and ultimately made the decision to attack its rival in the South' (ibid.: 236). North Korea was utterly devastated by the Korean War but subsequently made immense economic strides under the leadership of Kim Il Sung (Lankov 2002: 63-4). North Korea explains that the war was started by South Korea, and that it was a righteous struggle to save the Korean peninsula from its American colonisers and unite it under a new socialist regime dedicated to establishing a united nation free of its colonial vestiges.

4.1 *The Korean War in text*

Children's literature is often deeply implicated in the establishment of a new nation's identity, especially in the case of totalitarian states that place utmost emphasis on ideological education (see Balina 2008). Yi Yŏng-mi states that Kim Il Sung, inspired by Lenin, believed in the propaganda properties of children's literature, and that the latter must be used as a direct channel for conveying hegemonic political discourse (Yi 2006: 227). Children's literature in North Korea sees itself as responsible for building politically minded citizens in accordance with *juche* (chuch'e) philosophy (Kim Mansŏk 2003; Yi Sun-uk 2007). The post-1950s was a period of great activity in literary circles, during which the content of children's literature was discussed and child readership defined. Yi Yŏng-mi notes that in 1956, the literary critic Kang Hyo Sun pointed out that children's literature must strive to raise children's awareness about the class system, cultivate socialist thinking, instil correct ideas about the working class, and equip children with scientific knowledge, all with the purpose of infusing children with the passion for unification (Yi 2008: 335).

One of the recurrent themes in North Korean children's fiction is the Korean War. It appears in hundreds of stories in the children's magazine *Adong Munhak*, and in books by children's book publishers. The Korean War lends itself particularly well to the narrative of transcendental bravery and self-sacrifice that is an essential part of the heroism discourse in North Korea; it is also an ideal site from which to promote anti-American propaganda. The texts, which follow schematic and predictable narratives, are accompanied by violent illustrations, in particular from the 1970s onwards. The article will examine the violence in the illustrations and analyse these depictions through a consideration of propaganda and theories of fascist cultural ideology and aesthetics.

4.2 The young hero: transcendental courage and martyrdom

North Korean children's literature enforces young readers' understanding of the world through its particular ideological lens. Children's fiction about the Korean War from the immediate post-war period to the present consistently depicts the Korean conflict as an uncompromising struggle against the US and its puppet Korean army. At the same time, it provides a stage upon which the boys and girls of North Korea can vicariously perform their loyalties to their nation's leaders. This heroism is supported by the North Korean celebration of war heroes. Kim Chong-su notes that after the war, North Korea named 549 war heroes who had faced mortal challenges through transcendental actions (Kim 2008: 183). He argues that this institutionalised heroism played an important role in mobilising the youth of North Korea for economic efforts as well (ibid.: 184). The persistence of this discourse, now buttressed by military-first politics, is indicative of the successful role that it continues to play in the control of the youth of North Korea.

Several themes recur in the schematic texts of Korean War children's literature: the celebration of children's passionate patriotism and self-sacrifice; the reminder of the benevolence of North Korea in its role as a surrogate family, and an invocation of the debt to Kim Il Sung; and painful recollection of the Japanese occupation as preparation for national independence.

4.2.1 Bravery and self-sacrifice

Stories from 1954 until the late 1960s commonly narrate an act of bravery of North Korean children avenging the death of their parents. In the August 1957 story by Ryu To Hŭi, 'Ppŭraga'esŏ on p'yŏnji' (A letter from Prague), young Sŭngch'ŏl and his sister bite the American soldier that shoots their father in their presence; the boy is then taken to a South Korean POW camp and tortured. He stays loyal to his ideological convictions until he is liberated by the prisoner exchange and is allowed to go to North Korea. And in 'Namhaeng ryŏlch'a' (Southbound train) (1963) by Kim Kwang Hyŏk, young Minch'ŏl risks his life at gunpoint to save two North Korean soldiers. His dream to join the North Korean forces and avenge his parents, who were executed by an American soldier, comes true. The children-turned-soldiers that appear in the stories of the 1950s and 1960s are driven by a personal vendetta, and are fearless in their commitment to their ideological beliefs.

Many stories celebrate the ultimate patriotic act of self-sacrifice. In *P'yŏngyang hanŭrŭl chik'yŏ* (Protecting the skies of Pyongyang) (1985), edited by An Chŏng Hwan, a decorated but modest pilot is shot down, and deliberately crashes his plane into enemy ships crying 'Hail Kim Il Sung!'. In 'Majimak p'okumi ullilttae kkaji' (Until the sounds of the last explosion) (1986), also edited by An, a young soldier collects grenades from the bodies of dead American soldiers in the heat of the battle; when his comrades come to rescue him, he hands them his ID and attacks an American soldier with a grenade in his mouth, killing the soldier and himself to save them. And in Kim Chong Chŏng's 'Han sonyŏne taehan ch'uŏk' (Memories of a boy) (1997), Kŭmsŏk withstands torture and public execution rather than reveal any information to the South Korean enemy.

4.2.2 *North Korea and Kim Il Sung: family and saviour*

Korean War stories emphasise the great relief with which children, made orphans by the American forces, find their way to the loving embrace of North Korea. In Ryu's 'Ppŭraga'esŏ on p'yŏnji,' Sŭngch'ŏl feels excited to be repatriated to North Korea, as if he were 'coming home to his mother and father' (Ryu 1957: 14). Yongnam, in Kim Wŏn Chong's 'P'okp'ungŭi adŭl' (Son of the whirlwind) (1964), forms a fierce attachment to a division commander who nurtures and cares for him after the Americans kill his parents. And when Kŭmsŏk from 'Han sonyŏne taehan ch'uŏk' (see above, Section 4.2.1), is tied to a tree and tortured, the entire village steps forward claiming to be his relatives. The loss of family, caused by American and South Korean brutality, is made up for by North Korea's warm embrace.

Many stories open and close with a mention of the Great Leader: take, for example, *Nanŭn kim ilsŏng changgunnimŭi chŏnsada* (I am

General Kim Il Sung's warrior), published by Sarochŏng ch'ulp'ansa in 1975. The title already invokes the leader, and the battles inside are fought for the sake of Kim Il Sung. In this picture book, North Korean soldiers ambush South Korean soldiers in order to uncover their plans of attack. Once they get their military intelligence, they climb into a captured South Korean vehicle, and the North Korean soldiers' faces are described as follows:

> The faces of the soldiers, who had sworn their uncompromising loyalty and readiness to sacrifice their lives for the sake of their leader, glowed with a devotion that can overcome any obstacle (Sarochŏng ch'ulp'ansa 1975: 11).

Longer novels about the war invariably open with a glorifying introduction and reminder of Kim Il Sung's crucial leadership. The Great Leader's presence is maintained if not within the body of the work then in an introductory section, which provides the child reader with information about Kim Il Sung's role in the war.

4.2.3 *The Japanese occupation*

While the Americans and South Koreans are the unequivocal enemy, some texts evoke the Japanese colonial period. This creates a direct connection between the colonial period and the Korean War in order to emphasise the continuation of the struggle for Korean independence. For example, Chui Ryŏl ajŏssi in *Kojiue ollyŏp'ŏjin kimilsŏngŭi norae* (The song of Kim Il Sung that spread over the highlands), published in 1974 by Sarochŏng ch'ulp'ansa, recalls the humiliation dealt to him by the Japanese. He invokes memories of his mother doing the laundry for their landowner, and these memories invigorate and prepare him for the fight against the American enemy. Kang Hoyŏng also recalls the Japanese occupation in *P'yŏngyang hanŭrŭl chik'yŏ* (An 1985). Kang was a shepherd who was beaten by his Japanese landlord, and who joined the North Korean army to avenge his family's humiliation. Another soldier, Han Kye Ryŏl, recalls the exodus forced upon his family by the Japanese, and thanks Kim Il Sung for returning his land (Yu 1985).

4.3 *The Korean War in illustrations*

War art is 'a work of art, regardless of medium, that deals with war' (Brandon 2007: 5), and it contributes to the repository of visual representations that shape the way we remember war. Art can also support historical accounts of war; war-related images, especially photographs, have an assumed documentary value.[8] The colour and black-and-white illustrations in children's books, which provide a visual narrative, also contribute to and reinforce the way events are remembered. In North Korea, where information is tightly controlled, these visual images acquire an added force of propaganda. According to Jowett and O'Donnell, the purpose of propaganda is 'to control information flow and manage a certain public's opinion by shaping perceptions through strategies of informative communication' (Jowett and O'Donnell 2006: 44). Indeed, the illustrations in North Korean children's literature reinforce the interpretation of the Korean War as a war of liberation. In addition, however, the illustrations have been marked since the mid-1950s by a graphic violence that heightens the emotional response of the reader by dehumanising the enemy and desensitising the child reader to the illustrations' inherent brutality and the consequences of violence and hatred.[9] In addition, scholarship on fascist aesthetics illuminates the way in which violence promotes national unification and regeneration rhetoric, with such ideologies then inscribed on young readers.

4.3.1 *The juche soldier and his enemy*

One of the ways an illustration elicits the reader's disdain is by contrasting the exuberant, virile image of the North Korean soldier with the despicable, heinous face of the enemy. A common theme is North Korean soldiers' cunning use of their appearance to sneak into South Korean military bases. In the illustrated novel by Kim Sun Yŏng, *P'okp'a chakchŏn* [Mission demolition] (1990), for example, North Korean scouts impersonate South Korean soldiers in order to intercept

---

[8] Brandon notes that 'the concept of war artists as eyewitnesses is strong, and people expect their work, like journalists' reports, to be in some degree truthful' (Brandon 2007: 96).

[9] Another reference to violence in Korean War-related imagery can be found, according to Ross King, in North Korean stamps, the first of which appeared in 1960 (Ross King, nd, 'Monuments Writ Small: The Politics of North Korean Philatelic Imagery', unpublished paper).

the delivery of military cargo. The fact that the soldiers look sufficiently alike to be able to fool one another can potentially present complications for the reader, but the visual representations make them distinguishable. The North Korean soldier often stands tall and square on both feet (Figure 9), and when in action he is poised in graceful motion (Figure 10). Colour pictures often bring out the rosiness of the North Korean soldier's cheeks, the fullness of his flesh, and the determination in his eyes (Figures 10, 11):

Figure 9
(Kim 1990: 2-3)[10]

Figure 10
(Cho 1988: 33)

Figure 11
(Sarochŏng 1975: front cover)

Figure 11 shows a North Korean soldier with strong features, a commanding nose and full but determined lip and a misty yet focused gaze looking away, that allows the viewer to study his face without feeling threatened by his authority. And when North and South Korean soldiers appear together, they are easily told apart:

---

[10] The North Korean soldiers in this illustration are disguised as South Korean soldiers for the purposes of their mission: 'The Reconnaissance Team changed their uniforms and weapons and stood in line. Team leader Kim Kwan Mun faced his file of men disguised in the puppet army uniforms' (Kim 1990: 2). Note the uniforms in the other illustrations from this story in figures 12, 13 and 14. I am grateful to Rüdiger Frank for his insightful observations about these images.

THE KOREAN WAR IN CHILDREN'S LITERATURE 293

Figure 12   Figure 13   Figure 14
(Kim 1990: 28)   (Kim 1990: 15)   (Kim 1990: 16)

The South Korean soldiers are always dwarfed by the North Koreans (Figures 12, 13). When drawn together, the North Korean soldiers are positioned above so that they can peer down at the South Koreans (Figure 13), or are seated so that they need make no eye contact (Figure 14). The South Koreans' faces are pictured as ugly and contorted with fear. They often huddle clumsily, or are portrayed as uncoordinated and cowardly (Figures 15, 16).

Figure 15 (Sarochŏng 1974: 60)   Figure 16 (Sarochŏng 1974: 29)

American soldiers' racial differences are expressed markedly in their faces (Figure 17), and their moral degradation is represented both in their cowardliness and their propensity for drunkenness. In Figure 18, North Koreans discover American soldiers in a drunken stupor; even the photo on the wall is askew, and seems to be a nude portrait. The Americans run at the first sign of trouble; in Figure 19, the wreckage of the room also reflects the moral decay of the American officers.

Figure 17 (An 1985: 63) Figure 18 (Sarochŏng 1975: 24) Figure 19 (Cho 1988: 29)

The lack of morals of the Americans is also reflected in their faces. In Figure 20, the captured American's eyes and mouth are black, and a shadow hovers in the background to emphasise the darkness of his soul. And in Figure 21, a group of miscreants including the commanding officers of the army and air force have been completely destroyed. Their clothes are in tatters and their faces are bandaged. In the background, their decay is symbolised by the shattered image of Jesus on the cross.

Figure 20 (Sarochŏng 1975: 25)   Figure 21 (Cho 1988: 20-1)

The moral righteousness of the North Koreans is reflected in the soldiers' poses, shining eyes, robust figures and handsome faces. The South Koreans are short and cowardly, and are often shown being bullied by the Americans, who are depicted as the embodiment of moral decay. Figure 22 shows an American officer cursing at his inferior South Korean officer. In Figure 23, the American soldier strikes the

South Korean soldier for not having succeeded in catching any *ppalgaengi* (Reds).

Figure 22 (Hong 1980: 18)   Figure 23 (Hong 1980: 19)

4.3.2 *Brutal violence*

The cumulative effect of these images—the creation of an affective response in the reader—is enhanced by the repeated and graphic violence that appears throughout. Beginning with the early stories in the 1950s and peaking in the mid-1970s and 1980s, the illustrations highlight both the brutality of the opposing forces and the violence with which North Koreans dispose of their enemy. An early example comes from 'Saessak' (Sprout) (1956), by Ch'oe Hak Su (Figure 24).

Figure 24 (Ch'oe 1956: 76-7)

The American soldiers announce that they will be taking over the North Korean school for their purposes,[11] and when the North Korean children revolt they are shot. By the 1970s, however images of victimisation are replaced with graphic depictions of North Korean soldiers' brutal victory over their enemies. The soldiers appear usually as the agents of action: they wield axes, bayonets, rifles, clubs, rocks and knives, and the illustrations capture them in mid-action. These illustrations are characterised by the coolness and aloofness of the North Koreans. There is an eerie emotional detachment in their faces and poses as they go about their business of killing.

A number of illustrations make the point. A North Korean officer, disguised as a South Korean, has stolen into the South Korean military base office with the purpose of obtaining top secret documents. When a South Korean soldier refuses to co-operate, the North Korean stabs him (Figure 25), steals the documents, and then sets fire to the office (Figure 26). What is striking, besides the stabbing and burning of the South Korean, is the stoic expression on the North Korean soldier's face; he displays no emotion. On the contrary, his eyes look into the distance, and his body is posed in movement away from his victim. His hair seems to be perfectly set, as if the struggle never happened at all.

Figure 25 (Sarochŏng 1975: 58)   Figure 26 (Sarochŏng 1975: 60)

Figures 27-29 offer further violent illustrations: the soldier in Figure 27 is piercing his enemy with his bayonet; the one in Figure 28 is

---

[11] Armstrong notes that '[o]ne notable example of [the US forces'] insensitivity was the use of school buildings for billeting occupation personnel' (Armstrong 2003: 75).

about to knife his American enemy to death; and in Figure 29, the young man has just murdered his opponent with an axe. Once again, very little emotion is depicted in the faces of the North Korean soldiers. The man in Figure 27 is grim, and movement is indicated by the background lines drawn from left to right in a downward angle. In figure 28, the American is terrified while his North Korean captor looks cross in concentration; but the handsome North Korean face at the forefront of the illustration draws attention away from the killing. The soldier appears focused and determined, as if already looking ahead to the next mission. Finally, the body language between the young men in Figure 29 gives no indication that one of them has just killed a soldier with his axe, and only the broken body of the soldier in the corner gives any indication of the action that has occurred.

Figure 27 (Sarochŏng 1974: 15) Figure 28 (Sarochŏng 1975: 23) Figure 29 (Hong 1980: 14)

Illustrations often picture the moment of impact and death of the enemy. Figure 30 captures the American target dying with one surprised hand in the air while the North Korean soldiers open fire at short range. Figure 31 depicts the moment of contact when the North Korean soldier shoots an American at close range. And Figure 32 captures the moment after a North Korean officer executes an unarmed South Korean who refuses his command to dismantle the train tracks. Moments later, the train with military cargo for the South Korean army is derailed and the South Korean soldiers working on the railway plunge to their deaths.

Figure 30　　　　　Figure 31　　　　　Figure 32
(Sarochŏng 1975: 29) (Kŭmsŏng 1976: 27)　(Kim 1990: 30)

Figure 33 depicts an American dying with a painful scream on his face. Figure 34 captures a battleground in which the North Koreans are butchering their enemies; on the left-hand side a man is about to deal a deadly blow to his opponent with an axe.

Figure 33 (Sarochŏng 1974: 8)　　Figure 34 (Yu 1985: 34-5)

5　Aesthetics of Violence

Illustrations in children's picture books demand our attention because they enhance the cultural literacy of young readers. Peggy Albers notes that the 'artwork of picture books greatly influences how children begin to perceive, read, and reinterpret their worlds through art' (Albers 2008: 179). Kimberley Reynolds comments that '[t]he word-image dynamic is particularly adept at giving expression to meanings and concepts that reside at the edges of language—things for which the vocabulary and grammar that regulate verbal communication may currently be inadequate' (Reynolds 2007: 17). But the artwork above does more than communicate concepts that 'reside at the edges of language': the dehumanisation and degradation of the enemy aestheticises violence in a way reminiscent of scholarship on fascist aesthetics. Writing about Japan, Alan Tansman notes that fascism 'provided the possibility for an experience of immediacy and unity that countered the alienation and fragmentation of the modern individual, and it promised an end to class division by promoting the myth of a nation unified by the natural bonds of its blood and spirit' (Tansman 2009: 3); one way that a sense of unity and natural bonds was felt was through the regenerative experience provided by violence. Mark Antliff notes that many fascist artists shared a desire for regeneration that was 'simultaneously spiritual and physical, moral, social and political' as well as a totalising 'revolt against decadence' (Antliff 2007: 5), and he notes that violence was 'the authentic source of creative energy … with the ability to transform the individual' (ibid.: 6). Tansman argues that 'according to the logic of fascist aesthetics, violence … can heal the fractured intellect by engaging all the senses while producing an experience of sublimity' (Tansman 2009: 26). He goes on to explain that being a spectator to violence, as a reader viewing images that capture moments of dying, pain and destruction, is a means of experiencing the sublime:

> Wonder, or the abstract experience of the sublime, mutes the actual effects of violence, allowing viewers or reader a spectatorial remove or an abstract distance from the corporeal register of sublime experience … sublime aspects of the Japanese fascist moment share both the individuating *and* the socializing power of the sublime and the beautiful. They harbor the potential to inspire both the individual's domination by the aesthetic moment and his being lured to feel pleasure in violence (ibid.: 26-7).

While North Korea cannot be defined as fascist, certain elements of the fascist aesthetic—namely, violence as a driving force of regeneration—can be found in North Korean illustrations. Those in North Korean picture books about the Korean War do more than provide a supplement to the text, or celebrate the bravura of the North Korean soldiers: they perform on an aesthetic plane that connects the viewer to larger ideals of regeneration and empowerment through violence. The sublime is epitomised in the handsome, beautiful and detached faces of the North Korean soldiers as they rise above or look past and beyond their actions, carrying the viewer with them to experience a transformation: a new society, born out of the ecstatic destruction of the enemy. Take, for example, Figure 35.

Figure 35 (Hong 1980: 41)

The young North Korean soldier, Sŏnghwan, is pictured moments before his death. He has withstood the torture visited upon him by the Americans as they loom over him, their shadows extenuating their claw-like fingers. Sŏnghwan goes to his death with rosy cheeks, a wistful look in his eyes and perfectly set hair: he is the epitome of beauty. His physical and spiritual core transcends the reality of his experience; and his sacrifice embodies the national renewal and unity that is celebrated by the fascist aesthetic. The graphic violence of the illustrations—both the violence that is dealt to the enemy and the violence that is experienced by the North Korean martyrs—becomes part of a violent performance whose ultimate goal is regeneration and the celebration of the rebirth of the North Korean nation.

REFERENCES

An, Chŏng Hwan (ed.) (1985), *P'yŏngyang hanŭrŭl chik'yŏ* [Protecting the skies of Pyongyang], P'yŏngyang: Kŭmsŏng ch'ŏngnyŏn ch'ulp'ansa

An, Chŏng Hwan (ed.) (1986), *Majimak p'okŭm'i ullilttae kkaji* [Until the sounds of the last explosion], P'yŏngyang: Kŭmsŏng ch'ŏngnyŏn ch'ulp'ansa

Albers, Peggy (2008), 'Theorizing Visual Representation in Children's Literature', in: *Journal of Literacy Research*, 30, pp. 163-200

Antliff, Mark (2007), *Avant-Garde Fascism: The Mobilization of Myth, Art, and Culture in France, 1909-1939*, Durham NC: Duke University Press

Antze, Paul and Michael Lambeck (eds) (1996), *Tense Past: Cultural Essays in Trauma and Memory*, New York and London: Routledge

Armstrong, Charles K. (2002), *The North Korean Revolution, 1945-1950*, Ithaca NY and London: Cornell University Press

Armstrong, Charles K. (2003), 'The Cultural Cold War in Korea, 1945-1950', in: *Journal of Asian Studies*, 62 (1), pp. 71-99

Balina, Marina (2008), 'Creativity Through Restraint: The Beginnings of Soviet Children's Literature', in: Marina Balina and Larissa Rudova (eds), *Russian Children's Literature and Culture*, New York and London: Routledge, pp. 1-18

Brandon, Laura (2007), *Art and War*, London: I.B.Tauris

Chang Su-ch'ŏl (1958), 'Ŏndŏkkiresŏ maejŭn ujŏng' [Friendship forged on a hill path], in: *Saebŏt* (August), pp. 53-9

Cho, Pyŏng Kwŏn (ed.) (1988), *P'aechŏn changgunŭi mallo* [The defeated general's claims], P'yŏngyang: Kŭmsŏng ch'ŏngnyŏn ch'ulp'ansa

Ch'oe, Hak Su (1956), 'Saessak' [Sprout], in: *Adong Munhak* (October), pp. 66-78; (November), pp. 16-26

Ch'oe, T'ae-ŭng (1954), 'Oksaek chogae kkŏpjil' [The jade seashell], in: *Sonyŏn segye* (February), pp. 10-13

Cumings, Bruce (1981), *Origins of the Korean War: Liberation and the Emergence of Separate Regimes*, Princeton NJ: Princeton University Press

Cumings, Bruce (2004), *North Korea: Another Country*, New York: The New Press

Hong, Chong Wŏn (1980), *Yŏngkwangŭro pitnanŭn sonyŏn kŭnwidae* [The glorious children's guard], P'yŏngyang: Kŭmsŏng ch'ŏngnyŏn ch'ulp'ansa

Jenkins, Henry (ed.) (1998), *The Children's Culture Reader*, New York: New York University Press

Jowett, Garth S. and Victoria O'Donnell (2006), 'What is Propaganda, and How Does It Differ From Persuasion?', in: Garth Jowett and Victoria O'Donnell (eds), *Propaganda and Persuasion*, 4th edition, Thousand Oaks CA: Sage, pp. 1-48

Kim, Chong Chŏng (1997), 'Han sonyŏne taehan ch'uŏk' [Memories of a boy], in: *Adong Munhak* (September), pp. 8-10

Kim, Chong-su (2008), '6.25 chŏnchaenggwa pukhan "ch'ŏngnyŏn yŏngung"' [The Korean war and North Korea's "youth heroes"], in: *Chŏngsin munhwa yŏnggu* 31 (1), pp. 161-88

Kim, Kwang Hyŏk (1963), 'Namhaeng ryŏlch'a' [Southbound train], in: *Adong Munhak* (August), pp. 24-45

Kim, Mansŏk (2003), 'Chuch'e sidaeŭi chosŏn adongsigie taehan koch'al' [An examination of childhood during the period of juche], in: *Munhak kyoyukhak* 12, pp. 195-220

Kim, Sun Yŏng (1990), *P'okp'a chakjŏn* [Mission demolition], P'yŏngyang: Kŭmsŏng ch'ŏngnyŏn ch'ulp'ansa

Kim, Wŏn Chong (1964). 'P'okp'ungŭi adŭl' [Son of the wildwind], in *Adong Munhak* (February), pp. 5-23; (March), pp. 70-85

King, Ross (nd), 'Monuments Writ Small: The Politics of North Korean Philatelic Imagery', unpublished paper

Kŭmsŏng ch'ŏngnyŏn ch'ulp'ansa (1976), *Chŏkhuesŏ ssawŏigin sonyŏntŭl* [The victorious children fighting in the rear lines], P'yŏngyang: Kŭmsŏng ch'ŏngnyŏn ch'ulp'ansa

Kwŏn, Chŏng-saeng (2007), *Komiwa op'undori ajŏssi* [Komi and Mr Op'undori], Seoul: Pori

Kwŏn, Chŏng-saeng [1984] (2001), *Mongsil ŏnni* [Sister Mongsil], Seoul : Ch'angjak kwa pip'yŏngsa

Kwŏn, Chŏng-saeng (1985) *Ch'ogajipi ittŏn maŭl* [The village of thatched houses], Waegwan: Pundo ch'ulp'ansa

Lankov, Andrei (2002), *From Stalin To Kim Il-Sung: The Formation of North Korea 1945-1960*, New Brunswick NJ: Rutgers University Press

McCallum, Robyn (1999), *Ideologies of Identity in Adolescent Fiction*, New York and London: Garland

Nikolajeva, Maria (2003), *The Rhetoric of Character in Children's Literature*, Lanham MD: Scarecrow Press

Nodelman, Perry (1988), *Words About Pictures: The Narrative Art of Children's Picture Books*, Athens GA and London: University of Georgia

Pak, Kye-ju (1953), '38 sŏnsangŭi so' [The cow of the 38th parallel], illustrations by Kim Yŏng Ju, in: *Sonyŏn segye* (August), pp. 20-23

Park, Sunyoung (2006), 'The Colonial Origin of Korean Realism and its Contemporary Manifestations', in: *Positions* 14 (1), pp. 165-92

Reynolds, Kimberley (2007), *Radical Children's Literature: Aesthetic Transformations in Juvenile Fiction*, Basingstoke, Hampshire UK: Palgrave Macmillan

Rose, Jacqueline (1984), *The Case of Peter Pan, or, the Impossibility of Children's Fiction*, London: Macmillan

Ryang, Sonya (ed.) (2009), 'Introduction: North Korea: Going Beyond Security and Enemy Rhetoric', in: *North Korea: Toward a Better Understanding*, Lanham MD: Lexington Books, pp. 1-21

Ryu, To Hŭi (1957), 'Ppŭraga'esŏ on p'yŏnji' [A letter from Prague], in: *Adong Munhak* (August), pp. 4-15

Saroch'ŏng ch'ulp'ansa (1974), *Kojiue ollyŏp'ŏjin kimilsŏng ŭi norae* [The song of Kim Il Sung that spread over the highlands], P'yŏngyang: Saroch'ŏng ch'ulp'ansa

Saroch'ŏng ch'ulp'ansa (1975), *Nanŭn kimilsŏngŭi chŏnsada* [I am Kim Il Sung's soldier], P'yŏngyang: Saroch'ŏng ch'ulp'ansa

Shin, Gi-Wook and Michael Robinson (1999), 'Introduction: Rethinking Colonial Korea', in: Shin Gi-Wook and Michael Robinson (eds), *Colonial Modernity in Korea,* Cambridge MA and London: Harvard University Asian Center, pp. 1-18

Smith, Katharine Capshaw (2005), 'Forum: Trauma and Children's Literature', in: *Children's Literature*, 33, pp. 115-19

Sŏ, Tong-su (2006), 'Hanguk chŏnjaenggi munhak tamron yŏngu: pangong t'eksŭt'ŭŭi kiwŏnkwa kobaekŭi chŏngch'ihak' [Research on literary discourse in the war period: the origins and politics of confession of anti-communist texts], in: *Uri ŏmun yŏngu*, pp. 385-418

Sŏn, An-na (2007), *Ch'ŏnŭi ŏlgurŭl kajin adong munhak* [One thousand faces of children's literature], Seoul: Ch'ŏngdong kŏul

Sŏn, An-na (2009), *Adong munhakkwa pan'gong ideollogi* [Children's literature and anti-communist ideology], Seoul: Ch'ŏngdong kŏul

Stephens, John (1992), *Language and Ideology in Children's Fiction*, London and New York: Longman
Stueck, William Whitney (2002), *Rethinking the Korean War: A New Diplomatic and Strategic History*, Princeton NJ: Princeton University Press
Tansman, Alan (2009), *The Aesthetics of Japanese Fascism*, Berkeley CA: University of California Press
Tatar, Maria (1992), *Off with their Heads!: Fairy Tales and the Culture of Childhood*, Princeton NJ: Princeton University Press
Thacker, Deborah (2000), 'Disdain Or Ignorance? Literary Theory and the Absence of Children's Literature', in: *The Lion and the Unicorn* 24 (1), pp. 1-17
Wŏn, Chong-ch'an (2001), 'Han'guk adong munhakŭi ŏjewa onŭl: pansŏngkwa kwajerŭl chungsimŭro' [Past and present of Korean children's literature: reflections and tasks], in: *Adong munhakkwa pip'yŏng chŏngsin* [Criticism and children's literature], Seoul: Ch'angjakkwa pip'yŏngsa, pp. 13-26
Yi, Ho-baek (2007), '"Kusuhan illŏsŭt'ŭreisyŏn" ŭi segye' [The wonderful world of illustrations], in: *Urinara ŏrini ch'aekŭi yŏksa: haebang hu 1960 nyŏndae kkajirŭl chungsimŭro* [History of Korea's illustrated books: from liberation until 1960], Seoul: Kungnip ŏrini ch'ŏngsonyŏn tosŏgwan, pp. 10-20
Yi, Sun-uk, (2007), '4 wŏl hyŏngmyŏngkwa pukhan adong munhak' [North Korean children's literature and the April Revolution], in: *Hanguk munhak nonch'ong* 46, pp. 373-98
Yi, Wŏn-su (1995), *Supsok nara* [The forest country], Seoul: Ŭngjin ch'ulp'an chusik hoesa
Yi, Yŏng-mi (2006), 'Pukhan adong munhakkwa kyoyuk yŏngu' [Study on North Korean children's literature and education], in: *Han'guk munhak ironkwa pip'yŏng*, 30 (10.1), pp. 225-57
Yi, Yŏng-mi (2008), '1950 nyŏndae pukhan adong munhak kyoyangjang yŏngu' [Study on 1950 North Korean children's literature], in: *Hanguk ŏnŏ munhak*, 66, pp. 329-58
Yu, Hyŏn Sam (1985), *Chogukŭi koji naŭi koji* [My motherland's highlands are my highlands], P'yŏngyang: Chosŏn misul ch'ulp'ansa
Zipes, Jack (1991), *Fairy Tales and the Art of Subversion*, New York: Routledge

ABOUT THE AUTHORS AND EDITORS

Sabine Burghart
is research assistant to the chair of East Asian Economy and Society at the East Asian Institute, University of Vienna. She holds a M.A. in political science from the University of Leiden. Between 2004 and 2007, she served as programme officer at the Korea office of the German Friedrich Naumann Foundation for Liberty in Seoul. She was in charge of the foundation's training programmes and capacity-building projects in the DPR Korea.
Email: sabine.burghart@univie.ac.at

Annette Erpenstein
is currently completing her dissertation in geography at Westfaelische Wilhelms-University in Muenster on 'Urban conflict studies in Korea'. From 2004 to 2007 she worked as adjunct professor in the Department of Urban Planning at Seoul National University. Since July 2004, she has been the official representative for the German Chamber of Architects Germany in Korea and the US. She worked in Germany from 1991 to 2004, first in public service and later in private architectural and city planning firms, and also as an urban planner and project developer for all kinds of urban planning projects.
Email: annette_erpenstein@hotmail.com

Rüdiger Frank
is professor of East Asian Economy and Society at the University of Vienna and vice-head of the Department of East Asian Studies. He is also an adjunct professor at Korea University and the University of North Korean Studies in Seoul. He holds an M.A. in Korean Studies, Economics and International Relations and a Ph.D. in Economics. Visiting professorships have included Columbia University New York and Korea University Seoul. He is a council member of the Association for Korean Studies in Europe, vice-director of the Vienna School of Governance, and deputy chief editor of the *European Journal of East Asian Studies*. His five-month first visit to North Korea took place in 1991 as a language student at Kim Il Sung University. His

major research fields are socialist transformation in East Asia and Europe (with a focus on North Korea), state-business relations in East Asia, and regional integration in East Asia.
Email: ruediger.frank@univie.ac.at

James E. Hoare
Ph.D., retired from the British Diplomatic Service in 2003. He was posted to Seoul and Beijing, and his last appointment was as British Chargé d'Affaires and Consul-General in Pyongyang. He now writes and broadcasts about East Asia. Among his recent publications are *A Political and Economic Dictionary of East Asia* (Routledge 2005) and *North Korea in the 21st Century: An Interpretative Guide* (Global Oriental 2005), both written with his wife, Susan Pares. He is a senior teaching fellow at the School of Oriental and African Studies, University of London, where he teaches a course on North Korea, and an honorary departmental fellow in the Department of International Politics, Aberystwyth University. He lives in London.
Email: jim@jhoare10.fsnet.co.uk

Thomas Kern
is professor of sociology at Heidelberg University. He holds a Ph.D. and a *venia legendi* in sociology. From 2000 to 2003, he was a visiting research fellow at Yonsei University in Seoul, and received grants from the Humboldt Foundation and the German Research Foundation. From 2003 to 2008, he was a senior research fellow at the Institute of Asian Studies, GIGA German Institute of Global and Area Studies in Hamburg. From 2008 to 2009, he was affiliated to the Max Weber Center for Advanced Cultural and Social Studies in Erfurt on a Heisenberg Grant from the German Research Foundation. He has published several books and articles on civil society, cultural sociology, democratisation, religious change, and globalisation.
Email: thomas.kern@soziologie.uni-heidelberg.de

Patrick Köllner
is acting director of the Institute of Asian Studies, GIGA German Institute of Global and Area Studies. He holds a Ph.D. and a *venia legendi* in political science. Between 1996 and 2006 he was sole editor of the German-language *Korea Yearbook*. His research focuses on Japanese and Korean politics and political parties more generally. Recent publications includes a monograph on the organisation of Japanese

political parties, *Die Organisation japanischer Parteien* (2006), and articles in journals such as *Japanstudien, Journal of East Asian Studies, Politische Vierteljahresschrift*, and *Social Science Japan Journal*.
Email: koellner@giga-hamburg.de

Mark Morris
is university lecturer in Japanese Cultural History at the University of Cambridge and a fellow of Trinity College. His main teaching and research interests concern Japanese modern fiction and film, and Korean film. Work in progress includes a study of South and North Korean film which locates films and film genres in their social and historical contexts and also in a more general, comparative film-historical context.
Email: mrm1000@cam.ac.uk

Susan Pares
has worked in the Research and Analysis Department of the Foreign and Commonwealth Office and, since 1987, as an editor and writer on East Asian subjects. She edited *Asian Affairs*, 1997-2001, and between 2000 and 2007 the *Papers of the British Association for Korean Studies*. She served in the British Embassy in Beijing, 1975-6 and accompanied her husband, James Hoare, on postings to Seoul (1981-5), Beijing (1988-91) and Pyongyang (2001-02). They are co-authors of several books dealing with East Asian and specifically Korean affairs. The most recent is *North Korea in the 21st Century: An Interpretative Guide* (2005).
Email: spares@myway.com

Werner Pascha
is professor of East Asian economic studies at Duisburg-Essen University, Germany, director of its Institute of East Asian Studies (IN-EAST) and board member of its Research Training Group 'Risk and East Asia', funded by the German Research Foundation. He has been a visiting fellow at various organisations, including the Academy of Korean Studies (1996) and the Korea Institute for International Economic Policy (2007). His research interests include the political economy of institutional change in Japan and Korea, and international economic relations within and with the East Asian region. Recent publications include the book, co-edited with Jörg Mahlich, *Innovation and Technology in Korea: Challenges of a Newly Advanced Economy*

(2007), and the paper 'Financial Cooperation in Northeast Asia after the Global Financial Crisis', in *The Journal of East Asian Affairs* (Winter 2009).
Email: werner.pascha@uni-due.de

Durgesh K. Rai
is research associate at the Indian Council for Research on International Economic Relations (ICRIER), New Delhi. He holds an M.Phil. in economics from Jawaharlal Nehru University, New Delhi. His areas of interest include global trade, FTAs/RTAs, multilateralism vs. regionalism, regional economic integration and co-operation, trade and development, migration, human resources and economics of education. He has several publications, including a recently co-authored article on 'Gains from India-Korea CEPA' in *Foreign Trade Review*, a peer-reviewed journal published by the Indian Institute of Foreign Trade, New Delhi.
Email: drai@icrier.res.in

Alexander Ruser
graduated in Sociology, Philosophy and the History of South Asia at Heidelberg University in 2004. He currently works at the Department of Sociology at Heidelberg University. His work has focused on social policy, pension policy and critical discourse analysis. His thesis compared the transformation of the welfare state in Great Britain and Germany. His article 'More than tea or curry? Do we have to fear India' (with René Schultens) was recently accepted for publication by the SARAI Programme of the Centre for the Study of Developing Societies, Delhi.
Email: alexander.ruser@soziologie.uni-heidelberg.de

Daniel Schwekendiek
is a scholar with an interdisciplinary interest in social, economic and health development in the two Koreas and their diasporas. He is author of numerous journal articles and books. He holds a German B.A./M.A. and Ph.D. in economics from the University of Tuebingen —where he has also been a visiting lecturer since 2009. He has been a researcher at the University of Oxford and at Seoul National University, and moved to the University of California (Berkeley) in June 2010.
Email: info@daniel-schwekendiek.de

David Shim
is a Ph.D. candidate at the German Institute of Global and Area Studies. He is interested in critical approaches to International Relations theories. In his dissertation he examines the problematisation of the Democratic People's Republic of Korea from a discourse theoretical perspective. He has published working papers and articles on South Korea's foreign policy and its innovation system and on North Korea.
Email: shim@giga-hamburg.de

Dafna Zur
received her M.A. from the University of British Columbia, Vancouver, where she is now is completing her Ph.D. dissertation on the formation of national identity in North and South Korean children's literature, 1920-1960. She received her B.A. from the Hebrew University in Jerusalem. Her interests lie broadly with colonial-period children's literature magazines, North Korean science fiction, and war literature.
Email: dafnaz@interchange.ubc.ca

MAP OF THE KOREAN PENINSULA

Design and Imaging Unit, Durham University.